CHICAGO

and the

American
Literary
Imagination
1880-1920

CHICAGO

and the

American

Literary

Imagination

1880-1920

Carl S. Smith

UNIVERSITY OF CHICAGO PRESS
CHICAGO AND LONDON

The University of Chicago Press, Chicago   60637
The University of Chicago Press, Ltd., London

The Carl Sandburg poem, "Prayers of Steel," is
from *Cornhuskers* by Carl Sandburg, copyright
1918 by Holt, Rinehart and Winston, Inc.;
renewed 1946 by Carl Sandburg. Reprinted by
permission of Harcourt Brace Jovanovich, Inc.

CARL S. SMITH is associate professor
of English and urban affairs at
Northwestern University.

Library of Congress Cataloging in Publication Data

Smith, Carl S.
  Chicago and the American literary imagination,
1880–1920.

  Bibliography: p.
  Includes index.
  1. American literature—Illinois—Chicago—History
and criticism.   2. Chicago (Illinois) in literature.
3. American literature—19th century—History and
criticism.   4. American literature—20th century—
History and criticism.   5. City and town life in
literature.   I. Title.
PS285.C47S6   1984   810′.9′3277311   83-9311
ISBN 0-226-76371-4

To Jack and the memory of Stish

Contents

Preface

This book examines major thematic and formal patterns that appeared in a range of literary works which discussed in a serious and substantive manner life in the City of Chicago during the decades surrounding the turn of the century. The purpose of this examination is to analyze a major episode in the aesthetic response to the rise of the modern industrial city in America, of which Chicago was by wide agreement a leading example, if not *the* leading example. This is, then, a literary study with ties to social and intellectual history—a history marked by sudden, sometimes violent and disturbing changes that resulted in the emergence of new settings, habits, personalities, institutions, and values that both coexisted with and displaced older ones. Literature and other art forms themselves changed as they in different ways endorsed, criticized, reflected, or even attempted to ignore the alterations in American life. In this period, life and art become modern.

The nineteenth century invented Chicago and did so with such dispatch and vigor that any attempt to define what is most characteristic about the city's history must deal above all with rapid growth and change that seem miraculous even to a twentieth-century mind. Although the site of what was to be Chicago was first explored by Jolliet and Marquette in 1673, the city as it is known today did not exist before the early 1830s; when the World's Columbian Exposition opened in 1893, there were over 20,000 Chicagoans who were older than the town they inhabited. Chicago was not the only city that grew so rapidly, but none came so far so fast.

Preface

The city's distinguishing features were the result of the intersection of a number of circumstances that were so interconnected that it is difficult to separate them. The all-encompassing fact is that Chicago was in the right place at the right time, and its citizens were capable of taking advantage of their opportunities. The right place was a flat and unenclosed position near the southwestern tip of the Great Lakes, accessible through the Erie Canal to the Atlantic Ocean and, after the Illinois and Michigan Canal was opened in 1848, to the Mississippi River. Once the railroad entered Chicago in the 1850s, Chicago's place as the central nexus linking the manufacturing East and the agricultural West was assured. In addition, the city was situated near sources of lumber, coal, ore, and water sufficient to make it a major industrial as well as trading center. The right time was the high tide of a free enterprise economy, an unrestricted immigration policy, and a series of revolutionary inventions in building, transportation, and communications.

The driving strength of these several combined factors is reflected in the scale of the statistics of Chicago's growth. In 1830, Chicago included some fifty settlers. There were over four thousand by 1837, the year of the first charter. Some 300,000 people dwelled in the city the Great Chicago Fire destroyed in 1871, their numbers having increased tenfold since 1850. There were over a million by 1890, and twice that number by 1910, making Chicago second in population only to New York. In 1890 about forty percent of the city's citizens had been born abroad, while almost twice that many were, if not immigrants themselves, children of foreign-born parents. These joined an increasing flow of newcomers of American parentage who came primarily from the farms, towns, and smaller cities of the Middle West, the Middle Atlantic States, and New England. By 1910, their total had swelled to over two million. No deterrent, man-made or natural, could slow the city's expansion: not prolonged periods of financial depression that plagued the American economy in the late nineteenth century, not strikes and social violence, not even the fire that leveled the heart of the business district and left a third of the population homeless.

The period between 1880 and 1920 was a critical time in Chicago's brief history. In this interval the city was rebuilt from the fire and, after a half-century of chaotic growth, settled into the geographical limits and the social and economic patterns with which it is identified—with some variations—to this day. Barely emerged from its frontier past, Chicago had a vision of an unlimited future in which it would become the leading city of the American republic. Other young cities shared this dream, but in no other place did it come so close to coming true. Chicago in this era was the setting of many of the outstanding failures and successes of

x

urban cultural life. If the Haymarket Riot and the Pullman Strike seemed to question the basic moral and economic bearing of the city and the nation, the opening of Adler and Sullivan's magnificent Auditorium Building, the new Art Institute, Hull-House, and the World's Columbian Exposition suggested that the potentially destructive energies of industrial capitalism might be directed into the service of a more elevated, harmonious, and beautiful world than had ever been known before.

The literature of Chicago speaks eloquently if inconsistently of these major national and local developments. Those who wrote about Chicago recognized its rise as one of the emblematic events of the age, and several of them perceived this development not only as a significant event in its own right but also as a phenomenon with special meaning for them as literary artists. As a result, among a large and varied body of literature dealing with Chicago as a central subject, there are many texts which speak to the issue of the uncertain status of art and the artist in the modern city. This book investigates these texts in order to discover what they perceived was happening to literature and society, and the wider implications of these changes.

Before going further, it would be helpful to define what kinds of works are studied here and what is meant by "literary imagination." My concept of the literature of Chicago is broad, including almost any attempt to discuss the city qualitatively in words. By "discuss qualitatively" I mean speak thoughtfully about the distinctive nature of Chicago and what it was like to live within it. To do so required a careful process of observation, reflection, and expression. My definition encompasses histories, guidebooks, travel accounts, autobiographies, journalism, and criticism, though I concentrate most heavily on fiction. I discuss a diverse assortment of writers whose literary intentions and talents varied considerably. When I say that they all had a "literary imagination," I mean simply that these authors had the kind of mind that responds to experience by writing about it. Though the writers I treat often disagreed on aesthetic standards, they all valued literature as a conveyor of important truths, as a bearer of ideas and ideals, and as a potentially powerful cultural force.

The rise of Chicago was accompanied by an enormous literary response. In a University of Chicago doctoral dissertation on "Chicago and 'The Great American Novel'" that he completed in 1935, Lennox Bouton Grey counted some five hundred novels about Chicago. My choice of texts is necessarily limited, focusing on some better-known writers and including some obscure selections. My general principle has been to choose those texts which I believe examined contemporary conditions in Chicago most seriously and effectively, and which directly and indirectly discussed the relationship of literature, art, and urban life. This principle, along with considerations of scale, has led me to make certain important exclusions, most notably some examples of Chicago journalism and early urban sociology. This study is intended to be broadly suggestive, however, and useful to considerations of other Chicago writing and of the literature and culture of the turn of the century.

While I use historical and biographical materials, I have not written a history of Chicago or even of Chicago writing, nor do I examine in depth the lives of the authors of most of the works cited or such important literary events as the Chicago Renaissance in the arts early this century. To do so would be both a greater and lesser task than concerns me in this book: greater because it would require a survey of many more texts and biographical details than are included here, lesser because the analysis of certain texts and authors would be briefer. Besides, much of the ground I do not cover has been studied by other scholars, whose considerable assistance—along with that of many others on whose work this book is based—I acknowledge in the notes and bibliography.

Acknowledgments

I have several institutions and many individuals to thank for their assistance. Northwestern University has consistently provided support and encouragement, beginning with a faculty summer fellowship for a smaller project on which this book is based. Shortly after that, I was aided by a joint appointment at Northwestern's Center for Urban Affairs and Policy Research. I am grateful that two CUAPR directors, Louis Masotti and Margaret Gordon, have seen the work of humanists as directly relevant to the center's central interest in research in the social sciences. The center also made it possible for me to have the help of Harry Ross, who was an exceptionally insightful and energetic graduate assistant. This project was also indirectly benefited by a fellowship from the National Endowment for the Humanities that enabled me spend the academic year 1977–78 at the National Humanities Institute at the University of Chicago. A special word of gratitude is due to Edward Rosenheim, director of the institute, and to several other members of the faculty and staff of the University of Chicago. I am very thankful also for the resources of a number of libraries and librarians. These include most notably the Northwestern University Library, with special thanks to Russell Maylone; the University of Chicago libraries; the library of the Chicago Historical Society, and especially Larry Viskochil and Archie Motley; the Newberry Library; and the Chicago Public Library. During a leave in Berkeley I found the Chicago holdings of the University of California quite impressive.

Acknowledgments

I have been fortunate that several people gave so much time to read and comment on earlier drafts. Burton Bledstein, Carl Condit, and Robert Wiebe, whose enthusiasm for this project has been equal to their remarkable expertise, have been most helpful, but I am also very thankful for the responses of Howard Becker, Henry Binford, Gerald Graff, Neil Harris, Albert Hunter, Harold Kaplan, Russell Reising, and Robert Streeter. I also learned a great deal from discussions with, among others, Daniel Aaron, Reid Badger, Josef Barton, Richard Blau, T. H. Breen, Sidney Bremer, John Cawelti, David Donald, Perry Duis, Paul Glad, Harrison Hayford, William Hesketh, John and Joy Kasson, Lewis Kreinberg, A. Robert Lee, Richard Luecke, Sidney Monas, John Stilgoe, Eric Sundquist, and John Thomas. I might never have finished without the untiring commitment and good cheer of Marjorie Weiner.

The Dreiser section of Chapter 4 is a much-revised version of an article that appeared in the *Canadian Review of American Studies* 7 (Fall 1976), 151–62, and I thank that journal for permission to use it here. I also wish to thank the University of Chicago Library for permission to quote from the Robert Herrick Papers, which are in the University Archives.

I am most indebted at all stages of the conception, research, writing, and rewriting of this book to Jane S. Smith, a wise and trusted colleague in every best sense of the word.

1

Introduction: toward a literature of Chicago

We struck the home-trail now, and in a few hours were in that astonishing Chicago—a city where they are always rubbing the lamp, and fetching up the genii, and contriving and achieving new impossibilities. It is hopeless for the occasional visitor to try to keep up with Chicago—she outgrows his prophecies faster than he can make them. She is always a novelty; for she is never the Chicago you saw when you passed through the last time.

—*Mark Twain*, Life on the Mississippi

THE RIGHT WORDS

George Warrington Steevens was only a few years out of Oxford when the London *Daily Mail* assigned him to tour America and report on the presidential campaign of 1896. In his brief career (he died in 1900 at age thirty of a fever contracted in South Africa during the siege of Ladysmith), Steevens specialized in covering impassioned and often exotic conflicts. His posthumously published account of the Boer War was preceded by other collections of his newspaper correspondence, including *With Kitchener to Khartum*, *With the Conquering Turk*, and *The Tragedy of Dreyfus*. What the young journalist found in America was a conflict of another kind, equally impassioned and exotic. When he gathered his impressions in *The Land of the Dollar* (1897), he depicted the cultural life of the United States as a mass of warring contradictions. Appropriately situated at the center of all this confusion lay Chicago, where he arrived early in October. The city, like the country as

1

Chapter One

a whole, struck him as a collection of startling contrasts. He called
Chicago "queen and guttersnipe of cities, cynosure and cesspool of the
world," and he marveled at its combination of beauty and squalor, parks
and slums, "keen air" and "stench of foul smoke," and "public spirit and
municipal boodle."

Steevens's description is striking in its vigor of style, but it is otherwise hardly exceptional. Since the middle of the nineteenth century,
visitors had spoken of Chicago in terms of its raw vitality and cultural
paradoxes, so that by the late 1890s Steevens's approach was thoroughly conventional.[1] But his remarks are noteworthy in that he
framed his response to Chicago in specifically literary terms. In his
opening paragraph, he began by confessing, "Not if I had a hundred
tongues, every one shouting a different language in a different key,
could I do justice to her splendid chaos," and he ended by asking,
"Where in all the world can words be found for this miracle of paradox
and incongruity?"[2] Steevens was a skilled author who here used hy-
perbole for effect in trying to convey a sense of Chicago's overwhelming
energy by claiming that it left him at a loss for words. In so doing,
however, he was also admitting his inability as a writer to penetrate very
deeply into the subject of Chicago. Indeed, he even questioned whether
the city could be explained in a system of signs and meanings such as a
standard language.

Other observers used a similar technique in describing Chicago, organizing their impressions of the city around their inability to articulate
them. Julian Street, a native Chicagoan who returned as part of a tour of
America that was the basis of his travel book *Abroad at Home* (1914),
raised the same issue of the inadequacy of words in dealing with Chicago when he commented in mock exasperation, "Call Chicago mighty,
monstrous, multifarious, vital, lusty, stupendous, indomitable, intense,
unnatural, aspiring, puissant, preposterous, transcendent—call it what
you like—throw the dictionary at it! It is all that you can do, except to
shoot it with statistics."[3] Steevens and Street were exaggerating, but
the matter they raised was important. What was involved was not simply a question of "words." It was the possible ways in which a person
who analyzed experience and ideas in sentences, paragraphs, and
whole works of imaginative literature might respond to the city and
record this response in a form that was truthful, comprehensible, and
aesthetically appealing. When Steevens wondered what words could be
found, he was considering how he might know Chicago and communicate his knowledge. What words, carefully chosen, would explain Chicago and his reaction to it?

The two tourists were articulating better than they knew the central
artistic issue of Chicago literature of the late nineteenth and early twentieth centuries. This issue is the clash of aesthetic forms and ideals with

2

the modern urban industrial environment. Much of the best and most important literature of Chicago—that is, the literature which attempts to describe and analyze the quality of life in the city in thoughtful depth—is the work that reflects the difficulties authors encountered as imaginative artists writing about Chicago. They were trying to use words to encompass a city which strained their aesthetic vocabulary, a vocabulary which included inherited forms and conventions that were based on assumptions about literary art and social reality that were perhaps no longer relevant. The challenge which Chicago raised to the literary imagination was to find modes of artistic control that would make it possible to write about the city in a way that revealed its essential nature.

What was happening in Chicago was happening everywhere urbanization occurred, and Chicago literature is one part of the larger intellectual and aesthetic response to the rise of the industrial city. Chicago writing is especially interesting, however, because it reveals so starkly the problems writers faced and the solutions they found in creating a literature of modern urban life. Chicago's growth was so rapid that the new city seemed foreign even to those writers who spent a great deal more of their lives and their intellectual and emotional substance in Chicago than did Steevens or Street. In a certain sense, all of those who wrote about it were tourists. Fascinated with this "foreign" place that did not seem to speak in terms they understood, they were still so struck with its significance that they tried to learn its language and read it, so that they could translate its meaning into their words and those of their audience. This audience was a broad group of middle-class readers who were well aware of Chicago and other cities like it and eager to interpret their significance—or have someone they trusted do it for them.[4]

Those who wrote about Chicago included several figures—such as Hamlin Garland, Theodore Dreiser, Henry Blake Fuller, Robert Herrick, Frank Norris, Carl Sandburg, Sherwood Anderson, and Willa Cather—who were central to the development of American literature. They formed no unified school, but they all saw Chicago as a place of primary cultural consequence, a new kind of capital of American civilization (for better and for worse) born out of the heartland of the continent and the Industrial Revolution. As a phenomenon of such broad importance, Chicago seemed to them to demand treatment by those concerned with the future of art and society, and they believed that those who treated it masterfully would be the leading writers of the day.

PROMISE AND PROBLEMS

From the late nineteenth century into the first decades of the twentieth, several programmatic statements appeared that reveal the enthusiasm writers and critics felt for Chicago as a promising literary subject. These statements are especially important because they also disclose some of the problems all authors, enthusiastic or not, faced in finding the right "words" with which to write about the city. In 1892, for example, Stanley Waterloo, one of Chicago's several novelist-journalists, wrote an angry letter to the *Dial,* the impressive national literary and cultural journal published in Chicago.[5] Waterloo criticized midwestern book reviewers for fawning on writers from the East and ignoring the innovations of new and better local talents. In his remarks, Waterloo was continuing the call for the support of a local literature of the region that was sounded earlier in such pronouncements as Garland's *Crumbling Idols* of 1884 and Edward Eggleston's 1871 preface to *The Hoosier Schoolmaster.* Eggleston had complained that the life of New Englanders dominated American literature, "while our life, not less interesting, not less romantic, and certainly not less filled with humorous and grotesque material, had no place in literature. It was as though we were shut out of good society." He added that even western writers generally "did not dare speak of the West otherwise than as the unreal world to which Cooper's lively imagination had given birth."[6]

Waterloo, whose interests were more specifically urban, also argued for the literary significance of what he called the "great West" for American letters: "Those who have shorn away forests, and built railroads and huge cities, have had their hopes, their aims, their consciences, their passions, their temptations, and their loves; and the story of them is worth the telling." He pointed out also that this story was something qualitatively new, not "reflected or imitative," and that it would require a new form of telling. Waterloo expressed a contempt for older, "eastern" forms, which he felt were effete and contrived. The story of the West would "not be told in the soft, trig sentences of some distant essayist or laboring sonnet-writer," he explained, "but in a style adapted to the prospect and theme; and the relators will be of those born to the purple of the region." He admitted that the result "may be sometimes crude," but he stated that it would be "interesting." To make his case further, Waterloo cited both foreign and national literary precedents: "So crude but interesting were the Norsemen's Sagas. So the force of the ragged-versed Whitman is felt in its reckless naturalness. In this new story is the swing of manhood."[7]

In Waterloo's view, Chicago was a place of unprecedented energy, and it demanded an energetic literature equal to it. The measure of the quality of any literary form that dealt with Chicago would be how successfully its own force compared to that of its subject, and the truthfulness of the form was of greater concern than its beauty. Over two decades later, Sherwood Anderson made a similar claim in his essay,

"An Apology for Crudity," in which he berated American writers for praising "writers of the old world and the beauty and subtlety of the work they do," while "the roaring city" lay before them. Anderson argued that the most important subject for the American writer was the impact of industrialism, "and industrialism is not lovely." Beauty and subtlety might come to American life and literature in time, but for the moment American writers must face the reality around them.[8]

There were few assertions of this kind so striking as those made on several occasions by Theodore Dreiser, and none is so extraordinary as his uncontrolled tribute to Chicago at the beginning of *The Titan* (1914). Dreiser described the Chicago he saw as a boy some thirty years earlier, and he tried to recapture the excitement he later felt as an aspiring writer in the city. "To whom may the laurels as laureate of this Florence of the West yet fall?" he asked, doubtless assuming that in the act of writing he was placing the wreath on his own brow. He continued:

This singing flame of a city, this all America, this poet in chaps and buckskin, this rude, raw Titan, this Burns of a city! By its shimmering lake it lay, a king of shreds and patches, a maundering yokel with an epic in its mouth, a tramp, a hobo among cities, with the grip of Caesar in its mind, the dramatic force of Euripides in its soul. A very bard of a city this, singing of high deeds and high hopes, its heavy brogans buried deep in the mire of circumstance.

"Take Athens, oh, Greece!" Dreiser exclaimed. "Italy, do you keep Rome!" Chicago was nothing less than "the Babylon, the Troy, the Nineveh of a younger day," where "came the gaping West and the hopeful East to see. Here hungry men, raw from the shops and fields, idyls and romances in their minds, builded them an empire crying glory in the mud." Far from expressing any fears that Chicago was a difficult subject, Dreiser declared in this one reckless sweep that no other subject could be so promising. His allusion to Florence revealed his often-expressed belief that the rise of Chicago signaled a rebirth in arts and letters equal to that in fifteenth-century Italy.[9]

These passages reveal in various ways a strain of encomiastic boosterism which was encouraging to a writer's spirits but inadequate as a practical aesthetic program. They imply that, if one somehow opens his sensibility to the driving spirit of the region, *there* is a literary field as immense as the lake and prairie, from which an appropriate literature will spring like wildflowers. "The prairies lead to general conceptions," Garland asserted in *Crumbling Idols*, assuming that these conceptions would be unmistakably of the area and would readily find an appropriate form.[10] This boosterism was not limited to Chicago writers. In

1903, William Dean Howells, always eager to promote new native talent, wrote in the *North American Review* that Chicago authors of the day had captured the special democratic spirit that "was the faith of New England" and now was "the life of the West" and "the Western voice in our literary art." Howells spoke of "the atmospheric democracy, the ambient equality" of the region that somehow naturally found its way into Chicago literature.[11] But he never defined his terms very well, and he included a very broad range of writers, some of whom were sometimes openly critical of the social and aesthetic consequences of democracy, not to mention of Chicago itself.

Waterloo, Anderson, and Dreiser agreed that Chicago writing would be crude, but beyond that their descriptions usually indicated what it would *not* be more than what it would. Warner Berthoff notes that this kind of negative definition appears often when one looks for a coherent program among American literary realists, who were considerably surer of what they opposed than of what they favored.[12] Waterloo and Dreiser in particular confounded matters further by using the very kind of language they appeared to be attacking. Waterloo talked about "the Great West" in heroic generalities (e.g., "Those who have shorn away forests," "the purple of the region") and Homeric phrasing ("ragged-versed Whitman") that seem inappropriate to their subject and their literary ideology. Dreiser, like Steevens and Street, did not describe the city at the beginning of *The Titan* so much as, to paraphrase Street, hurl words at it in desperation, using terms whose meaning is unclear ("singing flame," "all America") or which are jarring in relation to one another ("Titan," "Burns," "king of shreds and patches," "Caesar," "Euripides"). He tried to hold all these together with turns of phrase and images ("laurels as laureate," a "bard" with "heavy brogans buried in the mire of circumstance," "maundering yokel with an epic in its mouth") that are ludicrous even by the standards of Dreiser at his worst. Trying to penetrate the sources of Chicago's undeniable energy and capture that energy in his writing, Dreiser here only flailed away. And, for all his commitment to a new literature of urban life, he talked of Chicago within a conventional literary framework of idylls and romances, evoking writers of distant times and cultures and, with his apostrophes and inverted word order, speaking in a stilted and stylized prose.[13] His paragraph records a losing struggle with the unrealized possibilities of his subject.

CREATIVE SOLUTIONS

The major achievement of those who wrote most effectively about Chicago—and Dreiser is certainly included—is that they did develop creative solutions to the stylistic and thematic problems they faced. They did so by confronting these problems directly in their effort to portray urban experience realistically. The most interesting Chicago works in the evolution of American and modern literature are those which, as Steevens and Street did in their minor way, attempted to find aesthetic terms in which to analyze life in Chicago and which, in this attempt, raised larger social issues. These works went well beyond the efforts of the two travelers in trying not only to capture the city's energy, its freshness, its crudity, and its power, but also to question the sources and implications of these qualities and the disruptions, both good and bad, that the rise of the city had caused in society and in the lives of individuals. To accomplish all this, Chicago writers used two major artistic strategies that are closely related and both of which are evident in otherwise very different texts. Both involved turning a problem into an advantage by making it a major thematic or formal device, as Steevens did when he discussed Chicago in terms of the impossibility of talking about it.

The first strategy was to dramatize the apparent opposition between life in Chicago and the practice and appreciation of traditional art forms. In many of the serious novels of the period between the mid-1880s and World War I, an important character—often the protagonist—is an artist of some sort (this category encompasses painters, musicians, journalists, architects, and aesthetes, as well as poets and novelists, and it includes the untalented along with the gifted)—and the proper place of art and the artist is a central topic. In most books, both the artist and his or her work fare badly. Even in those cases where he or she does well, the novels still reveal that, while the authors may have believed that Chicago was a place of artistic opportunity and a rich subject for literary art, they still felt threatened by this city which seemed inimical or, perhaps worse, indifferent to them, and that Chicago was a dispiriting place to live.

Instead of simply withdrawing from the field, however, these writers directed their efforts to explaining why—for the sake of the society that appeared to exclude them—they, their work, and the ideals they advocated could not be ignored. They commonly made their case by allying their activity as artists with humane values which they thought were endangered in Chicago. It is remarkable how the same terms come up repeatedly through the permutations of plot and character in Chicago writing, and in books whose final assessments of the situation differ. Chicago fiction of the late nineteenth and early twentieth centuries often reads like a debate on its own place in the world it explores.

This debate examines a good deal more than the place of art. Novel after novel of the period, and some important works of nonfiction, characterize Chicago as a place where choice and necessity have drawn people from all over Europe and America. These people—artists or not—struggle to find a meaningful way to live in this bewildering new metropolis where there are few useful precedents to guide the individual in formulating a set of personal values. Characters in Chicago fiction are uneasily preoccupied with their careers, their progress toward some undefinable goal in Chicago's undefined future. The idea of career is tied to a public notion of success, of which the best yardstick is money, and power and prestige based on money. Yet this form of measurement offers no final satisfaction, and the human cost of getting it is too high. The system in which the money is made often is exciting, but it consumes the individual and widens the divisions between all people in the city, even members of the same family. In the discussion of this struggle in Chicago literature, "art" is a vague but loaded term, a loose set of ideals that call into question Chicago's materialistic spirit. Art becomes associated with values such as freedom, imagination, and love, and with a moral order based on timeless principles of truth and right rather than the rule of the dollar. The discussion of art thus becomes a way of dealing with the issue of how one should and could conduct one's life in the city.

Part One of this book examines in separate chapters three major aspects of this discussion of art and life in Chicago. It begins by showing how Jane Addams explained perhaps better than anyone else the vital importance of art in the city. It then analyzes several leading examples of Chicago fiction. This fiction includes most notably works by Henry Blake Fuller and Robert Herrick, in which the regrettably sad state of art and the artist indicates much deeper social distress. The third chapter studies a group of female characters who are of special relevance because they appear as representatives of art and high culture in the city. Of particular interest is a small number of female artists in Chicago fiction, including Dreiser's Carrie Meeber and Willa Cather's Thea Kronborg, whose careers differ in significant ways from those of their male counterparts. Part One concludes with an analysis of the works of three novelists—Norris, Anderson, and Dreiser—who wrote books which portray the businessman, of all people, as the leading artist in Chicago. These novels were the boldest attempt in Chicago fiction to reconcile the apparent opposition between the commercial culture of the city and humanistic values associated directly with art.

Most serious Chicago fiction that deals directly with the place of art in the modern city is not optimistic. Even the more enthusiastic Chicago realists were finally skeptical of the ability of modern urban life to nurture the human soul, and they depicted the failure of the promise which the vitality of the urban setting seemed to hold. In Chicago novels, as in much urban writing of the period, disappointments await everywhere: competition and a sense of isolation qualify the prospect of urban community, the hoped-for liberation from the limiting conditions of life elsewhere encounters new kinds of entrapment, and the apparently endless variety of urban experience soon becomes routine and tedious. The theme of art was a way to dramatize these conditions as a means of explaining the nature of a widespread social distress, but it did not offer any immediate hope of relief.

The second major strategy of writers struggling with the enormity of the metropolis was to take the most overwhelming physical features in Chicago and deal with the city by converting these features, in all their richness, to literary tools. If a writer could not find the right words with which to speak of Chicago as a whole, he might still seize upon those elements of the cityscape that struck his imagination as most salient and expressive, and then use them to analyze the city in its entirety. Those who wrote about Chicago most successfully used such elements to develop a striking group of images, symbols, and dramatic motifs in their writings. These formal devices together constitute an aesthetic vocabulary particularly suited to Chicago that reveals and explains the city in ways that are imaginatively arresting and convincing.

In itself this literary approach is not particularly innovative. The imaginative apprehension of almost anything centers around the selection and interpretation of its salient features. As John F. Kasson notes, this method is common in the prose of those who wrote of the new industrial conditions of the nineteenth century. "Describing the 'facts' of the city," Kasson explains, "they chose those facts most expressive and often shaped them for greatest emotional impact in the effort to comprehend and convey a situation at once 'immediate and all but unimaginable.'"[14] But the effectiveness of this strategy in the literature of Chicago at the turn of the century is noteworthy because of the magnitude of the urban elements involved. Chicago writers located on three indisputably major "facts" in particular: the city's railroads, its large buildings, and its stockyards. These were not the only facts that were observed and depicted, of course, but they were the most important and expressive. In their handling of these features Chicago writers came as close as they ever did to a mastery of the city as subject. Part Two of this book devotes a separate chapter to the treatment of each of them.

The preeminence of these three elements in Chicago writing is hardly surprising. Chicago owed its growth and economic well-being to the development of the interstate railroad network and a city-wide intraurban system, and the extent of the city's dependence on the railroad was highly visible. Likewise, Chicago was the site of major technological innovations that made large-scale commercial building, most notably the skyscraper, a practical reality. With the possible exception of the modern buildings in New York, Chicago's new construction projects were the most impressive in the world. Finally, the stockyards had perhaps the closest identification with Chicago of any feature in the city. Though the slaughtering operations have long since vanished, there are still many people for whom "Chicago" and "the stockyards" are synonymous.

The historical importance of the railroad, Chicago architecture, and the stockyards explains why they were described or referred to in many ways in Chicago writing, but the fact that they often appeared is of less note than the matter of their significance from the writer's point of view. The physical qualities of these three elements were promising to the literary imagination. Above all, each provided a solution to the problem of comprehending the sprawling and chaotic city, since each contained several of the important characteristics of Chicago in a more condensed and apparently rational form than did the city as a whole. The tall office buildings and the stockyards, for example, were "cities" in themselves, complicated concentrations of carefully organized yet also random activity that reflected the life of the entire town. All three dramatically displayed the idea of the City of Chicago as center of power. The locomotive, as Leo Marx has pointed out, was the major power symbol of the nineteenth century. The large building, and the skyscraper in particular, demonstrated the triumph of man's ambition over gravity and the possible transformation of his role as mediator between the earth and the heavens. And the stockyards were a vast interlocking process that seemed to be capable of feeding the entire world.

Each of these was the result of recent developments not only in machine technology but also in the organization of work. They were manifestations of the new kind of authority that built Chicago and were impressive testimony to industrialism's ability to remake the natural world. In addition, all three marked a scale of enterprise unprecedented before the rise of the late nineteenth-century city. The sheer mileage of tracks, the height of the new buildings, the acreage of the stockyards, and the capital behind these enterprises involved statistics that only began to suggest the awesome effect of a first-hand experience of any of them.

The train, the large building, and the stockyards also embodied some of the most important abstract characteristics of the city. These characteristics related to movement of both a literal and a figurative kind. In addition to being clusters of human activity, all three were either machines of locomotion or contained within themselves such machines, such as the elevator in the skyscraper and the conveyor in the stock-

10

yards. They created and confirmed the image of Chicago as a place of constant motion. On another level, they were expressions, sometimes ironic ones, of the notion of democratic social mobility.

Finally, and this was particularly important to an artist seeking the right words to capture modern urban experience, the railroad, the large building, and the stockyards each could be seen as the objective counterpart of some basic language pattern of the city. The rhythmic commotion of the train along the track was a monologue of dogged purpose, the upward thrust of the tall buildings was an explosive exclamation of an age of energy, and the bleating of the animals in the stockyards was the voice of Chicago as a modern Babel. Like the city itself, these kinds of expressions were ambiguous, making them all the more useful for the skillful writer. They spoke simultaneously of aspiration and greed, freedom and imprisonment, creation and destruction.

The use of the railroad, commanding architecture, and the stockyards in Chicago writing was an important event in the history of the relationship of the literary imagination with the subject of Chicago. The city demanded attention, and it did so through such urban realities as trains, tall buildings, and slaughterhouses. These features could not be overlooked any more than the city itself because as both fact and symbol they *were* the city. An individual did not decide to write about Chicago and then inevitably discuss, say, the stockyards; rather, he or she chose to write about contemporary Chicago *because* of the stockyards. Chicago's railroads, its large buildings, and its stockyards reshaped their world so thoroughly that they forced the imaginative writer to look upon life in new ways, but their expressive qualities at the same time offered him a means with which to formulate his perceptions.

The literary works examined here are hardly uniform in their precise choice of theme, their method, or their quality. Those who wrote about Chicago differed in their attitudes toward the city, their definition of certain common terms, and their talent. What unites them is their belief that the starkness with which Chicago revealed the appeal and, to a greater extent, the difficulties of modern urban life made it all the more important and attractive to them as a subject. Many Chicago writers came from the towns and villages of the Middle West and the East, and they were convinced that the future of American civilization, such as it was, rested with the city. Among their criticisms of urban life, there are only a few fond backward glances. The major contributions of two of Chicago's leading literary figures, Edgar Lee Masters's *Spoon River Anthology* (1915) and Sherwood Anderson's *Winesburg, Ohio* (1919), are eloquent but bitter attacks on the small towns of the Midwest—and all small towns—as places of slow and sure physical, intellectual, and spiritual death.

11

To the committed realist in particular, what was so riveting about Chicago was that it seemed somehow to set the norm for reality since it was the result of the major shaping forces of the nineteenth century. The dirtier and uglier it was, and the more alien to conventional notions of beauty it appeared, the more authentic did it seem and the more did it demand acknowledgment by the honest artist. Chicago was, as the common phrase goes, the *real world,* and, like it or not, it could not be ignored. A character in one novel expresses a widely shared attitude when, reflecting on a pleasant extended vacation away from Chicago in rural Wisconsin, she likens her surroundings to "a lovely fairy story." By contrast, "it's so real in Chicago, you know; so brutally real."[15] The action soon returns to the city, where it remains.

To a large extent, writers were trying to do contradictory things in talking about Chicago, and sometimes the faults of their work reflect this. They seemed to be intent primarily on knowing the real world of Chicago and capturing it precisely in their words. That is, they desired to be true to their subject and to submit their talent to its meaning. And yet they were ambitious not only to understand and explain the city, but also somehow to transcend and redeem it with their expressive power, even if only by showing what was wrong with it. They wanted their work to be both of the city and of the imaginative spirit which they felt that the city threatened. Their best writing would thus be a direct confrontation with the real world and an alternative vision of a better one. Finding the right words with which to couple these impulses would take some doing. A Dickens, a Dostoyevsky, or a Joyce might accomplish it, but could a Hamlin Garland or a Henry Blake Fuller?

Part One

The artist
and the city

2

Signs of distress

Democracy in literature . . . wishes to know and to tell the truth,
confident that consolation and delight are there: it does not care to
paint the marvellous and the impossible for the vulgar many, or to
sentimentalize and falsify the actual for the vulgar few. Men are
more like than unlike one another: let us make them know one
another better, that they may all be humbled and strengthened with
a sense of their fraternity. Neither arts, nor letters, nor sciences,
except as they somehow, clearly or obscurely, tend to make the race
better and kinder, are to be regarded as serious interests; they are all
lower than the rudest crafts that feed and house and clothe, for
except they do this office they are idle; and they cannot do this
except from and through the truth.

— *William Dean Howells,* Criticism and Fiction

The deepest problems of modern life derive from the claim of the
individual to preserve the autonomy and individuality of his
existence in the face of overwhelming social forces, of historical
heritage, of external culture, and of the technique of life.

— *Georg Simmel,* "The Metropolis and Mental Life"

THE EXAMPLE OF JANE ADDAMS

It was not a novelist or a poet but Chicago's most prominent social
reformer who best defined the basic terms of the discussion of the
relationship between art and life that was a central concern in Chicago
literature. When twenty-nine-year-old Jane Addams permanently settled in Chicago in September 1889, she brought to the once-elegant but
now commercially subdivided Near West Side home of Charles J. Hull a
combination of liberal reform ideology and a pragmatic willingness to

15

learn about city life. *Twenty Years at Hull-House* (1910), her history of the settlement she founded and memoir of her own life from her girl-hood in the hilly prairie town of Cedarville, Illinois, to her move to Chicago, is one of the most extraordinary personal narratives in American letters. Like Addams's whole public career, it speaks directly to the problem of the demoralization of the individual in the city, recounting with quiet passion the ways in which Addams and her colleagues tried to solve the dilemma of how one might live a worthwhile life in Chicago.

"The social organism has broken down through large districts of our great cities," Addams wrote early in her tenure at Hull-House. Middle-class citizens as well as the poor recognized the troubled conditions of the modern industrial city but could see no way to alter things. This fragmentation and feeling of helplessness were deeply distressing to Addams, for they threatened her cherished belief in the necessity of an organic connection between all parts of society and her conviction that the world could and must be made better. She feared that educated and well-intentioned people like herself, who were the best hope of social reform, "feel a fatal want of harmony between their theory and their lives, a lack of coördination between thought and action."[1] Her use of the word "fatal" points out how serious she thought the problem was.

Addams's main goal was to make real her ideal vision of the city as organic democracy by instilling in those whom Hull-House served—both rich and poor—a belief that through organized social and political action they might create a world in which they would feel a sense of satisfying belonging rather than alienation. She believed that this ideal vision of society as a unified whole, if convincingly communicated to city dwellers so that they felt its value, could at once contribute to the realization of that vision and restore a sense of meaning and purpose to their lives. Unless the individual could find a way to live which helped create a healthy society, each individual's humanity would be reduced by the extent of the failure of the vision, and the body of society would suffer.

Addams's idealism, which was founded in the social ideology most fully enunciated in America by Emerson, was fundamental to Progressive thought. It emphasized the necessity of turning the individual's intuitions of the need for social unity into practical power. The Hull-House settlement struck Addams as the best means by which to translate the "subjective necessity" for social action into a workable project. "The Settlement, then," she remarked, "is an experimental effort to aid in the solution of the social and industrial problems which are engendered by the modern conditions of life in a great city." Hull-House's effectiveness as a solution to urban problems depended on its ability to benefit all citizens in Chicago. Addams pointed out that the settlement house as a social force "insists that these problems are not confined to any one portion of a city."[2] The activities that Hull-House offered were intended to suggest to everyone who came in touch with this institution how one might best live in Chicago.

Hull-House itself expanded organically. By 1907 there were thirteen buildings interconnected over a full city block, including a coffeehouse, a gymnasium, and a residence for working women. From the beginning, the activities of the settlement revealed the great extent to which Addams and her associates believed that art, loosely defined, was an essential means of improving and redeeming the quality of life in the city. Hull-House residents were concerned with juvenile courts, public health, and union organizing, but also with the settlement's theaters, art exhibitions, craft studios, music school, and Shakespeare and Dante clubs. Addams saw no division between these kinds of cultural activities and apparently more direct attempts to establish social justice and improve living conditions in Chicago.

From the very first days of Hull-House, the settlement stressed the importance of literature and the fine arts. In the weeks after the opening of the settlement, Addams's close associate Ellen Gates Starr led a group reading of George Eliot's *Romola*—in Italian translation—for Italian immigrants in the neighborhood, and she showed slides of Florentine painting. An elderly woman who had lived at Brook Farm read from Hawthorne; and a young volunteer named Jenny Dow started a boys' club, enchanting its members with stories of Prince Roland. In addition to such readings and the establishment of several literary clubs for adults, Hull-House later hosted writers, sponsored lectures and discussions of art, and offered art history courses. Behind all these activities lay the conviction that the experience of art was one of the best ways in which to overcome isolation and the devaluation of the self in the modern city. Acquaintance with the richest art forms, Addams felt, would nurture the individual's sense of society as an organic whole of which each person was an important part. Addams's definition of great art included above all those forms which, in the process of their creation or in their effect on an audience, made society more humane.[3]

Hull-House encouraged immigrants to rediscover the arts and traditions of their native countries with which they had lost touch in the struggle of earning enough to eat and the effort to become assimilated into American life. In Addams's opinion, the revival of ethnic arts and customs was important to both immigrants and their American-born children, helping recover in the former "something of that poetry and romance which they had long since resigned with other good things," and instilling in the latter "a respect for the older cultivation, and not quite so much assurance that the new was the best."[4] In the process, the generations that the city's economic pressures and gaudy attractions had driven apart would be drawn back together.

Addams was particularly sensitive to the appeal of the theater. Hull-House undertook all sorts of dramatic projects, from Thanksgiving pageants to productions of Sophocles and Ibsen, all in the belief that the drama "shall express for us that which we have not been able to formulate for ourselves, that it shall warm us with a sense of companionship with the experiences of others." Addams asked, "Does not every genuine drama present our relations to each other and to the world in which we find ourselves in such wise as may fortify us to the end of the journey?"[5] The "companionship" of the theater, both as a group experience for actors and audience and as an opportunity for the individual to see that others shared his hopes and fears, thus was a particularly effective counterforce to a feeling of isolation.

On one extraordinary occasion, Addams tried to demonstrate quite specifically how important literature could be in understanding and resolving social conflict. In 1894 she prepared a talk on the Pullman Strike which she read before several audiences, including the Chicago Woman's Club and the Twentieth Century Club of Boston. In "A Modern Lear" she invoked Shakespearean tragedy to help explain the deadlock between George M. Pullman's enforced paternalism and the rebellious response of his apparently ungrateful employees. "If we may take the dictatorial relation of Lear to Cordelia as a typical and most dramatic example of the distinctively family tragedy," she suggested, "one will asserting its authority through all the entanglement of wounded affection, and insisting upon its selfish ends at all costs, may we not consider the absolute authority of this employer over his town as a typical and most dramatic example of the industrial tragedy?"

In conceiving of society as a family like Lear's, and by pointing out with Shakespeare's help that the conflicts of the strike went beyond the economics of industrialization, Addams hoped to share an insight into the situation that would help avert the catastrophes that destroyed Lear's family and his kingdom. At the end of her talk, she asserted, "If only a few families of the English speaking race had profited by the dramatic failure of Lear, much heart-breaking and domestic friction might have been spared." She then asked, "Is it too much to hope that some of us will carefully consider this modern tragedy, if perchance it may contain a warning for the troublous times in which we live?"[6]

Addams was aware, nevertheless, of another kind of problem that Chicago novelists also explored. While her faith in the ability of great literature to express ideals and make them live in society was unsurpassed, she feared that art—and literature in particular—might in some cases contribute to the social divisions she saw about her. Art could obscure as well as reinforce the individual's perception of society as a unified whole. In *The Spirit of Youth and the City Streets* (1909), her eloquent and persuasive study of children in the city, she condemned the vaudeville theater and the burlesque shows, which, she believed, dangerously captivated the imaginations of adolescents with their false glitter and cheap sensuality.

Addams believed that even fine art could become too much of a refuge, insulating the individual from the realities of the world around him and undermining his sense of moral obligation to others. She was particularly concerned with the way individuals of her privileged background might use art to hide from the duties of a useful life. This problem was one she had wrestled with before founding Hull-House. During the eight years between the time she finished her work at Rockford College in 1881 and she moved into Hull-House, she felt herself "absolutely at sea so far as any moral purpose was concerned, clinging only to the desire to live in a really living world and refusing to be content with a shadowy intellectual or aesthetic reflection of it."[7] In other words, she feared that she was substituting reading about life for living, and making believe she was alive by inhabiting a world whose only reality was aesthetic.

In a noted passage in *Twenty Years at Hull-House*, she made this last point vividly. In the section in which she discussed how she was affected by viewing the terrible slum conditions of London's East End in 1883, she explained that she "had been sharply and painfully reminded" of Thomas DeQuincey's "The Vision of Sudden Death," the second section of his essay, "The English Mail-Coach." In this section, DeQuincey recalled a harrowing experience that befell him one August night as he was riding on the mail coach through rural England. He was shocked to note suddenly that the coachman was asleep as the conveyance was hurtling down the wrong side of the road toward a "frail reedy gig" carrying two young lovers. DeQuincey gathered his wits sufficiently to shout out a warning, and the lovers barely escaped; but for a few precious moments he was unable to warn them because, in Addams's summary of the incident, "his mind [was] hopelessly entangled in an endeavor to recall the exact lines from the *Iliad* which describe the great cry with which Achilles alarmed all Asia militant."

Addams saw a significant lesson in the fact that DeQuincey's literary learning had temporarily prevented him from acting decisively when a much more minor deed of heroism than was asked of Achilles was required of him. Almost thirty years after she visited East London, there was still some bitterness in her application of the DeQuincey essay to her own situation and that of others like her who were "lumbering our minds with literature that only served to cloud the really vital situation spread before our eyes." Addams saw as preposterous and reprehensible the condition of literary intellectuals of her time, whose situation was made all the worse by the fact that their recognition of the problem did not help them solve it. Citing Matthew Arnold, she continued, "In my disgust it all appeared a hateful, vicious circle which even the apostles of culture themselves admitted, for had not one of the greatest among the moderns said that 'conduct, and not culture is three fourths of human life.'"[8]

Addams was not, of course, condemning the literary culture in which she placed so much hope, but only criticizing the way individuals used art to distance themselves from others. In so doing, they became passive spectators of experience, "readers" of life. Art was to be appreciated in itself, but also as a tool of social action essential to rehabilitating the broken-down social organism. In arguing for the importance of good theater in *The Spirit of Youth and the City Streets*, Addams asked rhetorically,

After all, what is the function of art but to preserve in permanent and beautiful form those emotions and solaces which cheer life and make it kindlier, more heroic and easier to comprehend; which lift the mind of the worker from the harshness and loneliness of his task, and, by connecting him with what has gone before, free him from a sense of isolation and hardship?[9]

Here she specifically repeated Howells's call for a democratic literature that tells the truth and makes the race somehow better.

In several ways, then, Jane Addams and Hull-House responded to the social fragmentation of the modern city with the special healing powers of art. This "art" took many forms in Addams's eyes, but it always had a visionary power capable of making the individual life meaningful by attaching it to the broader experience of the human community of the city and beyond. Both the creation and the experience of such art were important *social* as well as aesthetic activities that made both the individual and the community stronger. In the spirit of Emerson and Whitman and Howells, Addams believed that the high calling of the artist was to improve society, and it was her fond hope that even the slenderest acquaintance with art by the urban citizen, rich or poor, could help meet the considerable challenge posed by the modern city to humanity.

THE RUNAWAY PROCESSION

The relation between art and life is at the center of one of the earliest novels about modern Chicago, the Reverend E. P. Roe's *Barriers*

Burned Away (1872), which is also one of the most popular books ever written about Chicago. According to James D. Hart, an edition of 100,000 copies of the book published ten years after the original printing immediately sold out.[10] Roe's success encouraged him to trade the pulpit for the pen, and he went on to author a series of similar romances of faith and love that also found a wide audience. The faith and love in *Barriers Burned Away* are primarily those of hero Dennis Fleet, a moral Christian and democratic American, who falls in love with the beautiful Christine Ludolph even though she is an atheist and a coldly autocratic German.

Both Dennis and Christine are aspiring artists, but his paintings are clearly superior to hers since they are more original and have an uplifting emotional effect on the viewer that her work lacks. His art obviously reflects his piety and his sincerity, while hers betrays her cynicism and arrogance. Given her attitude toward God and man, Roe observes, "high, true art was beyond her reach." Realizing this, she hates Dennis and gets revenge by toying with his love for her. Then the Great Chicago Fire happily resolves everything. Dennis rescues Christine, and they take refuge with other survivors on the lakefront, where all are equal. In one grand conversion experience, she accepts God, America, and Dennis, at the same time renouncing the false beliefs that kept the two lovers apart. She tells Dennis, "Every barrier is burned away."[11]

Most Chicago realists of the turn of the century did not concur in Roe's belief that great art and Christian democratic ideals went naturally together, and that both would prevail in Chicago. Rather, they shared Jane Addams's view of the troubled state of urban society without expressing much of her hope. They observed as she did that the social organism had broken down in the city, and in their work they concentrated mainly on troubled middle-class people like themselves whose personal dissatisfactions were profound. They often expressed a belief in the humanizing qualities of art, but they did not feel that the traditional forms that Addams cherished were an effective counterforce to the divisive and dehumanizing materialism of the city.

The most skillful chronicler of this general condition was Henry Blake Fuller. Fuller was a rarity among Chicago novelists—and Chicago citizens—of the turn of the century in that he was a native of the city. He could trace his ancestry to the *Mayflower,* but more important to him were his ties to the community of pre-fire Chicago, where he was born in 1857. Unlike Roe, who saw regeneration in the fire, Fuller was a sensitive and disapproving witness to the city's rapid growth and radical transformation. His literary career was a peculiar combination of things. He despised Chicago, but he remained there virtually his entire life, observing contemporary society with a sharp eye while living alone and dreaming of other times and places. His work of the 1890s, which

was his best period, includes some of the outstanding escapist ro-
mances of the day, *The Chevalier of Pensieri-Vani* (1890) and *The
Chatelaine of La Trinité* (1892), as well as pioneering urban realism.
He drew the praise of both Charles Eliot Norton and Theodore
Dreiser.[12]

Fuller's deservedly best-known books are his two early Chicago novels, *The Cliff-Dwellers* (1893) and *With the Procession* (1895). Both are
intricately plotted and feature several major characters, almost all of
whom are drawn from the middle and upper-middle classes. In one way
or another, almost every individual in these books is pushing to get
ahead, usually at the cost of the literal and figurative bankruptcy of his
or her public and private life. Fuller's eye for the ridiculous in the
strivings of his characters provides many moments of social comedy,
but the overall tone of both novels is darkly ironic as he assesses the
costs of Chicago's commercial culture in personal terms. Those figures
who are not destroyed by some sudden outburst of violence or by a
gradual series of smaller setbacks are still in varying states of nervous
anxiety throughout the books, and they eventually settle sadly into lives
of diminished expectations. If they are newcomers to Chicago, they
soon no longer have the kind of hopes that brought them to the city in
the first place; if they are the "old settlers" with whom Fuller identified,
they miss the good old days. Those few who do succeed socially and
financially are only better off if they do not question the value of their
success and what compromises were made in attaining it.

Fuller, like many of his contemporaries, attributed this fragmentation, unrest, and depression to Chicago's worship of wealth. In one of
the most frequently cited passages in Chicago fiction, Fuller suspends
the major action of *With the Procession* to take the reader into a meeting
of a civic-minded group suitably named the Consolation Club, whose
members gather to discuss "the affairs of a vast and sudden munici-
pality." One member explains that by the 1890s the simple hopes that
lay behind the founding of Chicago have fallen into disarray in an age of
"[c]ontention, bickering, discontent, chronic irritation—a régime of
hair-cloth tempered by finger-nails." The central problem with Chicago, explains a character who works in a settlement like Hull-House, is
its materialism. "This town of ours labors under one peculiar disadvantage:" he claims, "it is the only great city in the world to which all its
citizens have come for the one common, avowed object of making
money." He goes on, "There you have its genesis, its growth, its end and
object; and there are but few of us who are not attending to that object
very strictly." Jane Addams's "sense of the whole" has been lost as every
man pursues his own advancement, forgetting "that the general good is
a different thing from the sum of the individual goods."[13]

Fuller repeatedly discussed the state of the arts in Chicago as a way of criticizing what he believed was wrong with the city. One of the secondary characters in *The Cliff-Dwellers* is a highly successful architect named Atwater, who does not seem to be particularly proud of his work. When he hears people praise the elaborate elevator systems of modern buildings, he complains, "That's all a building is nowadays—one mass of pipes, pulleys, wires, tubes, shafts, chutes, and what not, running through an iron cage of from fourteen to twenty stages." He adds, "Then the artist comes along and is asked to apply the architecture by festooning on a lot of tile, brick, and terra-cotta." Worst of all, the entire enterprise must be subordinated to the idea of a good return on the investment—"And over the whole thing hovers incessantly the demon of Nine-per-cent." Atwater claims that he tells any young architect just starting out, "My dear boy, go in for mining or dredging, or build bridges, or put up railway sheds, if you must; but don't go on believing that architecture nowadays has any great place for the artist."[14] The lofty aims of the visionary designer will be subordinated by business and held hostage to profit.

Fuller's definition of art was not precise, but clearly he saw the artist as one who serves some timeless ideal of beauty above all other ends, and he had little patience with the champions of "crudity." In a civilized society, the patron and public would follow where the artist leads. This does not happen in *The Cliff-Dwellers*. Erastus Brainard, a wealthy banker, treats his son Marcus with contempt partly because he wants to be a painter. Another character is a would-be poet who switches to real-estate speculation. There are strong hints that this is no great loss for literary art, but the transition she makes from one set of career ambitions to another is noteworthy in revealing Fuller's view of the directions the idealism associated with poetry takes in Chicago. In fact, the chief resident "artist" in Fuller's Chicago is a dishonest real estate agent named McDowell. "He was a poet—," Fuller explains sardonically, "as every real-estate man should be." In describing his swampy subdivisions, McDowell "shed upon them the transfiguring light of the imagination, which is so useful and necessary in the environs of Chicago." His view of his land is "not only serious but idealistic."[15]

McDowell's devotion to the art of selling worthless property dismisses the value of traditional cultural forms in Chicago. He tells George Ogden, a newcomer from Massachusetts who is the most fully treated of the many characters in the novel, that Ogden's East has no sense of the essential needs and spirit of a growing city. "It takes more than soldiers' monuments and musical festivals to make a town move," McDowell declares. Ogden's reaction is sharp and immediate, for he realizes that in this rejection of a public-spirited if unsophisticated art that honors the past and brings people together dwells the deepest kind of cynicism about the social compact. Ogden "seemed to see before him the spokesman of a community where prosperity had drugged patriotism into unconsciousness, and where the bare scaffoldings of materialism felt themselves quite independent of the graces and draperies of culture." Individual and group welfare are separated in McDowell's view. The unfortunate results of this outlook are the establishment of an inferior commonality based on the unquestioned pursuit of expansion and the institutionalization of a shallow selfishness incapable of perceiving its own shortcomings.[16]

Fuller's investigation of the opposition between art and life in Chicago is more complicated in *With the Procession*. The novel traces the dissolution of the Marshalls, an "old settler" family that is headed by the unpretentious, unimaginative David Marshall, a wholesale grocer who has made his modest fortune on the principle of serving his customers well. Marshall and his wife are bewildered by their children's eagerness to keep up with the financial, social, and cultural "procession" that is led by the most wealthy and fashion-conscious Chicagoans. His business is ruined by his scheming and overreaching partner Belden, but the greater tragedy that befalls Marshall is that he dies wondering whether anyone in his family understands and loves him, or if they simply have seen him as little more than someone who finances their selfish individual interests.

The meaning of the procession is best explicated by Susan Bates, an exuberant and good-hearted woman who, with her husband, has made her way from humble beginnings to financial and social triumph. The Bateses have a magnificent new mansion in the most prestigious South Side neighborhood, they are prominent figures at the charity galas, and she has worked her way into the leading clubs and the smart society columns. Mrs. Bates brags of her achievements and those of her husband to Jane Marshall, the one child David believes cares for him:

We have fought the fight—a fair field and no favor—and we have come out ahead. And we shall stay there, too; keep up with the procession is my motto, and head it if you can. I do head it, and I feel that I'm where I belong. When I can't foot it with the rest, let me drop by the wayside and the crows have me. But they'll never get me—never! There's ten more good years in me yet; and if we were to slip to the bottom to-morrow, we should work back to the top again before we finished. When I led the grand march at the Charity Ball I was accused of taking a vainglorious part in a vainglorious show. Well, who would look better in such a rôle than I, or who has earned a better right to play it? There, child! ain't that success? ain't that glory? ain't that poetry?[17]

Sue Bates seems to be unaware of the extent she sees society not as a world of culture and gentility but as a jungle where only the fittest survive. Her final words, in which she equates her "success" with "poetry," recall Fuller's description of the real estate speculator McDowell as Chicago's finest poet and reveal again how much he felt the idealism of art was missing in Chicago. Such vainglorious shows as the ball, which reflect the competition of the marketplace, are appropriately the supreme cultural achievement of the city.

Fuller uses Mrs. Bates to condemn the falsity and pretentiousness of such cultural efforts and to point out how they have divided rather than united the community. Mrs. Bates is an accomplished amateur pianist, but she dutifully practices her Grieg and Chopin not out of any special love for music but in order to gain membership in the exclusive Amateur Music Club. She buys books by the yard to have an impressive library she never reads; she attends lectures at the Fortnightly but is more concerned about her bonnet than with the subject of the talk; and she chooses paintings not as an expression of her personal taste but in order to keep her "right up with the times and the people." She tells Jane that she had her husband buy what they believed was a Corot, "for, after all, people of our position would naturally be expected to have a Corot."[18]

The question of *why* one must keep up with the procession is never asked or answered by anyone in the book. Fuller thought that the old ways of Chicago pioneers like the Marshalls were far more appealing than the customs of the present, for in the days before the fire, he believed, Chicago had a genuine community based on affection and respect, not on common allegiance to a destructive notion of progress. In a remarkable scene, Fuller points out how little Mrs. Bates's "cultural" interests satisfy even her. She invites Jane Marshall into a secret chamber of her new mansion where she is more comfortably at home among a few gathered remnants of the Chicago of her youth. Here are the bedstead, the dog-eared books, the wallpaper pattern from her former home, and an antiquated upright piano on which she bangs out "Old Dan Tucker" and other songs from the old days. Her other bedroom is for display; here is where she lives, trying to recapture a world lost in Chicago's rapid growth and her social climbing. The "culture" of the hidden retreat, just like the slang into which she occasionally slips, is decidedly provincial in comparison to the procession she aspires to lead, but it was vital in its day to Chicagoans' sense of themselves as a unified settlement.

Fuller's novel echoes some of the issues also raised in William Dean Howells's fiction, and the similarities and differences between the books set in Fuller's Chicago and those located in Howells's eastern cities are instructive. The Marshalls are a more sophisticated version of the Dryfooses of *A Hazard of New Fortunes* (1890), who, having acquired wealth, find only unhappiness in their move to New York. Just as the elder Marshalls miss their old Chicago home whose neighborhood has been fouled and made unfashionable by urban expansion and blight, the Dryfooses sadly yearn for the handsome Indiana homestead now irrevocably lost to the natural gas rigs that have made them rich. Fuller's David Marshall also shares with the hero of Howells's *The Rise of Silas Lapham* (1885) certain simple virtues (and a shady moral compromise with his partner that haunts him). If he lacks Lapham's social ambitions, his children make up for this, and the Marshalls' plan to build the new house in the "right" neighborhood is as ill-fated as the Laphams'. What Fuller's Chicago significantly lacks, however, is an old "cultured" family like the Coreys in *Silas Lapham,* who represent the stability of Boston as a community. They balance the rising Laphams and offer, despite their own shortcomings, some tested standard of civilized behavior. The "old" settlers of Chicago are not very old, and they, too, are run over by the procession, which sorely needs some intelligent guiding hand.

Fuller discusses art most specifically in *With the Procession,* as he handles the relationship between David and his younger son Truesdale (his older son Roger has gone into the business and has become, even in his father's eyes, noticeably coarsened). Truesdale is a mildly talented dilettante who has dropped out of Yale. At the beginning of the novel he returns from Europe, having exhausted his generous allowance and his father's patience. He is the character most like Fuller himself, who revered European culture and felt peculiarly exiled in Chicago, but the resemblance does not prevent Fuller from treating Truesdale as sarcastically as he does anyone else. Truesdale considers himself "as admirably and flawlessly a cosmopolite," and he tries to keep alive what faint flickers of the higher life he finds in the city. Since Parisian sidewalk cafés are not available in Chicago, he brings the would-be artists he encounters home to discuss their work. There they meet his father, the resident representative of Chicago's business community. "It was like thrusting a lighted candle into a jar of nitrogen," Fuller writes. "The candle went out at once. And never came back."

The problem is that, even to the pragmatic David Marshall, "art" in Truesdale's sense of elegance and beauty is "an inexplicable thing; but more inexplicable still was the fact that any man could be so feeble as to yield himself to such trivial matters in a town where money and general success still stood ready to meet any live, practical fellow half-way—a fellow, that was to say, who knew an opportunity when he saw it." Money, success, and practicality are the only standards Marshall feels such a man needs. Worse, the elder Marshall believes that the arts Truesdale follows have no organic relation to real life, and that a devotion to them reveals some personal weakness.

Truesdale in fact may be a silly poseur, but Fuller is still saddened that David Marshall's senses have been so deadened that he believes that the "desire of beauty" is "not an inborn essential of the normal human being." To Marshall, "Art was not an integral part of the great frame of things; it was a mere surface decoration, and the artist was but for the adornment of the rich man's triumph—in case the rich man were, on his side, so feeble as to need to have his triumph adorned." Marshall never thinks of himself as an artist, but he believes that men like him are the real creative force of Chicago: "He himself had taken hold of practical things at an early age; he had made something out of nothing—a good deal out of nothing; and compared with this act of creation the fabrication of verses or of pictures was a paltry affair, indeed.[19] His opposition of his "creation" to the artist's "fabrication" shows how much more he values his work as essential and real.

Marshall's attitudes, however, have made him a narrow, isolated, and miserable man, cut off from the happier world of his youth and unable to understand or accept Truesdale's ideas since he feels instinctively that they have no important relation to his life. The deeper problem, Fuller implies, is that Marshall is right. The community of old settlers is gone, and Truesdale's notions of society and culture *are* absurd in Chicago. The only "artists" Truesdale can find are pathetic and dreary misfits whom Fuller satirizes, including a "water-colorist with the portfolio of views from rural Missouri" and a "poet with his thin little volume so finely flattened out between the two millstones of journalism and literature. . . ."[20] A dedicated and talented artist would go elsewhere rather than try to worship the muse in Chicago. Fuller believed that the city desperately needed to be civilized, but he was very pessimistic about whether this enormous task could be accomplished.

Fuller also held out little hope for the success of an undertaking such as Hull-House. Jane Marshall is just the kind of lost middle-class soul Addams discusses in *Twenty Years at Hull-House,* and she pursues several projects of the sort which Addams saw as socially reconstructive. She lectures at the Fortnightly and speaks on Russian novelists (Addams was a great admirer of Tolstoy) at Hull-House. When she visits Mrs. Bates, she is trying to raise money for her pet cause, a club room in the downtown area where working women of all classes can buy or bring their lunch without resorting to less refined establishments that cater to men. Jane hopes that they can find refreshment in some variety of aesthetic experience in the club room, since it is to have a small library and musical activities. When the idea is put into practice, however, the fragmentation of the world outside the club penetrates its walls, and Jane's project only reinforces the divisions it aims to heal. The executive stenographer refuses to sit and eat with salesgirls, and the woman who sells gloves on the first floor of a department store does not want to have anything to do with the person who handles bolts and padlocks in the basement. When some of the club's wealthy benefactors show up to view Jane's work, they drive away members with their staring and their air of condescension.

In both *The Cliff-Dwellers* and *With the Procession,* Fuller treated the dilemmas of Chicago's citizens as a serious problem with sobering consequences. By 1901, the year he published *Under the Skylights,* he shaped his assessment of Chicago into social comedy that, at least at first look, is relatively free of the gloom that haunts his first two Chicago novels. At the same time, he concentrated even more on the subject of the place of art in Chicago as a way to discuss life in the city generally.

"The Downfall of Abner Joyce," the novella that opens the volume, is a surprisingly barbed treatment of the career of Fuller's friend, Hamlin Garland. It is also a pointed commentary on all the aspiring artists who came to Chicago from the farms and villages of the Middle West, the kind whom Truesdale Marshall brings home to his father's inhospitable table. The lesson of Abner's adventures is that the city which these zealous pilgrims hope to conquer invariably ends up subduing them and that they give in without much of a struggle. What makes Abner's "downfall" comic rather than tragic is that he lacks real talent for anything but pretension.

Abner is painfully serious. When he first arrives in Chicago he feels that the responsible artist must be political, and he confidently expects that the power of his fiction will make him an influential social leader. Fuller explains that "Abner's intense earnestness had left but little room for the graces;—while he was bent upon being recognised as a 'writer,' yet to be a mere writer and nothing more would not have satisfied him at all." Abner believes that aesthetic issues must be subordinated to social causes: "Here was the world with its many wrongs, with its numberless crying needs; and the thing for the strong young man to do was to help set matters right. This was a simple enough task, were it but approached with courage, zeal, determination."[21]

Abner's first book, *This Weary World,* which sounds very much like Garland's *Main-Travelled Roads* (1891), is a collection of a dozen stories which Fuller describes as "twelve clods of earth gathered, as it were, from the very fields across which he himself, a farmer's boy, had once guided the plough." He settles into a rooming house with others like himself who advocate a plan for readjusting the tax laws that resembles the proposals of Henry George. He also works on his new book, a novel called *The Rod of the Oppressor*, which Fuller says is "as gloomy, strenuous and positive as its predecessor."[22] At the same time he becomes friendly with a group of artists in a studio building called the Warren Block.

In all his insistence on the "verities" (a reference to Garland's championing of "veritism"), Joyce is fiercely uncompromising. But this literary Samson finds his unruly hair trimmed, as he yields to the wiles of the enemy without a real confrontation. He falls in love with and eventually marries a woman whose tastes are much more genteel than his own (Garland himself married the sister of Chicago sculptor Lorado Taft). She and other artist friends introduce him to well-to-do Chicagoans whom he believes are his ideological enemies, but he discovers with some misgivings that he likes them and their style of living. He soon leaves his boarding house. "Mere crudity for its own sake no longer charmed," Fuller comments. A sudden illness forces Abner to spend the night at the home of one of his new friends, and the angry Readjusters disown him. Soon he is dazzled by the "glamour of success and of association with the successful," and his wife is overseeing his writing.

The novella is finally a joke on this mediocre and trivial talent who would throw beanbags at plutocracy. Fuller's summary of Abner's latest project, *The Fumes of the Foundry*, not only makes light of the work itself, but attacks the whole "crudity" school of Chicago literature. Fuller scoffs at the idea forwarded by Waterloo, Dreiser, and Anderson that the city is a center of epic turmoil of a new and imaginatively exciting kind. Abner's book

> *would depict the modern city in the making: the strenuous strugglings of traditionless millions; the rising of new powers, the intrusion of new factors; the hardy scorn of precedent, the decisive trampling upon conventions; the fight under new conditions for new objects and purposes, the plunging forward over a novel road toward some no less novel goal; the general clash of ill-defined, half-formulated forces.*

As for the wealthy whom Abner once condemned, "Indulgence would come with understanding, and reconciliation to repellent ideals and to the men that embodied them might not unnaturally follow."[23] Fuller may have felt that a genteel literary aesthetic was inappropriate to the subject of Chicago, but his arch description of Abner's book shows his even greater disapproval of the imprecise and unreflective celebration of urban energy and the rejection of literary and social precedents.

In "Little O'Grady vs. the Grindstone," the second novella in *Under the Skylights*, Fuller further examined the ineffectuality of the artist in

Chicago. It is an ingeniously plotted tale that follows at a rapid pace the competition between two groups of artists for a commission to decorate a new building erected by the Grindstone National Bank, "a great edifice raised to the greater glory of Six per-cent."[24] Fuller's names for his characters indicate his inability to take them seriously. Little O'Grady is a painter and the leader of the artists who work in the Warren Block. They want to beat out Daffingdon Dill and his cohorts in a similar building called the Temple of Art. Daffingdon lacks ambition and is spurred on by his sweetheart, Virgilia Jeffreys; Virgilia is herself supported by her aunt Eudoxia Pence, who wants to be made a director of the bank. Making matters no simpler, Ignace Prochnow, the emigré leading light of the Warren contingent, is pursuing the affections of the fair Preciosa McNulty, who is torn between her love for him and her desire to find a more socially acceptable beau.

The result of all these machinations is a splendid jumble of the art-money-society connections that are so much more grimly depicted in *The Cliff-Dwellers* and *With the Procession*. The major source of comedy in the story is that neither the bank directors nor the artists can be taken seriously. The businessmen are boors who want their twelve lunettes simply because they feel obligated to adorn their beloved business with some form of decoration. The artists, desperate for any kind of public commission, cannot wait to prostitute themselves for this minor commission on a third-rate bank. They pander to their prospective patrons by offering ideas for murals illustrating such scenes as the Goddess of Finance "Declaring a Quarterly Dividend." O'Grady's shorthand description of another possible lunette belittles the academic style of the murals in turn-of-the-century American buildings, just as in "Abner Joyce" Fuller scorned the "crudity" aesthetic: "Stock-holders summoned by the Genius of Thrift blowing fit to kill on a silver trumpet. Scene takes place in an autumnal grove of oranges and pomegranates—trees loaded down with golden eagles and half-eagles. Marble pavement strewn with fallen coupons."[25]

The artists are fully aware that the businessmen consider them eccentric weaklings. The Warren group calls itself the "Bunnies," a name which befits their place as harmless, mindless pets of society. Virgilia believes that in order to impress the potential clients, her beloved Daffingdon and his allies must overcome their image of impracticality and approach the bankers as forthright businessmen themselves. She advises her swain, "Even if we are artists we mustn't give those hard-headed old fellows any chance to accuse us of wabbling, of shilly-shallying. We must try to be as business-like as they are." But neither group pleases the businessmen, who want the lunettes to celebrate their own achievements as pioneer Chicagoans. The competition becomes protracted. At one point O'Grady barges into a board directors meeting to complain that the bankers have given art little chance, to which a banker angrily responds, "To hell with art! What I wanted to do was advertise my business!"[26] Such is the Chicago view of the proper role of art. In a wild whirl of events at the end of the story, the bank fails, partly because of the scheming of the artists, and there are finally no building and no lunettes. The clear implication is that Chicago is no worse off for the loss of either. The lunettes are the only art the city might support, but such forms would do nothing except display the emptiness of modern urban culture.

"Dr. Gowdy and the Squash," the last and shortest work in *Under the Skylights,* is not as well-told as the first two entries, but it is another entertaining criticism of cultural conditions in Chicago. Dr. Gowdy is a worldly minister eager to spread his message to the thousands of potential listeners outside the walls of his church. Fuller characterizes him as a pompous popularizer of stale ideas. Gowdy is particularly proud of his book *Onward and Upward,* which Fuller cynically describes as being "full of the customary things . . . that get said and believed (said from mere habit and believed from mere inertia), . . . if the world is to keep on hanging together and moving along the exercise of its usual functions." At the center of Gowdy's message is the importance of art. Fuller's condensation of Gowdy's views on the subject ridicules the minister's kind of aesthetic idealism:

> *Dr. Gowdy was very strong on art. Raphael and Phidias were always getting into his pulpit. Truth was beauty, and beauty was truth. He never wearied of maintaining the uplifting quality resident in the Sunday afternoon contemplation of works of painting and sculpture, and nothing, to his mind, was more calculated to ennoble and refine human nature than the practice of art itself.*

Subsequent events expose the vacuousness of Gowdy's pronouncements. His publishers drum the book aggressively, so that copies of it "competed with the novel of adventure on the newsstands, and were tossed into your lap on all the through trains."[27] A copy reaches twenty-four-year-old Jared Stiles of rural Hayesville, Illinois, inspiring this son of the soil to take up the brush and palette. Jared finds further encouragement in the proselytizing efforts of an organization called the Western Art Circuit (which is directly based on a group called the Central Art Association, whose active supporters included Hamlin Garland), whose opinion it is that the lives of the farmers of Illinois would be enriched by creating and viewing art forms that depict their own world. To this end, the Western Art Circuit mounts at the county fair near Jared's home an exhibition of cornfields done by Indiana farmers.

31

Awakened to the aesthetic possibilities of Hayesville, Jared decides that the most accessible subject is the winter squash. In another obvious swipe at the "veritism" of Garland, Fuller has Jared remark, "Some of 'em do grapes and peaches, but round here it's mostly corn and squashes. I guess I'll stick to the facts—that is, to the verities."[28]

Jared spends the winter painting squashes, and he even exhibits one at a church gathering. His curiosity about the art world now aroused, he journeys to Chicago, where he discovers to his great surprise that people are willing to *pay* for paintings. He even finds a study of a squash at an exhibition. Suddenly his amateur interest in painting for its own sake vanishes, and with entrepreneurial ingenuity worthy of Chicago he goes home to paint the biggest squash portrait he has ever undertaken and frames it in weathered fence boards. When he brings his work to exhibit in the city, the directors of the Western Art Circuit frown on his overly literal style, but his work appeals to a wide audience. It is not that his painting is any good, but that it reminds the many city dwellers with rural roots of the life they have left behind in coming to Chicago.

This unexpected turn of events is an ironic affirmation of the soundness of Jane Addams's idea that art forms can serve an important purpose in reassuring newcomers to the city that their native culture is something to be cherished and not abandoned in the effort to succeed in the city. But the value of Jared's work has nothing to do with artistic merit or the expression of some humanizing sentiment beyond its evocation of a nostalgia for a simpler world. And this "art" is quickly subsumed into the service of profit. Hotel managers, hoping to attract trade, exhibit Jared's paintings in their lobbies. Eager to cash in further on Jared's paintings, the promotion-hungry department store of Meyer, Van Horn, and Company commissions Jared to paint a squash that it will place prominently in its windows. The store pays Jared five hundred dollars but advertises that the "masterpiece" by the new artistic sensation is worth ten thousand dollars. What now verifies that the painting is worth seeing is that it costs a lot of money, and so its imaginative appeal as a souvenir of the countryside is displaced by the fascination of its material value. In Chicago, the fact that it is an expensive painting is more important than any other quality.

Gowdy, not knowing that he started all this, attacks this publicity stunt and Jared's paintings, and he soon finds himself hopelessly involved in a complicated series of misunderstandings which eventually jeopardize his standing as a cultural critic. He finally befriends Jared, who at the story's close is booked into a theater where, as he explains, "I put the finishing-touches to a picture every night in full view of the audience, and frame it with my own hands."[29] His salary is three hundred dollars a week. The art and theater in which Addams placed so much hope have here become part of a get-rich-quick stunt in which the public is willingly diddled. Jared succeeds where the "Bunnies" fail, but only because his "art" finds its appropriate niche on the vaudeville stage.

Despite the clever and amusing qualities of *Under the Skylights,* the accumulated cynicism of the three tales suggests that they were born from a similar sense of defeat as that which colors *The Cliff-Dwellers* and *With the Procession.* The "artists" depicted have no conception of their own work that is to be taken seriously, and their "art" is undistinguished to the point of being ludicrous. Fuller did shift his thinking from the earlier novels in that he no longer described the drive for wealth and success as being so dispiriting. The wealthy do-gooders of Abner Joyce's acquaintance and the directors of the Grindstone National Bank are neither evil nor harmful; the ambitious Dr. Gowdy is self-important but innocuous. The city is perhaps more habitable than it is in the earlier books, but there is still little expectation that it will be anything but ugly and uninteresting. It is a city of fools, part of whose foolishness is revealed by their pursuit of worthless notions about art. Chicago is imaginatively and artistically inert. It is incapable of encouraging and sustaining the "higher" life, and there is little hope of escaping the general mediocrity that Fuller saw dwelling amidst all the go-getting.[30]

Several of Fuller's contemporaries who also analyzed Chicago through a discussion of the fate of art in the city drew conclusions that were similarly disturbing, even if they were not precisely the same as Fuller's. Their studies of hopeful Chicago artists were sometimes more fully drawn than those in Fuller's fiction. This is true in the work of Robert Herrick, whose skills as novelist and critic, like Fuller's, have been undervalued. Born in Cambridge, Massachusetts, in 1868 and educated at Harvard before teaching briefly at the Massachusetts Institute of Technology, Herrick was one of the many scholars lured to the new University of Chicago in the early 1890s by its legendary president William Rainey Harper. Between 1897 and the early 1930s, Herrick published almost two dozen novels, some quite controversial because of their candor, in addition to short stories, essays, and criticism. A half-dozen of these novels, particularly those written early in Herrick's career, directly concern Chicago life. Herrick was a difficult man whose general outlook was disapproving. Though he remained at least part-time at the university until 1923 (he published an unflattering roman à clef about the institution, titled *Chimes,* in 1926), Herrick never warmed to Chicago. As much as he disliked the city, however, he felt that living there was vital to his writing and that the social and literary values of the genteel New England in which he was born were out of date. In a letter of 1905, he observed, "My strength is lost as soon as I lift my foot from the prairie. Whatever I do will be done *there*."[31]

Herrick believed that the serious artist was obliged to confront and contribute some understanding of the social ferment of his time. Writing in the *Yale Review* in 1914, he explained that the most pressing challenge facing the novelist of his day was, "Given a highly diversified people in eager strife for individual survival, brought together in a materially rich environment, what are the results psychologically and spiritually?" He concluded, "That is the novelist's exciting problem. What is the consciousness of the new American, individually and in mass, resulting from this? How does he feel his world?"[32]

In his unpublished autobiography, Herrick claimed that throughout his novels he tried to examine the more specific issue of what to do both as novelist and as citizen about Chicago's materialism. The question that animated his Chicago fiction, he observed, was "'what is the greatest form of life?' the triumphs of the world, or the triumphs of the spirit?" This was the most important question to ask, he felt, at a time when these triumphs seemed so mutually exclusive, and when the victories of the spirit on any terms were rare. While he said that he never thought that Chicago was more greedy or corrupt than other cities, and though he claimed that he wrote about the city mainly because it was conveniently "near at hand," he still characterized it as a place where the dilemmas of modernity were especially evident, where the "greedy race for physical satisfactions . . . was staged . . . in an environment that did not relieve it of any of the sordid and mean aspects of the predatory individual game." Herrick went on, "Everybody knew more or less what everybody was after, and there was little of the beauty and old social customs that soften the harsher aspects of a people whose energies are centered upon 'SUCCESS.'"[33]

While Chicago art and culture are important in all of Herrick's novels, the work in which he most fully and directly studies the career of a Chicago artist is *The Common Lot* (1904), the story of a talented architect named Jackson Hart. Hart has the finest professional education and the best opportunities. Schooled in the East and in Paris, he has a job in the prestigious firm of Walker, Post, and Wright. But he desperately wishes to get out of Chicago. He despises the city and "the common lot" of "all the toiling, sweating humanity" who live and work within it. When the book begins he is eagerly awaiting the reading of the will of his wealthy uncle Powers Jackson, assured that it contains a bequest that will give him "freedom for his whole lifetime, freedom to do with himself what he pleased, freedom first of all to leave this dull, dirty city, to flee to those other more sympathetic parts of the earth which he knew so well how to enjoy!" He is not so fortunate, however. His uncle leaves his millions for the construction of an industrial school for the children of working people, and Hart is embittered. His fiancée Helen, who shares the idealism of Jane Addams, urges him to devote his skills to an architecture which will somehow serve those of the common lot, but he shocks her by denying that her high ideas have any relevance in Chicago. "It's only good when it succeeds," he tells her. "It doesn't live unless it can succeed in pleasing people, in making money. I see that now! Chicago has taught me that much in two years."[34]

Although he does not describe what a democratic architecture of the kind Helen advocates might look like, Herrick uses the buildings which Hart does design to attack the selfish values of Chicago which his hero has accepted. When Hart is commissioned to design the school his uncle endowed, he finds himself at a loss for ideas and puts together a stiffly monumental Beaux Arts structure of no distinction. To Herrick, there is no better symbol than this building of what Chicago does to talent and imagination. Living in Chicago has made Hart incapable of expressing through his buildings the very ideals Helen wants him to champion: "The clamor and excitement and gross delight of living had numbed his sense of the fine, the noble, the restrained." The final result is that "he had forgotten Beauty, and been content to live without that constant inner vision of her which deadens bodily hunger and feeds the soul of the artist."[35]

To make matters much worse, Hart's greed and his loss of his ethical bearings in Chicago encourage him to construct shoddy as well as ugly buildings. He gets involved with a crooked contractor and knowingly builds under code. Hart is fully aware of what has happened to him. Herrick writes that his hero "would much prefer a clean, honorable, 'high-class' career. If he could have secured money enough to satisfy his ambitions, to lead the kind of life he liked, without resort to such knavery as this, it would have been much pleasanter." Herrick then adds, "But in one way or another he must make money, and make it more rapidly and more abundantly than he had been doing. That was success." Herrick often sounds very much like Fuller in the scene at the Consolation Club in *With the Procession* in which Truesdale Marshall is told of the single-minded worship of money that suffuses all of Chicago. A character in *The Common Lot* remarks:

Time has been when it meant something of honor for a man to be a member of one of the learned professions. Men were content to take part of their pay in honor and respect from the community. There's

no denying that's all changed now. We measure everything by one
yardstick, and that is money. So the able lawyer and the able doctor
have joined the race with the mob for dollars.[36]

Unfortunately, once Herrick gets his hero deeply into his artistic and
moral dilemma, he himself retreats into mystical melodrama. A hotel
that Hart and the contractor have erected burns and collapses because
of its faulty construction. This tragedy begins to shock Hart back to his
senses. Distraught, he wanders in a daze, finding himself ultimately in
a wooded clearing that contrasts with the dirty urban landscape. The
month is April, and the feeling of regeneration that now overcomes him
in this natural spring setting, so distant in spirit from the deadening city
reminds Hart of an earlier experience. During his student days in Paris
he once put aside his work to wander "idly forth into the germinating
fields, which in some mysterious way had purified his soul of all petty
things."[37] This conventional pastoral retreat is highly improbable, but it
is interesting because it indicates how much Herrick believed that
Hart's creative spirit (and the values which he associates with it) cannot
be reborn in the city proper.

Reawakened, Hart slowly undoes the damage. He eventually returns
the money he made dishonestly and refuses to cover up the contractor's
schemes. Realizing that Helen was right, he goes to ask her forgive-
ness. She has since left him and retreated to an old family homestead in
Vermont, which in its isolation and simplicity stands for the integrity
that America has abandoned in the move from its Vermonts to its Chi-
cagos. Renouncing his former ambitions, Hart dedicates himself to the
love of his wife and child and rejoins his old firm in a humble position.
His work is still a barometer of his moral state. Once he cleanses himself
of the prevailing spirit of the city, his renewal becomes manifest in his
art. At the end of the novel, Herrick states that after "sluggish" years
"there has revived within Hart the creative impulse, that spirit of the
artist, inherent to some extent in all men, which makes the work of their
hands an engrossing joy."[38] He has been entrusted with the design of a
university in a far western state, a repository of culture and learning that
will stand as a bastion of incorruptible and enlightened democracy.

But Herrick's major contribution as a modern writer is that he has
made the case against an eventuality such as this too strong. The ending is a disservice to the seriousness of the rest of the novel, a bit of
wishful thinking tacked on to a pessimistic book which argues that in
Chicago success is a much stronger goddess than beauty or truth. The
pilgrimage of purification to Helen in Vermont must be balanced
against Herrick's own admission that the traditions of genteel New
England Puritanism in which he had been raised were unsuited for a

predominantly urban industrial world. Besides, the university Hart is designing is not to be located in Chicago, but in a presumably unspoiled setting in the West, and thus will not do Chicago much good. Hart's moral rebirth by no means implies that other architects will not build substandard and derivative buildings that reveal the deeper failure of Chicago as a humane settlement.

Instead, Hart's lesson is a personal one which has little bearing on the rest of the city. It would appear that he will never be an influential architect or social figure in Chicago because he will no longer pander to wealth and the cult of success, and there is no other way to become prominent and influential. At the end of the book the Harts disappear from the social scene, from the ranks of those who have the power to effect change but who are, through the very possession of this power, unwilling or even incapable of doing so. The final stage in Hart's redemption is his beatific vision of his wife and child in their home one evening. He has a mystical experience in which he virtually renounces temporal life. Herrick explains: "The woman and the child! These were the ancient, unalterable factors of human life; outside of them the multitudinous desires of men were shifting, trivial, little. . . . For the first time" in Hart's life, "an indifference to all else in the world swept over him in gratitude for these two gifts."[39]

Hart thus finally finds his deepest satisfaction and comfort in knowing that he has the idealistic Helen's approval and that this alone is his life's greatest reward. This calm and hopeful ending does not dismiss the fact that Hart's new faith cannot be translated into effective public action in Chicago. The truest and highest art that might represent this faith, in this case an architecture that somehow embodies democracy and love, will apparently never be seen in Chicago, which will remain a fallen world. The ending is at best a truce, not a victory, for Helen—a shaky truce at that. She has won back her husband, but she has given up her hopes of urban reform.

Will Payne's *Jerry the Dreamer* (1896) offers another variation on the themes developed by Fuller and Herrick. Payne was born in rural Illinois in 1865. He came to Chicago in 1890 and moved up from reporter to financial editor of the *Daily News* by the time he published *Jerry the Dreamer,* and his novel draws on his newspaper experience. His protagonist, Jerry Drew, himself comes to Chicago from Tampico, Illinois, a town that has failed because the railroad bypassed it by five miles. He has worked for the Tampico *Herald,* but he wants to be a writer in Chicago. As Jerry goes over the first hill outside Tampico, he has a gleaming vision of the city that awaits him, "off in the purple clouds, Chicago—life, fame, money, joy!" His plan is to make his literary mark by recording his impressions and selling them for publication, but much the same thing happens to him as happened to many another newcomer. Jerry is "vaguely oppressed and bored instead of elated" by his first encounter with the city. "He had got no impression of anything, but only a distressing feeling of isolation and aimlessness."[40]

Jerry does not give up easily on either his ambitions or his ideals. After some difficulty, he lands a job on the Chicago *Evening Call* and seems to be on his way to the fulfillment of his dream of becoming a successful writer in the city. But his belief that his work will somehow benefit the community is soon undermined. Journalism, he finds, is not an art but a business that serves Chicago's commercial interests and allows no creative freedom. The *Evening Call* office is just another kind of factory which hires workers like him to produce words as quickly and uniformly as possible. "The trouble is the stuff is so ephemeral," Jerry complains, adding, "I'd like to get a little quality of permanency here and there—something that lasted." He ponders whether he has lost something of value in keeping at his job, "whether he were not being changed from a reflecting man to a merely acting one. He knew that he had lost something."[41]

Payne implies that, unless a writer like Jerry uses his talents to attack the financial power structure of Chicago in behalf of the common citizen, his talents will deteriorate. As Herrick argues in *The Common Lot*, Payne seems to believe that a democratic ideology is a necessary basis for sound art. Jerry soon turns his literary skills to what he believes is a good cause when he moonlights on a small radical paper called the *New Era*, which is dedicated to attacking those he is expected to defend when he writes for the *Evening Call*. The crisis comes when Jerry must write an editorial for the *Call* criticizing the *New Era*. After much soul-searching, he does so on the grounds that the terms of his job have always been that he is paid to express other men's ideas. Besides, he sorely needs the money. He writes the editorial "with a sense of bondage and abasement" that he never anticipated he would feel when he first set out for Chicago in pursuit of a literary career.[42]

But Jerry soon decides that the *Evening Call* does not own him entirely, and on his own time he writes an exposé of the corruption in a nearby strike-torn industrial town. His story goes so far as to implicate his own father-in-law, Judge House. House is a businessman of a type that appears often in Chicago fiction, and in urban fiction generally (one thinks of Dickens), an unhappy man whose drive for power and wealth in the city have compromised his principles and destroyed his character. In writing his controversial story, Jerry declares the independence of his talents. In so doing he has burned his bridges to success in Chicago—and he quits the *Call*.

Jerry's professional troubles are compounded by his personal difficulties. He and his wife Georgia become estranged since he has taken her out of her social circle without providing any new friends, and because his work keeps him away from home a great deal. He hopes to win her to his reformist point of view, but he is increasingly haunted by the desperate fear that he can do nothing about the sordidness of the life around him. One after another of his schemes for social betterment fail, including the *New Era*. Jerry is further goaded by the fact that Sidney Bane, a well-to-do and underemployed architect (and Judge House's first choice as his daughter's suitor) calls on Georgia even after her marriage, treating her to some of the luxuries that Jerry is too poor or too busy to provide. Near the end of the novel, the gentle Jerry takes out all the frustration that Chicago has caused by striking Bane brutally, nearly killing him. Jerry has come a long way from his original hopeful vision of Chicago off in the purple clouds.

The ending of Payne's novel has some of the same weaknesses as the conclusion of Herrick's *The Common Lot*, as Payne, too, qualifies his realistic intentions in his desire for at least a relatively happy ending. He brings Jerry and Georgia back together, an unlikely development after all the bad blood that has been spilled. It is hard to believe that she would accept him after his article on her father and his thrashing of Bane. It is also not at all clear what the couple are going to do next, much less what their reconciliation might mean. Payne's artist-hero, badly scarred by his experiences, barely preserves the integrity that was once held captive by his job and his marriage, but he has ransomed it by abandoning his brilliant expectations of the possibilities of life in the city. In no way has he prevailed over his milieu. His only recourse seems to be to save himself from the brutality and corruption of public life by withdrawing from it, taking Georgia with him.

Unfortunately, this means that he must abandon the artistic ambitions that were central to his original idea of his career in the city. He will not let Chicago injure him further, but he will do nothing to affect it. He becomes another member of the scattered army of sad, defeated, urban folk who belong to no coherent community. He talks about getting the *New Era* started again, but this seems very unlikely. In the meantime, he barely supports himself, he explains, by "getting up stuff for a lurid weekly, printed on pink paper and circulated in the country." His creativity and journalistic skills are now devoted to "adding a few grewsome or scandalous details of my own invention" to stories of murder and divorce he clips from the daily papers. The city that has discouraged him, which has defeated him when he tried to use his talents to speak his conscience, is diminished by his silence.[43]

3

City women and urban ambition

The Woman had once been supreme; in France she still seemed potent, not merely as a sentiment, but as a force. Why was she unknown in America? For evidently America was ashamed of her, and she was ashamed of herself, otherwise they would not have strewn fig-leaves so profusely all over her. When she was a true force, she was ignorant of fig-leaves, but the monthly-magazine-made American female had not a feature that would have been recognized by Adam. . . . On one side, at the Louvre and at Chartres, as he knew by the record of the work actually done and still before his eyes, was the highest energy ever known to man, the creator of four-fifths of his noblest art, exercising vastly more attraction over the human mind than all the steam-engines and dynamos ever dreamed of; and yet this energy was unknown to the American mind. An American Virgin would never dare command; an American Venus would never dare exist.

—*Henry Adams*, The Education of Henry Adams

Characters like Helen Hart of *The Common Lot* and Jane Marshall of *With the Procession* are familiar types in Chicago fiction of the turn of the century. Of the realistic Chicago novels clustered around 1900 there are several books in which a woman is the central character, in addition to the many cases in which one takes a major role. These novels fall roughly into two broad types which overlap a good deal. The first includes books which center, as Sidney H. Bremer points out, on family relationships and conflicts between opposing social ethics rather than on the confrontation of the alienated and isolated individual with the hostile city. Most of the authors of these novels were middle-class

40

women, the wives and daughters of successful businessmen. They were generally more familiar with the continuities of domestic life in Chicago than were Chicago's leading male novelists, most of whom came to the city from elsewhere. Their work has been neglected both as a social record and as literary art. They authored children's books, drama, and highly formulaic sentimental novels, but also noteworthy fiction that treats, as Bremer notes, "complex personal experience, the frustrations and challenges of dealing with real families, groups, and social circles."[1]

The second, better-known group of novels is of more direct interest here. These books are usually by male writers or by female authors like Willa Cather who did not live for an extended period in Chicago. They also deal with "complex personal experience" and "real families" and "groups," but the analysis of the changes in human relationships in the new city, rather than social continuities, is a major topic. As is the case with the first group, most of the female characters in these books have traditional domestic roles—daughter, sister, wife, and mother—within the context of home and family. Outside of the home, their interests extend into institutions of genteel culture which are frequently in some way associated with art. These institutions include schools, clubs, museums and galleries, the symphony and the opera, charities, and retail shopping establishments. What happens to these characters, and to their ideas about art, dramatizes their creators' general observations on the nature of urban life.

Chicago authors explored the world of art and genteel culture commonly associated with women usually to illustrate how separate this "female" circle was from the masculine business world. That business is linked with ideas of male strength and worldly wisdom, while culture is tied to notions of feminine weakness and innocence, is less important than that business and culture are divided. This division is indicative of a deeper split that reaches into the most intimate domestic relationships. In ignoring the "artistic" interests of the women, the male characters reject those things that might contribute to a more satisfying private and public life. At the same time, however, the women sometimes retreat into culture as a response to their neglect and boredom. In such cases, the demands they make on their husbands in the name of art and culture become a form of retaliation for their powerlessness. Such gestures are meaningless in terms of creativity or liberation, and they can even be dangerous. As Jane Addams noted in her reference to DeQuincey, the pursuit of the pale aesthetic reflection of life was a potentially fatal trap.

The most intriguing novels which examine the male-female-business-art nexus are those books which study women who possess "male" ambitions of one sort or another. These are women who are determined to have their own careers, or at least to play some active role in public life, even if such a career or role must be combined with a traditional domestic one and must be something distinct from the male pursuits of wealth, power, and success. In such cases, writers found a particularly vivid way to depict the conflicts between different value systems in the city and the pervasiveness of the alterations in individual and social life brought about by urbanization and the commercial spirit.

Aspiring Heroines

Robert Herrick's second novel, *The Gospel of Freedom* (1898), is indebted to Henry James's *The Portrait of a Lady* for the conception of its central character. Its heroine, Adela Anthon, could be described as a Chicago Isabel Archer. Adela is young, beautiful, wealthy, intelligent, and headstrong, and she insists that she must "matter" in some way. She has little sense of social responsibility, but she is determined to spend her life and her fortune in the cause of imagination and freedom.[2] She soon finds two suitable projects, one in art and one in business. She becomes the patron of both an expatriate artist-critic named Simeon Erard (a particularly mean-spirited caricature of Herrick's friend Bernard Berenson) and a Chicago-based inventor, John Wilbur. She believes that in both instances she has discovered a highly creative use for her money, which was so mundanely earned by her father in the brick business, since it frees these two imaginative men to do as they please. But some difficult questions remain in her mind: "Would it free her? Enrich her? Cut through circumstances so that the restless, savage beast in her could grow and possess and be satisfied?"[3] Herrick's choice of language here shows how much Adela wants to go beyond simply helping others to be free; she wishes to liberate herself and become an active force in the male realm of real power.

Adela fears that an opportunity will not come, but then one seems to present itself when Wilbur proposes. She accepts him because she believes that this marriage will not trap her but that, through her influence on her husband, she will have some effect in the world of affairs. In her opinion, Wilbur's "every act" seems to be an indication of "freedom, a large, hopeful way of life, full of plans and the realizing of plans by constant, swift, clever calculation." His activities are imaginatively alive, while the aesthetic interests that preoccupy most women strike her as silly and purposeless. She reflects, "How much more vital *that*, than the dead groping into one's interior self after expression of some faint representation of that inadequate self,—called art!"[4] She hopes to advise her husband so that they can together discover a new and higher mode of living than is available to either of them alone. But the partnership she envisions does not work out. She finds that she is forced like other wives to attend mainly to the family's petty social obligations. She is expected to court the right people and perpetuate the sentimental pieties about home and family which she has rejected. She does not want a domestic life, and she despises the shallowness of all the ladies' clubs to which she belongs. Worst of all, while she still envies her husband's freedom, she is soon outraged by his compromises—so common in Chicago fiction—with big money. He becomes involved with a corrupt businessman whom she finds sordid and vulgar.

Shocked and angered that she has given up "her love of intellectual life, her longing for beauty" to be party to "a common swindle on the public," Adela tells her puzzled husband that they must leave this "prison" of Chicago. Finding Chicago's social and commercial life unredeemable, she no longer desires to participate in it at all. Like Jackson Hart of Herrick's *The Common Lot*, she becomes desperate to escape Chicago's commonness and to live abroad in an atmosphere where she can "think of *other things*" than power and money. The alternative is frightful, she contends: "If this goes on, we shall be like the others, . . . all of them, ploughing the mud for swill."[5]

Erard the aesthete then visits Chicago and fans her discontent. He scorns Chicago's boorishness, asserting that there is "not a building, not a dog-hutch, where there is an idea expressed beyond size, convenience, and either the possession of money or the desire for it."[6] He urges Adela to make a break for freedom while she can, or die disappointed. After telling her husband that their marriage lacks the necessary passion that might hold it together even in spite of her disappointment with Chicago, she finally does follow Erard. She travels to Florence, eventually divorcing Wilbur and scandalizing her family, though she does not become Erard's lover.

Adela soon recognizes that Erard is a selfish pedant, and she realizes that his personality has as many shortcomings as Wilbur's. She now understands what Helen Hart of *The Common Lot* tried to teach her husband, that wealth or beauty not directed toward human betterment is worthless. A Chicago friend committed to social work (he is about to head a school for blacks in the South) tells her that the one constant in her dalliance with both business and art has been self-indulgence. She has demanded more from life than she has given, and the ideal of freedom that she has been chasing is an illusion. The novel ends with Adela pondering how she can find some significant way in which she can combine her ambition to serve the world with the ideals she associates with beauty and intellect. In the last line of the book, Adela declares, "I must learn how to live."

So the *Gospel of Freedom* concludes unresolved, though not because Herrick tacked a false ending on a realistic plot. Having rejected conventional female society, Wilbur's materialism, and Erard's aestheticism, Adela has by no means resolved her dilemma. How can this woman, who has a cultivated sensibility and a hard-earned awareness of herself and the world, now act in a way that exercises her freedom constructively? Herrick gives no direct answer, but he does call for a dedication to those forms of social action that will improve the city. For someone like Jane Addams, social action meant opening a settlement in an industrial district. For Herrick himself, who was less a democrat than his books might suggest, it meant writing progressive novels that helped middle-class readers with their own moral choices by inspiring them to improve the conditions in which they and other men and women lived.

Herrick's later Chicago fiction features several ambitious women like Adela Anthon, most of whom are at sea because life has also disappointed them. Helen Hart, for example, is disturbed by the wastefulness of the wealthy few amid the struggles of the many, and she urges her husband to design buildings that will somehow improve this situation. Helen still acts through the traditional role of wife, however, and not as an independent woman. She is the social conscience of democracy, a good fairy who whispers in one of her husband's ears while the bitch-goddess Success screams in the other.

Herrick's best-known book, *The Memoirs of an American Citizen* (1905), is the fictive autobiography of a millionaire meatpacker named Van Harrington, but it has several important female characters. Most of them believe in ideals and cultural forms that Van thinks are irrelevant in Chicago. Van feels that art is to be taken seriously only if it can work to some business advantage. In a key scene, he grudgingly goes to the opera with his wife. He thinks that this fancy show belongs exclusively to her effete world, which has no importance to his "real" world of the stockyards. But he quickly becomes interested in attending the performance when he realizes how it might help him in the city's banks and boardrooms. He forgets the name of the opera (he calls it "some French thing"), but he remembers how "all the important people of the city" were there. "Even as a matter of business," he shrewdly concludes, "I saw it would be a good thing to know these people. Of course, the social side of life doesn't count directly in making money, but it may count a good deal in getting close to the crowd that knows how to make money." He even revalues his wife in terms of the marketplace: "Perhaps I began to have even a little more pride in Sarah than I had before, seeing how she knew people and counted for something with them. In the game that we were going to play together this social business might come in handily, perhaps."[7]

More important to Herrick's treatment of women and art in the commercial city is that Harrington's rise is overseen by Jane Dround, who is the wife of his boss. Mrs. Dround assumes much more successfully (though secretly) the influential role that Adela Wilbur wanted when she married. Excluded by her sex from business, and impatient with her weak-willed husband's caution in handling his affairs, Mrs. Dround finds excitement in her sponsorship of Van. Theirs is a strange kind of passionate yet sexless affair in which she gives him the financial backing he needs and thrills in his forceful assertion of power.

Mrs. Dround thus escapes wifely passivity, but she is no champion of idealism and reform. She is totally captivated by Van's ambition and by the savage business environment in which he exercises it. This is revealed by her attitudes toward the fine arts, of which she is supposed to be a leading patron. At a key point in the novel, Van explains to her how he can save her husband's tottering business by creating a nationwide marketing system. He takes down an atlas from the shelves of her library to show her what he means. She listens, looks up to a portrait on the wall, and replies, "'This—this scheme you have plotted, is life! It is imagination! . . . That art, . . . that is a mere plaything beside yours!'"[8]

Art by standard definitions is thus dismissed as trivial, while Van's financial manipulations, because they seem to involve imagination and creativity, are deemed art. Van's "art" runs directly counter to the social good since he is ready and willing to use unethical and even illegal means to gain an edge. He rationalizes his actions by citing the corrupt nature of the Chicago business world which he alone cannot change, and by claiming that he serves society by putting meat on the table. He argues his case repeatedly with another important female character, his sister-in-law May, who is a spokesperson for the old values of Jeffersonian democracy. Van explains that no modern business "could be done on her plan of life. That beautiful scheme of things which the fathers of our country drew up in the stage-coach days had proved itself inadequate in a short century." Chicago is not pretty, but it is real and alive, while May's ideas are an outdated dream. "But we men who did the work of the world, who developed the country, who were the life and force of the times, could not be held back by the swaddling-clothes of any political or moral theory," he declares. "Results we must have: good results; and we worked with the tools we found at hand."[9] The creative imagination in Chicago is a bottom-line mentality that must focus on ends, not means.

Herrick admires his hero more than he perhaps originally intended, but he still depicts Chicago as unattractive. The separation of men and women and the ideas for which they stand bodes ill for any reconciliation of the brutishness of industrial capitalism and the loftier ideals of art and culture that might keep the whole city from becoming a figurative stockyards. The guarded optimism of *The Gospel of Freedom* is not missed in *Memoirs* since Van's candor makes him a more attractive character than Adela Anthon. He argues convincingly that Chicagoans have no choice but to run their lives as business dictates because making money is what Chicago is all about. This money might go to supporting high art, but this art will neither humanize the city nor thrive on its own because it neither develops out of nor speaks to the conditions of urban life.

Like Helen Hart, Jane Dround, and others, Dora Glen of Robert Morss Lovett's *A Wingèd Victory* (1907) finds that her ambitions can only be realized through her ability to influence the men around her. She marries Vance Sterling, a gifted poet and playwright who believes in the necessity of radical social change. Vance tells Dora early in their relationship, "No one can be a poet who is not a revolutionist—no one else can have hope and faith and love."[10] This is as explicit a linking of art, democratic reform, and humanistic values as appears in Chicago fiction. Vance makes a reputation for himself quite quickly with such works as his "Chant for the Anarchists," a poem dedicated to the cause of the Haymarket accused.

Dora's faith that Vance "will be a great poet, and make songs for The People" slowly turns to despair, however. When Vance loses his job as a newspaper reporter because he insists on telling the truth about capital's abuse of labor, he suggests that it might be better after all to give up and leave the city. Dora tells him that that they cannot abandon the struggle. He, who has devoted himself to telling the truth about "modern things," is duty bound to remain, and he needs the city as both a source and market for his work. She reminds him of their earlier dedication and urges him to maintain his courage: "And we can't accept this as a defeat. We mustn't yield an inch. If we do, we shall both go to pieces. We must fight it out, here."[11]

But Vance does go to pieces, as is indicated by what happens to his art. He accedes to the commercial temperament of Chicago when he agrees with a publisher to release his first book of poems under a pseudonym, along with a headnote that states falsely that the putative author was "a young man of romantic temperament and revolutionary tendencies" who "shot himself at Florence." The publisher, eager to sell more books, thus exploits the stereotype of the artist as a flighty and self-destructive social and political deviant. A bit later Vance seems to be succeeding beyond Dora's dreams when he sells his prolabor play, "The Strike," to a New York producer. He goes to New York to help mount the show while Dora continues to support him by working as a nurse in Chicago. She soon hears from Vance that the play is a hit, but when she at long last sees it, she is appalled. At the insistence of the producer, the play has been stripped of its political thrust—the workers are made to look silly—and diluted into a pointless spectacle whose major appeal is its noise and excitement. This has all been done with Vance's cooperation.

To make matters even worse, the former radical tells Dora to quit her job of healing the sick because "[i]t's very inconvenient for me just now to have a wife who can't be received in society." This stuns Dora, who can only conclude sadly, "It was the world, the world which once they had dreamed of conquering for humanity, which had taken him captive." Vance is now "but another of the knights who had forgotten his quest under the spell of its [the world's] enchantment."[12] She tries to restore her husband to the cause, but fails. Vance is unstable, and when he finally realizes how he has betrayed Dora, he shoots himself (thus ironically making the false headnote true).

Vance's conception of Dora as his wingèd victory (he calls her this in one of his poems) is significant. He sees her as the embodiment of an ideal—indeed, of idealism itself. But she has the limitations of such a masterpiece in that she can inspire yet not directly act. And, as an inspirational force, she is overmatched in Chicago, a Virgin lost in the land of the dynamo. Until she can find an effective way to act without compromising her principles as Vance does, she is powerless. Dora herself asserts, "But we modern women can't do anything perfect. If we conquer we conquer for ourselves alone; and if we give ourselves we are defeated. We are like birds meant to fly, but with no wings—we must always run or hop about the ground."[13] This is obviously an unhappy condition for a would-be "wingèd" victory. Grounded with these women are the values of imaginative freedom and democracy which they champion.

Throughout the novel, Dora and one of her close friends, a woman aptly named Constance Dare, discuss the helplessness of women. Constance is one of the few conscious feminists who appear in Chicago fiction before 1920. Constance tells Dora that only men have real freedom: "It makes me furious that a woman can't go anywhere without a man to say 'Open sesame.'" She believes, furthermore, that marriage is an admission of defeat, the surrender of the one power, sex, which women have over men. After her husband's death, Dora muses on what has happened to her, and she sees her life as a representative case. As a group, she feels, women have been severely handicapped by the restrictions on their freedom to act. "There is something that we totally lack—," she remarks, "a possibility of perfect triumph, of splendour." She places her hope for the future in her unborn child (she is pregnant when Vance dies), who she hopes will be a boy. She still believes that her only chance for this vague and undefined thing called "perfect triumph" is through intimate attachment to a male who can live out her dreams for her. Dora gives birth to a girl, whom she pities. Lovett explains, "It was her own life that she saw perpetuated in that of the little girl beside her—a life in which there was love and faith and sorrow, but no splendour, not even that of renunciation."[14]

Having defined this dilemma, Lovett retreats from the hard issues he raises about men and women and idealism and art in Chicago. He, too, resorts to conventions of sentimental romance, which are never far below the surface in the book. Instead of striking out at her fate in some way, Dora becomes reconciled to it and moves to the outskirts of the city. She soon feels that bearing her daugher was "natural" and right. More surprising, Constance Dare renounces feminism and her wish "that we [women] had a world to ourselves, without men," now claiming that woman's highest purpose resides in motherhood. She tells Dora, "The baby has converted me. Henceforth I shall proclaim the faith: 'There is no God but life, and love is his prophet.'"[15] To put the final touches on this cloying ending, Dora (now madonna as well as wingèd victory) finds another and, the reader is assured, more lasting love in a dashing friend who nobly supported Vance and Dora through their tribulation. At the novel's close, her gallant lover gallops toward her on horseback in a scene which would satisfy any reader of pulp romance, but which undercuts the rest of the novel. Unable to offer Dora satisfaction as a thoughtful and ambitious woman dedicated to living an important life in a troubling world, Lovett turns her into a two-dimensional damsel in a dream landscape where she can live happily ever after.

LEADING LADIES

If only in a minor way, *A Wingèd Victory* does make a few suggestions about how the ambitious and intelligent woman can find a public career that gives her personal satisfaction and perhaps even improves the urban community. One suggestion is simply that she go to work, as Dora does. Her nursing not only earns money but makes her feel that she is reducing human suffering. But her career, like most work opportunities available to women, does not offer her anything approximating her desire for "perfect triumph." In any case, she gives this career up. Constance Dare presents a second alternative of greater potential social influence and personal liberation. She is an operatic performer, and she maintains that from the first her musical ambitions were allied to her desire to be free. She claims that "[t]he only women who escape [the social conventions that restrict most women] are the artist women—

those of us who win our freedom by our eyes, or our hands, or our voices."[16]

It is not clear what Constance Dare's renunciation of feminism means in terms of Lovett's discussion of art and the city or of her explanation of why she is an artist. She is a secondary character, and her singing is only briefly alluded to and never dramatized. By the time her renunciation occurs, the setting of the book has shifted to the prairie outside Chicago, and Dora has resigned from the struggle to which she once rallied her husband. The challenges that the commercial city posed to Dora and Vance as social reformers and artists have largely been forgotten—fortunately perhaps for Dora, if not for the reader interested in a fuller discussion of the dilemmas Lovett raises. But a few other important novels of the period do try to explore more fully the possibilities of a female artist as central character. In fact, the only Chicago novels of real literary quality with artists who achieve critical and commercial success have female protagonists. What their success implies about urban life and the possibilities of improving it, however, is not reassuring.

The most noteworthy of these books is the most famous and, by most critical judgments, the best example of Chicago fiction, Dreiser's *Sister Carrie*. With all of Dreiser's emphasis on Carrie's passivity, it is easy to underemphasize the fact that she does end up a leading lady of the New York stage, but to do so is a mistake. Though she falls into her acting career by chance when Drouet volunteers her for a production of *Under the Gaslight* that his lodge is sponsoring, and though she turns to performing professionally only when Hurstwood fails to provide for her after they run off to New York together, her dramatic achievement seems a fitting consummation of the journey that began when she left Columbia City, Wisconsin, for Chicago. In the opening chapter, Dreiser depicts her as being bent on success that she believes only Chicago can furnish. She is "quick to understand the keener pleasures of life, ambitious to gain in material things." The capstone of her ambition is a hazy vision of power: "A half-equipped little knight she was, venturing to reconnoitre the mysterious city and dreaming wild dreams of some vague, far-off supremacy which should make it prey and subject—the proper penitent, grovelling at a woman's slipper."[17]

Carrie is proud of her beauty, she enjoys the company of men, and she is delighted with all the fine things Drouet and Hurstwood provide; but the stage offers her something more commensurate to her yearnings. In the theater she can succeed on the city's terms of money and power, and she can do so independently, without men. Her great luck is that she is a natural actress, possessed of "an innate taste for imitation and no small ability," unconsciously performing every time she passes a mirror. When Drouet first suggests that she take a part in the amateur production, she tingles with an excitement and anticipation that Dreiser describes in the same terms as her vision on the train of the city's promise: "The glamour, the tense situations, the fine clothes, the applause—these had lured her until she felt that she, too, could act—that she, too, could compel acknowledgment of power."[18]

Carrie's winning performance in the lodge production is perceived largely through Drouet's and Hurstwood's eyes, and they both indeed fall under her spell. "The two men were in a most harrowed state of affection," Dreiser writes. "They scarcely heard the few remaining words with which the scene concluded. They only saw their idol, moving about with appealing grace, continuing a power which to them was a revelation." In this moment Drouet the eternal ladies' man resolves to marry her, vowing unilaterally to "be to Carrie what he had never been before," and Hurstwood decides that "he would have that lovely girl if it took his all." Later, after she has become a popular actress in New York, she receives a steady stream of notes from men who want only to surrender to her, like the one with "a million in my own right" who begs for a half hour to declare his love.[19]

More satisfying to Carrie is that her acting alters her status in the city. Even the second-rate amateur performance seems to give her something that otherwise has been missing from her life in Chicago. She has suddenly discovered an access to all the things which drew her to Chicago and which heretofore have been denied. In her mind, these things are represented by "the greatness of the names upon the billboards, the marvel of the long notices in the papers, the beauty of the dresses upon the stage—the atmosphere of carriages, flowers, refinement." The stage seems to be the fulfillment of everything her imagination could hope for. Carrie feels that her acting paradoxically makes her dreams real: "Here was no illusion. Here was an open door to all of that. She had come upon it as one who stumbles upon a secret passage, and, behold, she was in the chamber of diamonds and delight!"[20]

Dreiser later suggests that Carrie's newfound artistic power is something that can work to the benefit of others. In some ways he sounds like Jane Addams speaking of the ability of the theater to unite an audience. Near the end of the novel her friend Ames tells Carrie why she enjoys such popular appeal and advises her on how she must use it. His point is that she expresses a universal feeling of unfulfilled aspiration that is common to all humanity. Her performance, her every expression, somehow captures the hopes and feelings of those who see her and reminds them of the human feelings that they all share. "The world is always struggling to express itself—to make clear its hopes and sorrows and give them voice," Ames explains. "It is always seeking the means, and it will delight in the individual who can express these things for it." The artist is such an individual. "That is why we have great musicians, great painters, great writers and actors. They have the ability to express the world's sorrows and longings, and the world gets up and shouts their names."

But with this artistic power, he points out, comes the high obligation to uplift the public, and with the fulfillment of that obligation will come a fame and power of a more important and enduring kind than any common sort in Chicago or New York. "You must help the world express itself. Use will make your powers endure," he tells her. He also warns, "You will have them so long as they express something in you. You can preserve and increase them longer by using them for others. The moment you forget their value to the world, and they cease to represent your own aspirations, they will begin to fade." He soon sounds like Helen Hart of *The Common Lot*, "Serve the many," he urges. "Be kind and humanitarian. Then you can't help but be great."[21] He suggests finally that she move from comedy into serious, more realistic, drama that will better serve her audience. By the book's end the miller's daughter from small-town Wisconsin is sitting in her luxurious New York hotel suite reading Balzac.

Though some readers see Ames as a spokesman for Dreiser, it is not clear how much the novelist endorses his character's notions. Ames's ideas are more fully articulated in the "new" Pennsylvania edition of the text, which is based on Dreiser's original manuscript, than in the "standard" version. There is some evidence that the revision of the ending of the novel, in which Ames's importance is diminished (especially as a possible love match for Carrie), was the work of Dreiser's hand, and not that of his wife Sara or his friend Arthur Henry, who were responsible for many other changes.[22] Even if the decision to reduce Ames's presence in the novel did not originate with Dreiser, there is still other evidence in both versions of the novel that implies that Carrie's artistic power reflects rather than counteracts the sources of social fragmentation in the city that people like Jane Addams and characters like Bob Ames wished to overcome. Although Carrie's performances charm her audience and create moments of imaginative and emotional intensity in which social divisions are forgotten, her drive to attain success is selfish and willful. From the first, after all, Carrie wants "supremacy." One of the reasons she listens to Ames is because he tells her that her power is only temporary unless she learns to adapt her talents before she grows older and loses the advantages of youth.

Personal ambition is also the key motive of Elizabeth Ross, a secondary character in Will Payne's *Mr. Salt* (1903). Like Carrie, Elizabeth comes to Chicago from Wisconsin, but her goals are more specific. She wants to become an opera star, and she knows that the city can provide her with training and a stage. Her first visit to the opera at the Auditorium confirms her career choice. When the prima donna sings, she stirs a "subtle confluence of emotion" through the audience. Elizabeth desperately wants to possess this ability to move people with her voice. Gazing at the stage "with wide, dim eyes, her lips slightly apart" in wonder, she is full of envy. "What power! What triumph!" she marvels. "To seize this slow, voiceless multitude in her spell, lifting them up for once to the passion for which they yearned, fusing them into one exalted heart."[23]

Like Ames in *Sister Carrie,* Elizabeth here thinks about the power of art in terms very similar to those which Jane Addams used. Both Carrie and Elizabeth use their talents mainly to get inside what Dreiser calls in *Sister Carrie* the "walled city" of privilege, however, not to knock down the walls for the sake of others. Their audience is mainly those who can afford to see them, especially the socially and financially mighty. Elizabeth's highest goal is not to reform the urban community or even to be a great musician, but to "exercise an irresistible power in a golden hall filled with richly dressed people who were masters of the earth and who yet would acknowledge her spell, surrounded with the color and perfume of flowers, in an air throbbing with harmonies."[24] Her art may create a refuge from the harsher world outside the theater, but she does not affect this world.

Except for the flowers and the harmonies, Payne might be talking in this last passage about the businessman-hero of his novel on the floor of the Chicago Stock Exchange. A later scene is even more striking in this respect. After additional training in Europe, Elizabeth returns to Chicago for a triumphant concert. The description of her experience emphasizes the links between her feeling of power and that of businessmen like Salt. Payne speaks of the evening in terms of conflict and battle, not harmony. The audience is the great "monster," and the performance is a death struggle in which Elizabeth either will conquer the monster or be herself destroyed. As it turns out she wins her victory, and her "blood glowed with it." From her point of view her great achievement is not only that she has unified her audience in a moment of fine feeling, but that afterward "a little court of privileged persons was gathering behind the scenes to do her homage."[25]

The fact that Carrie and Elizabeth are women is very important. Men of equivalent (if not identical) talent, ambition, and yearning would have become businessmen, while these women find in art an access to the highest form of power available to them. But in subordinating art to the dream of success they have abandoned the high-minded intentions behind the cultural activities of most women in Chicago fiction, who are not themselves artists and who are, therefore, powerless. Carrie and Elizabeth have assumed male ambitions at the cost of losing the moral force of women like Helen Hart and Dora Glen. In the process, they have almost become unsexed. Carrie is a lonely figure by the end of the novel, uninterested in men generally and apparently beyond either the ideal of love or even sexual passion (this is less the case in the Pennsylvania edition, in which there is attraction between Carrie and Ames, although Dreiser still sees Ames mainly as a guide in Carrie's endless yearnings for something more). Payne describes Elizabeth Ross's sense of calling in decidedly phallic terms, as if she has undergone a gender change in the course of her artistic triumph. As she views her first opera in the Auditorium and resolves to take her place as a great artist, "her bright will grew keen and steely hard as a sword, flawless, erect, shining, cruel."[26]

Once again in Chicago fiction, things are left in something of a muddle. While on one hand Dreiser and Payne (especially in *Jerry the Dreamer*) agreed that art might serve the needs of the individual and the democratic community, on the other they never show just how this might happen. In addition, they point out quite convincingly that artistic power can corrupt those who wield it, much as any other form of power corrupts. The women they depict seem more capable than most men of becoming successful artists in the city, but their very success poses the danger that they will lose the special humanizing gifts of women as they subordinate their artistry to a male dream of personal power. Dreiser and Payne imply that as soon as art ceases to be associated with weakness it also ceases to be allied with the well-being of society. The successful artist joins the urban dream of domination rather than working to overcome it.

Willa Cather's *The Song of the Lark* (1915), the fullest study of a female artist that appears in Chicago fiction, extends and deepens the general discussion of art and the city. Cather's novel depicts the childhood and early career of opera star Thea Kronborg. Like other real and fictive American artists of the late nineteenth and early twentieth centuries, Thea follows the familiar progression from small village to Chicago to final triumph in New York. (Like Constance Dare and Elizabeth Ross, Thea also studies for a time in Europe.) The Chicago section of the novel depicts her first serious formal training as a musician, and it falls between her girlhood in the intellectually and geographically isolated town of Moonstone, Colorado, and her triumph with the Metropolitan Opera. The novel is more directly about the struggles and sacrifices of the great artist rather than about the city, but the quality of urban life is a major topic. Cather asserts that the city is the only place where high art such as opera can flourish—because only in places like

New York and Chicago are there music schools, patrons, and opera houses—but urban sordidness cannot be redeemed or in any other way affected by art. It can, however, be transcended in those moments of high emotion that only art makes possible.

From the time of her girlhood in Moonstone, Thea seems to project a special spiritual quality that draws a series of men to dedicate themselves selflessly to helping her attain whatever she wants. All of them have been disappointed or injured by the world. These include Ray Kennedy, a railroad man who wants to marry Thea but who is killed in an accident; Dr. Howard Archie, who is trapped by a terrible marriage in narrow-minded Moonstone; and Andor Harsanyi, her emigré piano instructor in Chicago, who first perceives that her real talent is her voice. Finally there is Frederick Ottenburg, an elegant young man of wealth, charm, and culture, who becomes Thea's lover. Like Archie, he has married badly, which makes him all the more determined to use his resources to make sure Thea is free to use her talent. For Fred and all the others, helping Thea is a way to fulfill their own dreams of escape from the things that restrict them. In Harsanyi's words, "She is uncommon, in a common, common world."[27]

Ray Kennedy's insurance money helps get Thea out of Moonstone to Chicago. Here she finds not only the training she needs, but also other important sources of inspiration. Thea discovers the Art Institute's magnificent collection, particularly the Jules Breton painting from which the book takes its name. Cather explained later that the title "was meant to suggest a young girl's awakening to something beautiful." More important, she attends the symphony, where a performance of Wagner's music moves Thea much as Elizabeth Ross's visit to the opera at the Auditorium affects her. The experience is a spiritual awakening, as "with a dull, almost listless ear she [Thea] heard for the first time that troubled music, ever-darkening, ever-brightening, which was to flow through so many years of her life."[28]

The paintings and the music are isolated oases in a hostile terrain. Coming out of the symphony, Thea encounters "cold, hurrying, angry people, running for street-cars and barking at each other." Her heightened appreciation of the splendor of art simultaneously makes her sensitive to the ugliness of her surroundings in Chicago: "For almost the first time Thea was conscious of the city itself, of the congestion of life all about her, of the brutality and power of those streams that flowed in the streets, threatening to drive one under." She feels a terrible opposition between this world and the one she has discovered in the music. The brutality and power of the city are "bent upon taking away from her that feeling with which she had come out of the concert hall," which is that sense of personal power and worth that music gives her. She be-

54

lieves that if one has that feeling, the city becomes one's enemy: "People, buildings, wagons, cars, rushed at one to crush it under, to make one let go of it."

In her defiance of all that would deprive her of this special feeling, she becomes an artist and an adult. She suddenly sees the world as a place of violent conflict that threatens her desire to escape this world into the special one that art can create. "All these things and people were no longer remote and negligible: they had to be met, they were lined up against her, they were there to take something from her." She vows to make them "trample her to death" before she gives up. "As long as she lived that ecstasy was going to be hers. She would live for it, work for it, die for it; but she was going to have it, time after time, height after height." Her resolution pushes the din of the city out of her consciousness and restores her to the ecstasy of the music: "She could hear the crash of the orchestra again, and she rose on the brasses. She would have it, what the trumpets were singing! She would have it, have it—it!" In this moment of intense internal conflict, Thea becomes a woman: "Under the old cape she pressed her hands upon her heaving bosom, that was a little girl's no longer."[29]

In spite of such overwritten passages, Cather does not sentimentalize the depiction of Thea's career. She points out that absolute dedication to one's art, like the pursuit of any great ambition, is personally costly. Cather shows the reader how much training Thea must undergo, how the strenuous effort of singing grand opera exhausts her, and how she virtually ceases to have any private life at all. Forced at one point to choose between returning to Moonstone for her mother's funeral and taking a major part that suddenly opens up, Thea chooses the latter. Cather argued in her 1932 preface to the novel that "[t]he life of nearly every artist who succeeds in the true sense" is a variation on the story of Dorian Grey. She explained: "As Thea Kronborg is more and more released into the dramatic and musical possibilities of her profession, as her artistic life grows fuller and richer, it becomes more interesting to her than her own life." Cather continued, "Her human life is made up of exacting engagements and dull business detail, of shifts to evade an idle, gaping world which is determined that no artist shall ever do his best."[30]

Cather implies that, as in the case of Elizabeth Ross and, to a large extent, Carrie Meeber, the successful female artist's ambitions and career do not have much to do with the idea that society can somehow be humanized by contact with great art. But things are not quite this simple in Cather's book. Thea does not attempt to dominate the city; she only tries to make certain that it does not rob her of the joy of her music. Her work is not an access to power but an end in itself. Despite her sacrifices, her life is far preferable to, in Cather's words, "a smug, domestic, self-satisfied provincial world of utter ignorance" in which most women live.

Cather stated that Thea's "artistic life is the only one in which she is happy, or free, or even very real," by which she meant that it is the only life which is vivid and satisfying to her. While she does not wish to use her talent to dominate others as Elizabeth and Carrie do, she also does not dedicate it to social improvement. Her art is a means of personal liberation from the city, which is an irredeemably hostile, restrictive, and commonplace world. She tells Archie that "what one really strives for in art is not the sort of thing you are likely to find when you drop in for a performance at the opera. What one strives for is so far away, so beautiful . . . that there's nothing one can say about it."[31]

Cather hints, however, that this striving can involve more than personal escape. In ways she herself does not expect, Thea rewards all those who come to hear her. If only briefly, she offers her listeners the kind of experience she felt at the symphony. Ottenburg tells Archie, "After you've listened to her for an hour or so, you aren't afraid of anything." She does light up the lives of others by showing them the uncommon and helping them, for a moment at least, see beyond the world outside the opera house. Her achievements are thus greater than any of those who work within the context of the commercial city which she escapes. Back in Moonstone, the reader is told in the Epilogue, people enjoy telling the two great success stories of the town. One is Thea's, the other that of a boy who left to build a great business in Omaha. The townspeople group the two together, in business terms, "as examples of Moonstone enterprise." But Thea's story is told more often: "A voice has even a wider appeal than a fortune."[32]

Thea is obviously an artist of a different sort from Sister Carrie. Thea's intelligence and ambition are more developed and more active, she sacrifices so much more of her life to formal preparation, and the appeal of her performance is not in its expression of common longings so much as in its proof that such a thing as ideal beauty exists in moments like the ones Thea creates with her voice. Cather argues that art in the city can be something other than either a resort of weakness associated with women or another chip in the power game associated with men, but it is not a means of social reform. If its power is opposed to the daunting energy of the industrial city, this does not mean that it is on the side of democracy and freedom. These are concerns that art transcends for the alternative world that it makes, and into which both artist and aesthete enter as individuals, not as citizens of the urban community.

4

Business and art

The difficult thing is to get at the life immediately around you—the very life in which you move. No romance in it? No romance in you, poor fool. As much romance on Michigan Avenue as there is realism in King Arthur's court. It is as you choose to see it. The important thing to decide is, which formula is the best to help you grip the Real Life of this or any other age.

—Frank Norris, "The True Reward of the Novelist"

Cowperwood was innately and primarily an egoist and intellectual, though blended strongly therewith was a humane and democratic spirit. We think of egoism and intellectualism as closely confined to the arts. Finance is an art. And it presents the operations of the subtlest of the intellectuals and of the egoists. Cowperwood was a financier. Instead of dwelling on the works of nature, its beauty and subtlety, to his material disadvantage, he found a happy mean, owing to the swiftness of his intellectual operations, whereby he could, intellectually and emotionally, rejoice in the beauty of life without interfering with his perpetual material and financial calculations.

—Theodore Dreiser, The Financier

"Buy May wheat. It'll beat art all hollow."

—Frank Norris, The Pit: A Story of Chicago

In 1899 a young Chicago woman created a stir when she published a sensational novel which portrayed Chicago society as shallow, deceitful, and morally bankrupt. Margaret Horton Potter's *A Social Lion* (published under the pseudonym of Robert Dolly Williams) is full of secret love affairs, crooked business deals, and scandalous hypocrisy. However shocking the book was in its time, *A Social Lion* justifiably rests in obscurity because its tone is radically uneven, its characterizations are implausible, and its plot is sometimes inscrutable. Still, it is noteworthy because of the way in which its author mixed several major themes involving life and art in Chicago.

Of special interest is her central character, Herbert Stagmar. Stagmar is a significant figure in Chicago fiction because he is probably the first of a handful of protagonists who successfully, if not happily, combine the careers of financier and artist. Stagmar is a self-made man who developed his talents as a literary realist simultaneously with his equally hard-headed business expertise. His business and artistic activities coexist remarkably well. Potter explains that on many occasions when Stagmar was dealing in wheat on the floor of the Board of Trade, he was also studying human nature: "It was on this very floor that two or three of the writer's best-known characters, and even the central theme of one of his books, had originated."[1]

The plot of the novel is so muddled that any assertions about Potter's general intentions must be qualified, but she does appear to imply that business and art in Chicago are not necessarily in opposition, even if neither makes life gentler and kinder. Stagmar's literary talents and his financial acumen are aspects of a single powerful imaginative faculty, one whose existence most of Potter's more gifted contemporaries spent a great deal of effort demonstrating was impossible. In Chicago, these writers agreed, business and art were irreconcilable. Artists and businessmen were openly contemptuous, suspicious, or even fearful of one another. These writers argued that this antagonism reflected the larger social and spiritual disjunctions of modern life.

To most serious Chicago writers, the situation called for radical social changes. In more optimistic moods, Chicago's defenders and apologists both pointed out that the city was still growing, and they compared it to a husky, confident, but ungainly adolescent whose great intellectual and spiritual potential would develop only after he had achieved full physical maturity some time in the future. This comparison of Chicago to a healthy and well-meaning youth appears well into the twentieth century, most notably in Sandburg's "Chicago." Such comparisons rationalize the city's undisciplined growth and crudity and neatly summarize the expectation that, once the body matures, the mind (i.e., the cultural amenities) will follow.[2] In pessimistic moments, novelists like Fuller and Herrick wondered whether the city would never be more than a boorish giant, incapable of spiritual and artistic cultivation. In both views, until the money-hungry and success-crazed citizenry with high ambitions for triumph in business would pursue the nobler possibilities of life which great art revealed, modern urban society would remain unsatisfying even for those who had won its highest material rewards.

But some prominent Chicago writers early in this century suggested, if only tentatively, that perhaps what was needed most immediately was a radical *literary* change. Could it be, they wondered, that the new industrial age demanded of novelists some major redefinitions of their basic assumptions about urban life? Had the artist—rather than the businessman—been recalcitrant, insensitive, and blind to contemporary social conditions, as well as to an extremely promising subject that was ripe for anyone with literary ambition? Could they dare to admit that if the city would not or could not foster and respect art as they understood it, was it not because a new kind of artist and new art forms had arisen in the modern financier and his enterprises?

Out of these questions came several major works of fiction and related writings that are distinct both from the simplistic success literature that goes back at least to Horatio Alger and from other "romance of business" of the early twentieth century, as well as from the critiques of business methods and values by muckraking journalists and by such realists as Fuller and Herrick.[3] They also mark the last point at which major American writers took the American businessman so seriously; Sinclair Lewis's *Babbitt* was published only a few years later, in 1922. These works argued that business could be "artistic" in itself, offering the creative, intelligent, ambitious individual an understanding of existence that could help him and those who saw his work in the proper light live a life of personal satisfaction and worldly achievement. At their boldest, these novels even claimed that the leading businessman was in demonstrable ways an artist himself, perhaps the preeminent artist of the time. In this view, the businessman was akin to and not opposed to the literary artist, whose task now was to acknowledge and celebrate the commercial leader as an urban hero. At the very least, the writer must fully and positively understand that modern life, especially in the city, *was* commercial life, which was, therefore, a most important subject for modern literary art. He had to realize the dramatic possibilities of urban entrepreneurial capitalism with an open mind if art was to have any place of importance in the city and if his own ambitions of writing significant works of literary art could be fulfilled.

The depiction of the great businessman as artist is a complicated phenomenon, and what follows is a scrutiny of three leading early twentieth-century examples. These novels require a close analysis for several reasons. The main reason is that they are the fullest attempts to reconcile, or at least understand, the art-business tension which runs through Chicago literature. Giving the businessman his due might show how the city was an exciting, imaginative, and creative place. In the process, the writer might also establish his centrality as the creator and interpreter of a new urban mythology that explained how the materialism of Chicago might be transcended by certain figures whose vision could be shared, or at least appreciated, by all.

There is a good deal of ambivalence, however, both in those books which intend to criticize the businessman and in those that try to praise him in some way. Some writers, including Herrick in *The Memoirs of an American Citizen,* who set out to expose the faults of commercial life, found themselves portraying businessmen as the most interesting, dynamic, and intelligent individuals around. Calling the businessman an artist raised other problems. For one thing, it blurred what was frequently already a hazy conception of what art and artistic talent are and how they figure in society. And no writer outside of a cynical or thoughtless booster could finally bring himself to say that even the greatest businessman bridged the art-business opposition and the deeper personal and cultural problems it involved. The writers who saw the businessman as artist were unsure of what they wanted to say, partly because they envied the power of their heroes yet finally wanted to claim a higher distinction for their own art than for that of the marketplace.

THE PIT: A STORY OF CHICAGO

Frank Norris's last novel is both a celebration of the thrills of speculation and a consideration of the rewards and costs of business life. The novel is close to the standard romance of business, but it is also a complicated and unresolved discussion of the place of art in the city. This discussion makes *The Pit,* in spite of its faults, more intriguing than almost any other novel of American commercial life and one of the very few which tries to demonstrate how the physical and intellectual activity of doing business is exciting.[4] Norris asserts that although the highly competitive business world of Chicago, which can be seen at its most intense in the Pit, the trading room of the Chicago Board of Trade, can undo even those who are successful, it is the most imaginatively alive place in the city and is especially appealing to the literary realist seeking to understand and explain the nature of modern experience.

Norris maintains that Chicago as a commercial center is one of the most invigorating places on earth, and he seeks to capture that excitement in his book. He establishes this point immediately through the response to Chicago of his heroine, Laura Dearborn, who has recently arrived in Chicago from Massachusetts. She has come to the city because she feels that in Chicago she can satisfy her vague artistic ambitions in a way she never can in the narrowness of small-town New England. In the opening scene, one of her dreams is fulfilled as she attends the opera at the glittering Auditorium. The scene seems very similar to those in *The Song of the Lark* and *Mr. Salt* in which Thea Kronborg and Elizabeth Ross, also newcomers with artistic ambitions, discover a heightened sense of calling at a musical performance.

Laura has a very different experience, however, as the commercial affairs outside the Auditorium intrude and arrest her attention. There is a distracting murmur among the men in the audience who are discussing the failure earlier that day of a speculator named Helmick, who was ruined in his attempt to corner the wheat market. At first Laura is annoyed, but soon all this talk excites her and unexpectedly makes her evening richer than she expected. Despite her love for opera, she finds that she is absorbed by the Helmick failure, and for aesthetic reasons:

And abruptly, midway between two phases of that music-drama, of passion and romance, there came to Laura the swift and vivid impression of that other drama that simultaneously—even at that very moment—was working itself out close at hand, equally picturesque, equally romantic, equally passionate; but more than that, real, actual, modern, a thing in the very heart of the very life in which she moved.[5]

Norris has Laura reach the same conclusion that led him to write about the action in the Pit and to remark that it was the artist's task to discover the romance of Michigan Avenue and "grip the Real Life of this or any other age."[6] As far as he was concerned, the business activity on LaSalle Street was the great drama of the time. It was more interesting and important than most traditional high culture forms of other times and places, like the opera, because it was more "real, actual, modern," and essential to contemporary experience.

Norris quickly expands this idea shortly after the opening scene. Laura finds the "Great Grey City" oppressively squalid even near its most splendid neighborhoods, but it is consistently fascinating to her. She believes that "the life was tremendous," and is impressed by the panorama of boats on the dirty Chicago River, the hectic activity of the South Water Street wholesale market, and the scale and complexity of the railroad system. Chicago, she believes, is the age's greatest display of creativity in the most basic sense of the word. "Here, midmost in the land, beat the Heart of the Nation, whence inevitably must come its immeasurable power, its infinite, infinite, inexhaustible vitality." Laura's thoughts continue: "Here, of all her cities, throbbed the true life— the true power and spirit of America; gigantic, crude with the crudity of youth, disdaining rivalry; sane and healthy and vigorous; brutal in its ambition, arrogant in the new-found knowledge of its giant strength, prodigal of its wealth, infinite of its desires."[7]

This overenthusiastic passage, another example of the Chicago-as-young-giant conceit, anticipates by a decade Sandburg's "Chicago" and Dreiser's effusive tribute to Chicago as a "rude raw Titan." All these texts assert that in the building of the city is a story equal to those told in classical epic or the Bible. "I suppose it's civilisation in the making," Laura reflects on her panoramic vision of Chicago, "the thing that isn't meant to be seen, as though it were too elemental, too—primordial; like the first verses of Genesis."[8] Art forms that the "cultured" world favors cannot begin to match this drama of power enacted by the city itself. The modern artist, Norris believed, must recognize this, and he must discover a way to "grip" it that offers a romantic vision of this real life.

Norris strains his rhetoric throughout the novel, but he does develop, with some inconsistencies, an intriguing viewpoint from which he sees the businessman as the author, producer, director, and leading actor in the urban drama which he finds so exciting. In so doing, he depicts the financier as a figure who shapes experience with an imagination that looks beyond matters of mere profit and loss. Rather than state his case directly at first, Norris continues to work through Laura, the devotee of high art. Her heart is soon unexpectedly won by Curtis Jadwin, "capitalist and speculator," though her other two suitors at first seem more appropriate. Sheldon Corthell and Landry Court are closer to her own age, and they—especially Corthell—share her interest in art. Jadwin's attraction rests in the fact that Laura sees him as a more masterful figure in the exciting "commercial Empire" she has discovered in Chicago. Sitting by Jadwin at the opera, Laura "could not help being a little attracted," since he obviously is a man used to controlling the turbulent world in which he moves. His business success seems to verify his sexual power: "Those broad, strong hands, and keen, calm eyes would enfold and envelop a purpose with tremendous strength, and they would persist and persist and persist, unswerving, unwavering, untiring, till the purpose was driven home."[9]

Norris depicts Corthell as a man of rare taste. His talent in the design of stained glass is "indisputable." But Norris establishes Corthell's artistic credentials to discredit the importance of his work in contemporary Chicago. Had he been a failed artist—like those Truesdale Marshall brings home in Fuller's *With the Procession*—Corthell would be merely pathetic and silly, and easily dismissed. That he is so gifted means that even a skilled artist is unimportant and out of place in Chicago, and that his ambitions are not those of a successful and admirable person in the modern city. A trusted older female friend tells Laura that Corthell is talented and agreeable, and continues, "But somehow it never impressed me that there was very much *to* him."[10] Presumably, anyone with "much *to* him" would have gone into business.

With his brittle sensibility and narrow purposes, Corthell is unequal to the challenges that Jadwin eagerly accepts when he later begins to speculate in wheat. Laura immediately appreciates this difference when she first meets her future husband at the Auditorium. In his presence, she sees the opera as she assumes he must, as "posing and attitudinising," and wonders to herself, "How small and petty it must all seem to him!" When Laura is torn between accepting Jadwin or Corthell, Norris writes, "Of the two existences which did she prefer, that of the business man, or that of the artist?" She would be expected to choose the latter, "to whom the business district was an unexplored country," whose experience is unsullied by great conflict, who "passed his life gently, in the calm, still atmosphere of art, in the cult of the beautiful, unperturbed, tranquil. . . ." After all, "Him women could know, with him they could sympathise. And he could enter fully into their lives and help and stimulate them."[11]

Laura's resolution of her dilemma surprises even her. She instinctively decides that Corthell's interests are finally *not* appropriate to a spirited woman like herself, "a daughter of the frontier," in whose veins flows "the blood of those who had wrestled with a new world." An artist like Corthell, in short, is alien to the aggressive spirit that is characteristically American. By the turn of the century, that spirit is most at home in commercial Chicago, whose heart is the Pit. Like Adela Anthon and Jane Dround, Laura cannot go onto the floor herself, but her natural desires draw her to "the strong and the brave" like Jadwin, who dare "the Battle of the Street." She realizes that "the figure that held her imagination and her sympathy was not the artist, soft of hand and of speech, elaborating graces of sound and color and form, refined, sensitive, and temperamental," but "the fighter, unknown and unknowable to women as he was; hard, rigorous, panoplied in the harness of the warrior, who strove among the trumpets, and who, in the brunt of conflict, conspicuous, formidable, set the battle in a rage around him, and exulted like a champion in the shoutings of the captains." This passage expresses Norris's contempt for fine art as a realm of retreat, self-indulgence, and sensuality of a very limited kind, and for the conventional artist of his day as someone whose refinement masks weakness and cowardice. The businessman's milieu is exciting and attractive as a subject because of its violence, and the Pit is the noblest battlefield of the conflict out of which Laura sees Chicago emerging.[12]

Norris tries hard to convince the reader of the correctness of Laura's choice of husband. In developing his argument, he makes his most important contribution to the broader effort to develop a literary form appropriate to Chicago. Others had suggested, as Norris does in the scenes in which Laura is first impressed by her adopted city, that Chicago was in some way or other "epic" or "titanic," but more than any other writer he attempted to demonstrate just how Chicago could be the subject of literary epic and to prove that all his references to bloody battle and superhuman struggles were appropriate and not exaggerated. Norris believes that Jadwin is heroic because he and the other leading speculators contend with each other on a scale of action defined by the law of supply and demand in its most elemental terms, with the fertility of the earth on one side and the empty stomachs of humanity on the other. He thinks that Jadwin's ambition, pride, skill, and arrogance in mounting his corner are colossal. By comparison, Corthell's rarefied studio world is indeed petty.

Norris repeatedly compares the fury of the Pit not only to a battlefield but also to a whirlpool or maelstrom (he specifically cites Scylla and Charybdis) as it channels all the grain of the world and crushes those who try to master the flow. When Jadwin's corner breaks, the onrushing wheat that drops the bottom out of the market seems to deafen the ears, blind the eyes, and numb the minds of those on the trading floor. It is "coeval with the earthquake and glacier, merciless, all-powerful, a primal basic throe of creation itself, unassailable, inviolate, and untamed."[13] There are few more heroic celebrations of American capitalism than this vision which equates the workings of the market system with the basic forces of nature.

Norris attempts to work this vision into a coherent mythology. Fighting to master the Chicago market in wheat, men become literally transformed into bears, bulls, and other beasts. Away from LaSalle Street, Landry Court is absentminded, impractical, and irresponsible. On the floor, he undergoes a metamorphosis, as "a whole new set of nerves came into being with the tap of the nine-thirty gong, a whole new system of brain machinery began to move," and no one else is so alert and shrewd. "The Landry Court the Dearborn girls knew was a far different young man from him who now leaned his elbows on the arms of the chair upon the floor of the Board, and, his eyes narrowing, his lips tightening, began to speculate upon what was to be the temper of the Pit that morning."[14]

Those who prevail in this setting, Norris maintains, are the modern equivalents of Hercules, Ajax, Hector, and Ulysses. A minor figure in the book is an old trader named Hargus, who failed to hold a corner on the market some twenty years earlier and who has become pathetically senile as a result. Despite his failure, the "Hargus corner" is the measure of all other commodities deals and of heroic action in Chicago. Hargus "had been in his day a king all-powerful," and he had entered into memory as "a sort of creature of legends, mythical, heroic, transfigured in the glory of his millions." Jadwin surpasses Hargus as an overreacher. While hiding his identity to cover his strategy, he is known in all the papers as the "Unknown Bull" or the "Great Bull"; when he makes his corner, he is called by the newspapers "The Napoleon of LaSalle Street" and becomes the central figure of new legends.[15]

The comparisons of Jadwin to Napoleon seem apt, for no one in his time exercises more temporal might. Even when he loses his hold, Jadwin retains his grandeur, for he has tried, as an associate warned him, to fight the earth itself. When the new large harvests his high prices have spurred come in and he faces ruin since he has no more money or credit with which to buy the new wheat, Jadwin still refuses to surrender. He storms into the Pit himself and tries to buoy the falling market. Many of those he once terrorized cheer his fall now that they are free of "the weight of the Bull's hoof, the rip of his horn," but the magnitude of his achievement is acknowledged by the leader of the Bear faction, who has nothing but contempt for the small traders who applaud Jadwin's defeat. "They can cheer now, all they want," Jadwin's rival observes. "*They* didn't do it. It was the wheat itself that beat him; no combination of men could have done it—go on, cheer, you damn fools! He was a bigger man than the rest of us."[16]

To underline the point here, Norris's major effort in *The Pit* is to make the reader feel that all he and his characters say about Jadwin is true, that this speculator is one of the few people who can dominate this city of power, and that what he is doing is epic adventure that requires bravery and daring. What complicates matters and makes the book more interesting is how Norris relates Jadwin's greatness to a personal quality that he sees as creative, even artistic. Jadwin's "art" is, of course, of a different kind from Corthell's, but in Norris's view it is more worthy of the name in Chicago. Jadwin's artistry is based in his aggressive, intelligent control of the Pit, the major marketplace in this major commercial city. As a champion of the depiction of "Real Life," Norris saw himself as the literary equivalent of Jadwin, and a far better artist than Corthell, because he also dealt with the Pit. He urged his fellow novelists to a "close study, not of books, but of people and actualities," and he stated that the modern artist needed that "sixth sense or sensibility" that he claimed was "possessed of the financier and poet alike—so only they be big enough."[17]

Norris can see Jadwin as an "artist" because he believes his hero has a conception of what he is doing that is unmistakably materialistic but also spiritual and unworldly. In several places he calls Jadwin "unimaginative," but he attributes the speculator's achievement to a visionary sensibility that attracts him to the "resistless force" that dwells within the Board of Trade. Jadwin wants to understand and master this force—as does Norris—more than he wishes to make money. He is the purest kind of businessman, the speculator who works only with his intelligence and his line of credit in trying to realize the abstract economic model known as a corner. Since he neither grows nor takes final delivery on his wheat, he has no business but money—no corporate structure, no shareholders, no office to speak of—and no motivation besides his dream of control.

Norris distinguishes Jadwin, who knows "every eddy" of the whirlpool of wheat, from "other men, men of little minds, of narrow imaginations," who "perversely, blindly shut their eyes to the swelling of its waters, neglecting the chances which he would have known how to use with such large, such vast results."[18] He works by what Norris variously calls "genius," "inexplicable instinct," "intuition," and "presentiment," all of which are tied in Norris's mind to artistic talent. Jadwin attempts to make his corner when he senses that there are great possibilities in the air for anyone bold and farsighted enough to see the opportunities and use them brilliantly. The corner is to be the work of a "master hand," the apotheosis of the artist-financier.

Jadwin has his own strong ideas about art, which, not surprisingly, differ considerably from Corthell's. His taste, like his whole outlook, is practical, and it reflects his unsophisticated evangelical Christian upbringing in rural Michigan. In conversations with Laura, he sounds like a less articulate and sophisticated Jane Addams as he argues for a realistic literature related to the life around it and aimed to improve that life in some way. He couches his aesthetic simply and directly in the language of the Pit. "I'm not long very many of art," he tells Laura, "[b]ut I believe that any art that don't make the world better and happier is not art at all, and is only fit for the dump heap." He dismisses her taste for Meredith and Middleton, and with her help discovers "his abiding affinity" in Howells.[19] *The Rise of Silas Lapham* pleases him no end because it strikes him as so true. Never mind that he seems to miss the ironies of Lapham's "rise."

The temperamental Laura at first seems to be converted to her husband's taste. Like Adela Anthon, she weds a businessman partly to be closer to the essential sources of urban power that intrigue her so much. Jadwin's proposal of marriage offers her what appears to be a very promising way to combine the interests of art and business. As Jadwin opens his heart to Laura, he speaks out against men losing themselves selfishly in business and women falling into a "sort of warmed-over, dilettante, stained-glass [an obvious reference to Corthell] world of seclusion and *ex*clusion," which is another name for the aesthetic trap which Addams discussed. He tells her, "The men have got all the get-up-and-get they want, but they need the women to point them straight, and to show them how to lead that other kind of life that isn't all grind."[20] Laura marries him, and for a while they are very happy sharing their interests. They appear to be perfect partners, reading her novels and his business dispatches together.

But the Jadwins' expectations that they will live a sane and happy domestic life linking his business practicality and her artistic refinement are unfulfilled. They build an ostentatious, overdecorated lakefront mansion at the south end of Lincoln Park. It contains an art gallery full of precious objects that have no integral relation to their lives or to Chicago except as a display of a *nouveau riche* elite's pretentious and half-formed notions of high culture. This gallery is two stories high, domed with colored glass, and lined with cabinets full of bibelots.[21] Laura and her husband drift apart, as couples often do in Chicago novels. Jadwin soon gets bored in this stuffy house, and he becomes increasingly active in wheat trading, much to Laura's displeasure. As Jadwin gets sucked into the whirlpool, his neglect of Laura drives her into the arms of Corthell. On one of the evenings when he has worked late downtown while she has entertained Corthell at home, he bursts in on them as they sit together in the gallery, teetering on the brink of a love affair. Jadwin is so excited by the fact that he has cleared a half million dollars in a deal this very day that he does not see that Corthell is trying to take Laura from him. In fact, his impulse is to help this hapless artist who has no sense of where the real opportunities are. It is at this point that Jadwin, with a condescending generosity born of his exultation, advises Corthell to buy May wheat because it will "beat art all hollow."[22]

Art and business now again seem hopelessly at odds, as do the contexts in which men and women move. Artists like Corthell, who associate with women, lack the virile dynamism that distinguishes the great businessman, but all of Jadwin's vast energy is expended on his work so that he becomes sexually impotent. By the time Jadwin sees his wife in the evening he is too exhausted to be aroused by her charms, or even to pay her much attention. Soon he is spending nights alone in hotel rooms more convenient to the Pit, while at home he and Laura occupy separate bedrooms.[23] As he nears total physical collapse, only the Pit—not Laura's beauty—can galvanize him into passionate action, and it leaves him more exhausted after every encounter. When his corner finally caves in, his health breaks with it. At the end of the novel he is invalided and prematurely aged.

Jadwin is not the only one to blame for the disappointment of the couple's hopes for life together in Chicago. Laura fails to "point him straight" and keep him from losing himself in business. Instead of trying to understand her husband's obsession with grain speculation, she luxuriates in the role of abandoned wife, "acting the part of a woman unhappy amid luxuries, who looked back with regret and with longing towards a joyous, simple childhood." This self-indulgence is understandable, but it does nothing to relieve their problems. She loses herself for a while in various "female" activities of charity and culture. She speaks of endowing a hospital or of doing church or settlement work, and then she suddenly sets off on a binge of conspicuous consumption, buying a new wardrobe and attending the races in her showiest hat and carriage. She also dabbles in collecting, but this, too, only thinly veils her anger and boredom.[24]

Her most elaborate response is to retreat into a neurotic aestheticism. She has a stage built in the unused ballroom of her mansion on which she performs, alone and in costume, such parts as Lady Macbeth, Juliet, Portia, and Ophelia. Then, in final desperation, she tries to reclaim her husband's attention by springing her performances on him. Jadwin promises her one morning that he will return by eight, and, when he does, servants lead him into the darkened art gallery. Suddenly, to his consternation, the fully costumed Laura stands before him in dazzling light and recites to her bewildered husband from Racine's *Athalie*—in French. She then quickly switches costumes to become Bizet's Carmen, and directs her husband to pump the player attachment on the built-in organ as she dances to the bolero "with the same wild, untamed spirit as a tongue of fire."[25]

Her bizarre performance stops when her husband, himself near nervous collapse, tells her correctly that she seems overwrought, that he prefers her "old self, quiet, and calm, and dignified"—and much simpler. Apparently returned to her senses, she soothes him by playing the old songs and hymns, like "Open Thy Lattice to Me," he loves best as he reminisces on the lost happiness of his youth that he wishes they could recapture.[26] But after realizing that this calm comfort is what he needs and what she must provide if she is to be close to him once more, Laura again becomes angry and distraught when her husband's broker appears and summons Jadwin back downtown to plan his defense against the Bear faction.

Laura's peculiar behavior dramatizes further Norris's ideas about art and modern life. She came to Chicago in the first place because she wished to become a great actress and felt that her ambitions were misunderstood and stifled in New England. Norris implies that in spite of Laura's appreciation of the "dramatic" qualities of Chicago-in-the-making and her wise choice of Jadwin over Corthell, her lingering faith in traditional high culture gives her a false view of life that makes her miserable. In the opening scene at the opera, for example, she imagines amid the music and the excitement of the theater that Corthell is a Renaissance artist-priest and Jadwin a merchant-prince. Her idea of a perfect world is one in which she, a beautiful heroine, should "die beautifully, gently, in some garden far away," and "all the world should be sorry for her, and would weep over her when they found her dead and beautiful in her garden, amid the flowers and the birds, in some far-off place, where it was always early morning and where there was soft music."[27]

Her desire for this perfect stasis contrasts sharply with her husband's hunger for the Pit, where thousands of major transactions are consummated between opening and closing on a single day. If Jadwin loses control of himself when he does "battle" downtown, Laura's moods seem flighty and escapist. Despite her apparent agreement with Jadwin's taste in art, she never fully loses her desire for life to be equal to the make-believe world that she sees singing to her from the Auditorium stage. Like Thea, she wishes "that she could loose her clasp upon the sordid, material modern life that, perforce, she must hold to," and drift into the realm the opera creates.[28] When her real marriage falls apart, she deals with this problem through a conception of herself as tragic heroine, and she performs her elaborate histrionics which celebrate her misery and undermine her marriage further.

The book's conclusion is still another case in which a Chicago novel evades its most interesting complexities. It cannot be said that the book retreats into romantic melodrama, since it is suffused with elements of this form from the start, but Laura's total renunciation of her independence is disappointing. She continues to vacillate between loyalty to her husband and some ideal of fulfillment loosely tied to her aesthetic ambitions. She forces Corthell to agree to run away with her, although how much she loves him and whether she intends to carry out this plan are not clear. Just after Laura and Corthell arrange their elopement, her husband, this very day completely ruined, staggers home. Laura immediately sees that her place is by her husband's side and that her love for him, "the supreme triumph of a woman's life," must be "less a victory than a capitulation."[29] Together they abandon both their artistic and their business ambitions. They settle Jadwin's affairs and leave Chicago forever.

The book, which seems otherwise so different, now suddenly resembles those of Fuller, Payne, and Herrick, which usually conclude with a character or characters realizing that there is no satisfactory way to live humanely in Chicago. One must seek the higher, personal rewards of family life (which is as highly sentimentalized here as anywhere), renouncing all worldly ambition and abandoning the notion of career and the hollow prizes of wealth and power to other misguided souls who will be similarly undone. Laura and Jadwin are reunited, but they withdraw from Chicago, two defeated souls bonded together more by the memory of their trauma than by their hope for the future.[30]

The major problem with this ending is that Norris undermines both his depiction of urban business life as a calling that energizes the bold and imaginative individual and his portrayal of Jadwin as the most creative person of his day. Instead, he reasserts the idea that runs through his "Epic of the Wheat" that the forces of nature dwarf even those who seem most able to control them. Jadwin is finally only the wheat's most dramatic victim in *The Pit* (several other victims in *The Octopus* are equally dramatic), and Norris's thoughts on urban artistry are lost by the time the daunted trader shuffles sadly out of his dismantled mansion and into the hired hack that will take him to the railroad station and out of Chicago. Corthell, too, has abandoned the field. Jadwin learns from Laura that the artist, his hopes of winning Laura now irrevocably lost, has departed for Europe.

Norris perhaps found a "formula" with which to "grip" the "Real Life" of Chicago, but there are definite problems with it. Having defined the violent conflict of the business world and the commercial life of the city as the principle of reality, he romanticizes it too ornately with all his talk of battlefields and whirlpools. He finds "Romance" on Michigan Avenue, but it is not as convincingly "real" as he wants it to be. He seems finally as beaten by the wheat as anyone in his books. His strategy in *The Pit* is to celebrate the vitality of the Pit as blind force, conceding that there is no way to master it. Whatever the excitement of the novel's best passages (and Norris's powers of description and storytelling are impressive), the reader cannot help feeling troubled by the uncritical worship of power, with its accompanying unmourning dismissal of sensitivity. The most imaginative and creative man in the city is the self-made master-capitalist, but he moves in a world with no significant creative choices except "buy" or "sell," and he is an "artist" who produces nothing but social and economic havoc as he inevitably *un*makes himself.

TRILOGY OF DESIRE

The three novels in Theodore Dreiser's *Trilogy of Desire* (*The Financier, The Titan,* and *The Stoic*) rank with *The Pit* as would-be epics of American business. All the books in the *Trilogy* are set at least partly in Chicago, though the author's favorite city is the primary setting only in the second volume.[31] Despite Norris's and Dreiser's common interest in determinism that leads literary historians to group them together as Naturalists, their purposes and methods in their business novels were quite different. Norris constructed his book around actions meant to show the titanic power of the wheat as a natural force outside man's control. Dreiser believed that the forces that determine existence were more manifold and subtle than did Norris, and that these forces varied a great deal in their effects on different personality types. He was particularly interested in the powerful businessman as a type because of his apparent mastery of experience.

Dreiser was also more committed than was Norris to furnishing documentary evidence and descriptions not only of people, places, and things, but also of the financial strategies and transactions of his almost superhuman hero, Frank Cowperwood. His portrait of Cowperwood, though it includes details from Dreiser's own life as well as wholly fictive elements, was based primarily on his extensive research on the career of Charles T. Yerkes, who was especially prominent in the last two decades of the nineteenth century in the ownership of Chicago's streetcars and elevated railways.[32] In choosing Yerkes as his model, Dreiser deliberately selected a protagonist who was notorious for his unscrupulous business practices and his adulterous affairs. He was much more concerned than was Norris with the relationship between morality and success in life, as well as with the possibility that certain rare individuals could defy the rules and limits that governed most people.

Dreiser's *Trilogy*, like Norris's novel, is an important commentary on American culture and urban life because it argues that the meaning of art in the city has to be redefined. Dreiser's work unfortunately also resembles Norris's in that his handling of this question is at times contradictory and uncertain, and his books require close examination in order to determine just what he is saying. It is evident that Dreiser agrees that the often viciously materialistic world of urban finance that Cowperwood rules is one of the most promising subjects for the novelist. He explicitly asserts that the financier is the most creative figure of the late nineteenth and early twentieth centuries, that business and art in America in this period must be understood in relation to one another, and that what the financier does should be considered in aesthetic terms.

Throughout the *Trilogy* Dreiser repeatedly calls Cowperwood an artist. But just what kind of "artist" is he? Dreiser's opinion about this seems to vary. In the passage cited as epigraph, which appears early in *The Financier*, Dreiser first states flatly that finance is an art, then quickly distinguishes mere business from the "artistic" realm of nature and the appreciation of beauty and subtlety. He implies that the highly skilled financier, even if he is not expressly opposed to beauty or subtlety, is not one with the poet or painter who, in Dreiser's view, appreciates such things. He believes that the conventional financier would be distracted from his work if he paid too much attention to art. Cowperwood is extraordinary in that he can devote himself to fine art without interfering with his business, but he must exercise care to keep the two worlds separate lest he undermine his pleasure and success in each of them.

Although Dreiser at this point respects those who excel at business or art (by which he usually means painting or writing), he does not maintain that matters of high finance are the same as abstractions of philosophy and æsthetics; he never quite equates the problem of controlling a city's transportation system with the question of determining what is truth, or with the processes by which the artist creates a masterpiece. Still, he does see certain links between Cowperwood and some of the great artists of his time. On a trip to Europe, for example, Cowperwood meets several painters, including Rossetti and Whistler, and recognizes in them "the emotional, egotistic, and artistic soul." While he senses immediately "that there could be little in common between such men and himself in so far as personal contact was concerned," he also feels that "there was mutual ground on which they could meet."[33] He will not be their slavish admirer, but he does appreciate their special powers and discovers deep satisfaction in becoming a knowledgeable collector.

As Dreiser develops his portrait of Cowperwood further, he begins to blur the distinctions between a Cowperwood and a Rossetti or Whistler. He calls his financier an artist more frequently, emphasizing his sensitivity and creative power. Cowperwood's nerve and skill as a businessman become inseparable from his aesthetic sense, and Dreiser attempts to dramatize how this is so.[34] Central to this dramatization is a conception he shared with Norris, that Chicago is an emerging center of civilization worthy of appreciation by the most demanding sensibility. Of all the city's "hungry men" with "idyls and romances in their minds," the great businessman is the most attuned to the city's glorious possibilities.

Cowperwood's artistic sense, Dreiser argues, is the key to understanding his business career. In *The Financier,* young Frank is originally drawn to the commercial center of Philadelphia for aesthetic reasons. The financial district is described as if it were a Brueghel painting or a Hogarth drawing, full of comic-grotesque commotion as the traders swarm over each other: "At first it seemed quite a wonderful thing to young Cowperwood—the very physical face of it—for he liked human presence and activity." Only later does "the sense of the thing as a picture or a dramatic situation" fade, and Cowperwood comes "down to a clearer sense of the intricacies of the problem before him." Even then the issue of art is still relevant. "Buying and selling stocks," Cowperwood soon learns, "was an art, a subtlety, almost a psychic emotion. Suspicion, intuition, feeling—these were things to be 'long' on."[35] The terms "intuition," "feeling," "subtlety," and "psychic emotion" (used also by Norris when he discusses Jadwin's skills) imply that Cowperwood's business talents are similar to those of the artist.

The visual impression of the commercial heart of the city inspires Cowperwood again when he approaches Chicago for a fresh start after his infamous career in Philadelphia. Chicago, a much newer and more malleable city, is more attractive than Philadelphia to the ambitious Cowperwood. Its appeal to him is described as that of a great painting or musical composition: "This raw, dirty town seemed naturally to compose itself into stirring artistic pictures. Why, it fairly sang!"[36] These "stirring artistic pictures" are, however, only a rough sketch to be altered and filled in. During the course of his career in Chicago, Cowperwood remakes the face of the city with his streetcars. He is the ultimate urban realist because he works with elements of the city itself, not words or paints. Cowperwood's relationship with the city as artist-financier is complicated and paradoxical, for the city is both his subject *and* his medium, the source *and* the product of his inspiration.

Perhaps the best demonstration of Cowperwood's urban artistry is his use of the tunnels under the Chicago River in *The Titan*. One day, while again encountering the recurrent problem of having to wait for one of the many bridges on the Chicago River to turn so that he can cross, Cowperwood begins to ponder how a transit system might avoid such delays. Once again he sees the scene before him as a work of art. The tangle of teams and boats is chaotic, but also "lovely, human, natural, Dickensesque—a fit subject for a Daumier, a Turner, or a Whistler."[37] It is also a "fit subject" for Cowperwood, who moves from the problem to its possible solution, conceiving another "picture" that can make him wealthier. He assembles his raw materials. He recalls the unused and rat-infested tunnels under the river that were graded too steeply for the wagons for which they were originally constructed, and he realizes that the recently developed technique of cable traction now makes these tunnels practical. Bold and ingenious maneuvers win him rights to the tunnels, and in relatively short order the artist-financier builds a new transit line under the river. The men who own the tunnels could have exploited them as Cowperwood does, but they lack his courage and imaginative vision.

Dreiser's portrait of Cowperwood carries the idea of the self-made man to its limits. Cowperwood's finest artistry is that he creates himself and the conditions and rules by which he works.[38] He believes that the only person he needs and the only one he hopes to please is Frank Cowperwood. To be sure, his work does require a setting like Chicago. He and the city mutually develop and limit one another, but he changes Chicago far more than it affects him. This is true even when he is thwarted at the end of *The Titan*. He loses his battle for long-term streetcar franchises in spite of his wholesale bribery of the state legislature and the city council, but the coalition of financiers, politicians, and citizens that defeats him is an alliance only he could have aroused.

Dreiser explained his view of the businessman as artist in "The American Financier," published in 1920 in his collection of essays, *Hey Rub-a-Dub-Dub*. Dreiser again moves from the idea that the businessman at best is a metaphorical "artist" to an assertion that he is an artist by any standards. Dreiser states that although the financier is selfish and immoral, his "aggressive organizing mind" resembles that of the epic poet or painter. It "finds itself blazing with an impulse to get some one new thing done: it conceives some great scheme, is inspired with some great enthusiasm for something; and thereafter all else is as nothing." The financier may be unethical, but "his revolt against the commonplace fixity, rigidity and the like of the slower-moving man cannot be looked upon as either wholly evil or in vain." Dreiser expands his main point near the close of his essay. "At best," he observes, "all we have is the individual, not always financial, by any means, or artistic, but one who has dreamed out something: music, a picture, poetry, a machine, a railroad, an empire—anything, in short, that man as race or nation can use or rejoice in."[39]

In this essay, as within the *Trilogy*, Dreiser described the financier in terms that are as Romantic as they are Spencerian and Neitzschean.[40] Perceived as a Romantic artist, Cowperwood becomes a charismatic figure possessed of creative power equal to that of the greatest artificers. Writing in a newspaper article in 1914, the year of *The Titan's* publication, Dreiser called his central character "[a] rebellious Lucifer this, glorious in his sombre conception of the value of power," and he regretted the passing of the age of business titans such as Cowperwood. To some, Dreiser said, the financier's world will seem a "night-black pool . . . , played over by the fulgerous gleams of his own individualistic and truly titanic mind," but "[t]o the illuminate it will have a very different meaning, I am sure, a clear suggestion of the inscrutable forces of life as they shift and play—marring what they do not glorify— pagan, fortuitous, inalienably artistic."[41]

No study of the *Trilogy* can ignore Cowperwood's affairs and his art collecting, which further reveal how he is a financier-artist. Dreiser sees Cowperwood's women and his precious possessions as necessary in the development of a larger perspective on life by which the financier can transcend the limits of his materialistic world through the pursuit of the beautiful. Cowperwood's abilities to make money, to alter the city, to seduce attractive women, and to assemble an art collection are tied to one personal quality that Dreiser calls "artistic."

Each of Cowperwood's lovers is described as an art object in herself and as a stage in his education as a connoisseur. There is a general logic of aesthetic progression toward greater refinement as he moves from one woman to the next. At the opening of the ostentatious mansion Cowperwood builds on South Michigan Avenue, his wife Aileen, red-haired and radiant, is herself the central feature of the grand art gallery, contending with an "intensely nude" Gerôme painting of odalisques of the harem at bath and a brilliant portrait of herself that face each other from opposite ends of the room. His last mistress, Berenice Fleming, is a pure ideal in the form of a woman, and a very improbable character. She desires to live in such a way, Dreiser explains, "so that her life as well as her personality should be in itself an art form."[42]

Cowperwood's increasingly "aesthetic" relationship with women parallels his art collecting. He does make several purchases mainly for the sake of publicity, either because he wants to make a splash in society or because he wishes to demonstrate to the other would-be titans his impressive combination of financial and imaginative power. But just as Cowperwood's taste in women moves from the voluptuous Aileen to the ethereal Berenice, so his interest in art becomes more spiritual; material things eventually are important mainly as Cowperwood's access to some eternal ideal of beauty, and less essential as an end in themselves. Early in *The Financier*, Dreiser describes this progression "Wealth, in the beginning, had seemed the only goal, to which had been added the beauty of women. And now art, for art's sake—the first faint radiance of a rosy dawn—had begun to shine in upon him, and to the beauty of womanhood he was beginning to see how necessary it was to add the beauty of life—the beauty of material background—how, in fact, the only background for great beauty was great art." Cowperwood's mind at this point, "in spite of his outward placidity," is "tinged with a great seeking."[43]

From *Sister Carrie* on, Dreiser spoke more urgently than any other writer of this "seeking" and what he called the "lure of the material." In the *Trilogy* he most fully discussed where the lure leads. Cowperwood's commercial success enables him to understand as few men can the limits of this success. He woos his women and collects his paintings against his increasingly firm belief that the urban world he dominates is of little worth, that the basic terms of common experience are the meaninglessness of life and the mystery of death. The ideal of beauty becomes for him a means of defying the great material fact of human mortality. What he wants from women is their youth, freshness, and vitality, and what he desires in art is its timelessness. He rejects most modern art because it is "dated" by its newness in a way Old Masters are not since they have survived the test of time. He is disloyal to all his women—even Berenice—because they cannot stay young in years or in his affections. "Truth to say," Dreiser explains, "he must always have youth, the illusion of beauty, vanity in womanhood, the novelty of a new untested temperament, quite as he must have pictures, old porcelain, music, a mansion, illuminated missals, power, the applause of the great, unthinking world."[44]

The financial "art" that Cowperwood creates has none of the timeless spiritual qualities of the art he collects, which, he explains, "helped me to live through the endless practical problems to which I have had to devote myself."[45] Dreiser concludes that a financier like Cowperwood is an artist, and a far more significant figure than any conventional artist in his day, but his material success is important mainly as a necessary precondition of his spiritual refinement. At the same time, Dreiser implies that Cowperwood's "artistic" sensibility is what enabled him to make so much money in the first place. Cowperwood transcends the commercial urban culture of his time not, as Thea Kronborg does, by blocking it out and avoiding it, but by moving head-on and mastering it, which paradoxically seems to be the only way to escape it.

Frank Norris made a similar argument in *The Pit*. Jadwin is no longer a businessman but an epic hero and artist when he attaches the common act of buying and selling wheat to the idea of a corner. Less reflective than Cowperwood, Jadwin is still unconsciously haunted by the meaninglessness of a life which bores him. His response is to confront the Chicago best embodied in the Pit by attempting to dominate it with his nerve, imagination, and skill. Once he begins to do this, Jadwin seems to be freed from the conventional notions of wealth and career that entrap other figures in Chicago fiction.

Like Jadwin, Cowperwood is sometimes described more as a man of destiny than as a businessman. When during his years in Philadelphia he is imprisoned for larceny and embezzlement in the Eastern District Penitentiary of Pennsylvania, "Something kept telling him that whatever his present state he must yet grow to be a significant personage, one whose fame would be heralded the world over—who must try, try, try." Dreiser's account of this annunciation of the businessman as Romantic artist continues: "It was not given all men to see far or to do brilliantly; but to him it was given, and he must be what he was cut out to be. There was no more escaping the greatness that was inherent in him than there was for so many others the littleness that was in them."[46]

But Cowperwood's "artistry," like Jadwin's, is even more personal than Thea's, whose performance magically enchants her audience. By its very nature, the "art" of the financier is intensely selfish, something very far from the democratic and reform-minded art that Jane Addams advocated. Jadwin's work wrecks others (a close friend of his kills himself after being ruined by "the Unknown Bull") and dehumanizes this kind man, who exults demonically in his triumph as his character unravels. Cowperwood cares mainly for the triumph of his will and thinks little about the welfare of other Chicagoans, whether they are allies, competitors, or those his streetcars serve. He helps build modern Chicago, but he extracts more than he gives and does nothing to lessen social divisions.

Though Dreiser closely followed the details of Charles Yerkes's life in his depiction of Cowperwood, his romanticization of the financier, like Norris's, stretches the reader's credulity. One must keep in mind the muckrakers' views of figures such as Cowperwood as modern brigands rather than as creative intelligences. In *Lawless Wealth*, for example, Charles Edward Russell admitted that Yerkes possessed "a certain combination of hardihood, audacity, dexterity, and persistence that was rather out of the common," but asserted that the riches of men like him "represent no service to society, no reward for any one thing bettered, no creation, no development, but only the means to seize and to retain the resources of the country."[47] It is finally too hard to accept that gaining control of Chicago's streetcars by threats, thefts, bluffs, and bribery is "artistic," especially when one is never very sure what Dreiser means by art. Like Norris, he can define it only in extremes, either in terms of Cowperwood's and Chicago's creative vitality or as a reclusive aestheticism. Norris at least made a choice as to which world was the more "artistic," even if to do so he caricatured the aesthete as effeminate and glorified the businessman as much as Dreiser did. Dreiser wished to be a hardheaded realist, celebrating the "creative" will-to-power in crude, crass Chicago. But he also wanted to say that there was something finer than this crassness. In the *Trilogy* he is never sure which goal, wealth or beauty, is more important, or exactly how they are tied to one another.

Both Norris and Dreiser depict an urban world in which art by any definition has little promise to make everyday life more satisfying for the many. The conclusions of their novels of business are quite similar in some ways to those of the books that center around female artists. *The Pit* and the *Trilogy* seem to advocate escaping the city or avoiding its malaise by dominating it through the exercise of power—be it financial or dramatic or musical—and Norris and Dreiser call this power "artistic." The alternative for Cowperwood is an incapacitating nihilism. Aware that he is dying, he tells Aileen that in building his art gallery, "I have tried to bring into my life and yours the beauty which is entirely outside of cities and business."[48] Successful as he is, he is as alienated from his milieu as Thea or Carrie, or any other Chicago protagonist.

Although it is the city that first inspires him as a creative artist, the triumph of his sensibility distances him from that first, now too concrete, field of creation.

Windy McPherson's Son

Sherwood Anderson's first published novel is an odd book at war with itself. While it clearly is a critique of the romanticization of the businessman and an attack on the cult of success, *Windy McPherson's Son* (1916) offers a highly developed and sympathetic portrait of the great businessman as artist. Anderson's opinion of his businessman-hero and what he should do changes back and forth a great deal as the novel unfolds, no doubt partly because of Anderson's still undeveloped literary skills, but also because he, too, had trouble making up his mind.[49] For all its faults, the book is intriguing for what light it sheds on Anderson and his subject, and on the engagement of other writers of the period with the commercial culture.

Sam McPherson is a turn-of-the-century corporate leader as successful as Cowperwood, although he is never described in the same Nietzschean terms. He is a more modern businessman who works his way through a large organization, an arms trust. While he is more sophisticated than Jadwin, he has comparatively little of Cowperwood's passion for the fine arts. He is, furthermore, more sensitive than either of them to the opinions and feelings of others. What most distinguishes him from them is his ability to extricate himself from business at the peak of his success. While still a relatively young man, Sam dramatically drops everything to wander across the country in a holy search (he is compared to Saint Jerome and even to Christ) for Truth which is only partly successful and totally unlikely. This search begins with an act which Jadwin and Cowperwood, who thrive on conflict, would never even consider. Sam's renunciation occurs in a Chicago boardroom during a stock control fight which Sam wins in violation of a promise to his wife that he would not unseat her father as nominal head of the company. During a recess in the meeting, Sam notes that he had been scribbling absentmindedly over and over again the words, "The best men spend their lives seeking truth."[50] He subsequently becomes a major power in the firearms industry before giving it all up to go on his quest for enlightenment.

Throughout the novel Anderson ponders whether the individual of such intelligence and imagination should oppose the commercial culture that dominates the day, join it, or somehow do both. He considers these alternatives in *Windy* with a plot that combines several formulas that recur in Chicago writing. The first of four parts of the novel is a narrative of Sam's boyhood in Caxton, Iowa. This section is very similar to other Chicago versions of the tale of the young man (or woman) from the provinces awakening to the visions of artistry and fame that he can only fulfill in the city.[51] There is a distinct Horatio Alger cast to Sam's story, for this sensitive young hero is also a voracious go-getter with a hunger for making money and moving ahead.[52] The second part of *Windy* describes Sam's public triumph and personal travails in Chicago, recalling certain aspects of *The Pit* and some of Fuller's, Herrick's, and Payne's fiction. The third part is Sam's search for truth, a mission with ancient antecedents if no precise parallel in Chicago literature, even in books in which the protagonist retreats from the city for a time. The novel ends with a brief concluding section.

In Book I, Anderson establishes that business and art in late nineteenth-century America are closely related. Young Sam McPherson is an energetic money-maker, but he also is driven by an intuitive sense that there must be something more to life than money and the petty concerns of Caxton. These intuitions draw him to John Telfer, who seems to belong to another world. The son of a Caxton banker, the flamboyant Telfer had gone to New York and Paris as a young man to study art. But, "lacking ability or industry," he came back home with his goals unattained to live a smug and comfortable life as a waggish and somewhat embittered amateur philosopher.[53] Telfer recognizes Sam's superior ambition and intelligence, seeing in the boy a protégé who can succeed where he has failed in making something distinguished of his life. Most important, Telfer impresses upon Sam that there is this thing called art which gives life whatever meaning it has.

Very early in the novel, Telfer is offended when one of the other men in town describes a local woman who gives china-painting lessons as "a kind of an artist." His long, outraged, loosely Romantic disquisition on art that follows is very important to the rest of the book since it defines the kind of ideal experience to which Sam aspires. Telfer explains that great art is never subordinated to common use. An artist has "divine audacity" that transcends the common, a quality that is necessary because he is involved in "a battle in which is engaged against him all of the accumulative genius of the world." Telfer specifically differentiates the artist from the businessman, who contends with small-minded people, and the scientist, who studies inanimate matter. "But an artist tests his brains against the greatest brains of all times;" Telfer asserts, "he stands upon the peak of life and hurls himself against the world."[54]

Telfer tries to instill in Sam some larger vision that can survive against the prevailing ethos of materialism by incorporating it. He tells Sam that there is no virtue in poverty, for wealth applied intelligently "gives freedom and destroys fear," partly because it "brings into men's lives beauty and the love of beauty." He goes a step further and argues also that material success is a measure of the great artist, who shares certain qualities with the successful businessman, particularly an "eager hunger and shrewdness." Telfer implies that the drive to make money is an important counterbalance for the individual with an artistic sensibility. "The mind that has in it the love of the beautiful, that stuff that makes our poets, artists, musicians, and actors," Telfer says, "needs this turn for shrewd money getting or it will destroy itself." He adds, "And the really great artists have it," for it is only in "books and stories" that "the great men starve in garrets." While Norris and Dreiser claimed that some self-made men have a streak of artistry, here Anderson states through Telfer that the truly great artist will create, among his other work, a fortune.[55]

Sam quits school in his mid-teens, but Telfer's influence never leaves him. On his own the boy reads Whitman, and he sometimes awakens in the middle of summer nights to the call of a "strange longing." He creeps out of his bed to gaze through the window and meditate on his destiny. These incidents are similar to Frank Cowperwood's intimations of his own inevitable greatness even as he sits in prison, as well as to Sister Carrie's recurring sense that something better than what she has waits somewhere ahead. Like Frank Cowperwood and Carrie Meeber, Sam wants all that worldly success promises and some ineffable thing beyond that he feels is best expressed in the poetry Telfer gives him.

These desires are urban dreams that Caxton cannot fulfill. When Sam is only fifteen, he feels "the call of the city." He listens eagerly to the stories of the city told by traveling salesmen and, like Cowperwood and Laura Jadwin, develops a sense of Chicago as an exciting and aesthetically appealing setting in which he wants an active role: "In this *picture* [emphasis added] Sam thought he saw a place for himself. He conceived of life in the city as a great game in which he believed he could play a sterling part." Mary Underwood, Sam's teacher and confidante, advises him, "Go to your city and make your fight," her choice of words recalling Telfer's conception of life and artistry as a great struggle.[56] When Sam's mother dies, he is free to leave Caxton.

As Sam rises to the top of corporate life in Chicago, Anderson discusses his ideas on the relationship between business and art in the commercial city. There are many descriptive passages here which could have come out of *The Pit* or any of Dreiser's writings on Chicago. These echo Norris's and Dreiser's belief that Chicago at the turn of the century was an especially exciting place for the artist to be. Anderson reads the city as he would a poem or a painting, talking about the "meaning" and "message" of the South Water Street market area where Sam gets his start in Chicago. After describing the teamsters, the buyers, the colorful produce from all over the world that flows in and out, and the enormous scale of the entire operation, Anderson marvels at "the wonder of these things." Although Anderson points out that Sam is sometimes unresponsive to the excitement of the urban spectacle, his hero does view the city as an enthralling scene, a place that is thrilling for artistic reasons that are inseparable from its financial promise.

In a passage very similar to the one that describes the pleasure that young Frank Cowperwood takes at viewing the business heart of Philadelphia, Sam walks from Madison Street to State, "seeing the crowds of men and women, boys and girls, clambering aboard the cable cars, massed upon the pavements, forming in groups, the groups breaking and reforming, and the whole making a picture intense, confusing, awe-inspiring." Sam, Anderson says, "liked it all," and a basic part of its appeal, as in Cowperwood's case, is the way it attracts him to enter into the "picture" and remake it on his own terms: "The eager, straining rush of the whole, seemed no more to him than a kind of gigantic setting for action; action controlled by a few quiet, capable men—of whom he intended to be one—intent upon growth."[57]

In short, the city attracts, nurtures, and fulfills the talents of McPherson the artist-businessman, "who had the cold, quick business stroke of the money-maker combined with an unusually active interest in the problems of life and of living." From here on, Anderson really blurs the distinction between businessman and artist. He explicitly compares Sam's business sense with the creative intelligence of the artist: "The stroke that he [Sam] saw in the hand of the successful business men about him is the stroke also of the master painter, scientist, actor, singer, prize fighter. It was the hand of Whistler, Balzac, Agassiz, and Terry McGovern." This comparison with "Terrible Terry" McGovern, the famous prizefighter, and embattled artists like Balzac and Whistler, repeats Telfer's Romantic description of the artist as warrior.[58]

Anderson tries to demonstrate that the great businessman is worthy of the term "artist," at the same time pointing out that the same qualities that make Sam so eminent in the financial world inevitably lead him to realize that there is more to life than accumulating money and power. Though Sam's material success, like Cowperwood's, seems to be a precondition of his liberation, his business career and his longings for something more from life than wealth are more directly opposed than these things are in the *Trilogy of Desire*. The book changes direction several times, as Sam alternates between believing that whatever fulfillment he finds must be as a powerful businessman and thinking that the corporate world is eating him away.

Anderson examines the conflicts that Sam McPherson feels through his hero's relationships with a series of people he meets in Chicago who fill Telfer's and Mary Underwood's roles as spiritual advisers. The first is .

a minor character named Janet Eberly. Sam spends many evenings after work in her Wabash Avenue apartment, talking with her as he once discussed things with Telfer. Janet criticizes "Chicago men of money and action and growth" as being "blind, all blind" to what Anderson vaguely calls "a whole purposeful universe of thought and action." She "made it possible for him later to see life with a broadness and scope of vision that was no part of the pushing, energetic young man of dollars and of industry." The second and far more important person Sam meets in Chicago is Sue Rainey, the daughter of his boss. Sam is immediately drawn to Sue's independent spirit, intellect, and idealism, and he proposes not long after their first encounter. He envisions a life with her as the goal of his quest for something finer. She offers a strategy by which they can use their wealth and freedom to serve the world, although this plan, too, is imprecise. Her idea is to devote their main energies to raising children who, presumably, will help build a better future. This means, however, abandoning the ambition for business success that brought Sam to Chicago in the first place. Sue tells him explicitly that their union "means giving up your dreams of power."[59]

The McPhersons' marriage, like the Jadwins', tries to combine traditional domestic happiness with an active, equal, dynamic partnership oriented toward public life. Anderson at first seems to believe in it, stating that Sue's grand design "had stirred every vestige of sleeping nobility in Sam," thus implying that his "dreams of power" had eroded this nobility. Sam looks upon his business career as "nonsense and vanity," and his expectant vision of Sue with their babes in her arms is described almost as a religious experience of spiritual ecstasy.[60] Their love, Sam feels, will purge him of the greed that has characterized his dealings with men and the lust that had cheapened his attitudes toward women. For a while their partnership works better than the Jadwins' ever does. Sam still manages the company, even if his competitive drive loses its sharp edge, and he delights in Sue's company as they entertain her circle of intellectuals, artists, and social reformers. But three pregnancies end without a live birth, and these tragedies deflate their sense of high purpose and their spirit of camaraderie.

In the face of their failure to create a family, the McPhersons' lives settle for a long period into another pattern familiar in Chicago writing. Sue slips into a variation of the aesthetic trap, supporting "causes" of all sorts of which Sam and Anderson are skeptical. After a half-hearted attempt to go along, Sam reverts to a Darwinian view of life as a creative struggle that challenges and rewards the strong. His response to his increasing alienation from Sue and the disappointment of his hope that something better is possible from life than the rewards of business in Chicago is to return to his former, less abstract goals. Sam decides, "I will do some real work and make some more money. That's the place for me."[61]

Sam then sets about forming the firearms trust, even though it entails violating his promise to Sue that he will not hurt her father by reducing his prominence in the business. She leaves him when she gets word that he has broken his vow. At this point, Anderson seems to endorse this betrayal of Sue. Before the crucial vote at the board meeting, Sam takes a meditative walk along the lake. He decides that he has denied some essential part of his being in making the pledge to Sue, that it was a foolish gesture, "a part of the ridiculous and sentimental attitude of her father, and the promise given her insignificantly and unfairly won." The promise has nothing to do with the reality of urban life, which is rewarding and exhilarating. Sam turns his back to the lake to face "the towering city before him" and declares, "It [the promise] was never a part of all this."[62]

Anderson even inserts an apologia for the "Captain of Finance" of the turn of the century, arguing that there is "a widespread misunderstanding" of the motives of many such men who became prominent in this age "of change and sudden bewildering growth." He again describes business leaders as Romantic artists looking for worlds to conquer, once more recalling Dreiser as he speaks of them as "men who thought and acted quickly and with a daring and audacity impossible to the average mind." If they were power hungry and unscrupulous, he contends, they were the best their milieu could expect. He criticizes the times for offering them "no better outlet for their vast energies," but this only bolsters his assertion that they are the artists of their day. Sam's creative powers need exercise, and business provides the best available opportunity.[63]

Then Anderson switches direction again, as Sam's new plan also fails. Now he calls "the McPherson Chicago crowd" a bunch of pirates "upon the high seas of finance," and even Sam comes to see his work as a series of shady deals. In his isolation and depression, Sam lives a "nightmare" of dissipation from which he awakens when the pathetic suicide of Tom Rainey and the lonely death of Mary Underwood, both of which arouse feelings of guilt, shake him deeply and lead to his unlikely search for Truth.

Sam departs for the countryside, looking for physical labor to repair his body and worthy causes to restore his soul. His journey involves a rejection of the city as it is, an attempt to discover what is wrong with it, and an effort to find a way that life within it might be improved. He takes odd jobs from bartender to construction worker, but he fails to find any answers, for wherever he goes he encounters greed, selfishness, and suspicion of his motives. Early in his journey he has a vision of "a city built for a people, a city independent, beautiful, strong, and free," but he soon doubts that most of mankind can ever be motivated by idealism.[64]

In those moments when Sam hopes to escape and reform his world, he again turns to art as a means of undoing what the vulgar commercial culture has done and of finding a practical idealism for modern life. Above all, he wants to create a realistic urban art that will somehow redeem the city by depicting masterfully what has gone wrong so that conditions can be corrected. Sam, like Anderson and many other ambitious Chicago artists, yearns for an effective form of expression. Looking at the faces he sees on city people, "his fingers ached to get a pencil in his hand, or to spread the faces upon canvas in enduring pigments, to hold them up before the world and to be able to say, 'Here are the faces you, by your lives, have made for yourselves and for your children.'" Sam, Anderson continues, "felt within him a yearning for the power of the artist, the power not only to see the meaning of the faces in the street, but to reproduce what he saw, to get with subtle fingers the story of the achievement of mankind into a face hanging upon a wall." Listening to Telfer and Sue, "Sam had tried to get an inkling of the passion of the artist," and "now walking and looking at the faces rolling past him on the long street he thought that he did understand."[65]

In the short and highly fanciful last section, Sam ends his wanderings when he adopts the three children of a woman who does not want them, thus 'recovering' the three babies he had fathered and lost in the days of his strongest idealism. Without warning to Sue, he takes his new family directly to her. She is at this point living in a cottage outside a New England village. His pilgrimage is like Jackson Hart's penitent journey to his wife Helen in Vermont in Herrick's *The Common Lot*, except that the McPhersons are not going back to Chicago. Sue accepts the whole brood, and at the book's close it seems that they will all live a quiet life together in this peaceful hideaway so far from LaSalle Street and Sam's grand notions of urban artistry.

This conclusion is more of a retreat even than the ending of *The Pit*, for the Jadwins go to the West and the land of the future, while the McPhersons draw the veil around their lives in the rural New England past and the shelter of calm gentility. Their house sounds like a rest home, inappropriate for either businessman or artist. Sam says that here he is facing the great issues of existence, but the cottage is described as "a shut-in place in which he was to live what was left of his life." And, in the last sentence of the book, Sam "stumbled up the steps and into the house," which hardly seems a confident act of affirmation.[66]

On one hand, Anderson agreed with Dreiser and Norris that the businessman was the figure who most shaped his culture and who captured the popular imagination. As *Windy McPherson's Son* also reveals, he believed that some of the best minds and most courageous spirits of the age were naturally drawn to business as the most exciting and rewarding activity of the day, and that men like Sam could be called artists, at least in some figurative sense. In addition, Anderson seconded Dreiser's assertion that material success is a precondition for understanding that there is more to life than making money, though Sam finds final consolation in the bonds of family rather than in the timeless realm of art.

On the other hand, if Anderson shared some of Dreiser's conclusions about the significance of the American businessman and the attractions of business life, he was not as excited as Dreiser (though Dreiser was to change his mind) that such conditions prevailed. Anderson's entire novel, from Sam's conversations with Mary Underwood to his odyssey for Truth, contains his earliest indictments of modern life. His major target was business (and, particularly, industrial) culture, which he believed robbed life of imagination and variety, separated work from craft, equated time with money, made fancy the victim of fact, and left man spiritually and physically maimed, dispirited, and impotent. To the extent that Sam's creative spirit is bound to the ideas of progress and profit, he is the first of many "grotesques" that Anderson defined as a type in *Winesburg, Ohio,* and who are central to all of his fiction. Though Anderson believed that much of the vitality of the nation had left the small towns of America along with the Sam McPhersons, in *Windy* he points out that the city, where this same vitality is channeled into industrialization, standardization, money hunger, and undirected nervous energy, offers small hope for the future.[67]

Anderson's novel is heavily colored by his own personal turmoil, and some of his experiences are especially interesting to a discussion of business and art because Anderson himself tried to make it as a businessman and did not begin his literary career wholeheartedly until he was forty. In the first years of the century he wrote advertising and public relations copy in Chicago, including some articles in a trade journal that boosted the American businessman in the kind of language Lewis later satirized in *Babbitt*.[68] By 1907 he was an independent businessman in Elyria, Ohio, running the Anderson Manufacturing Company, a mail-order concern specializing in a roof-extending paint called "Roof-Fix," and writing his own ad copy. He was apparently content in a middle-class round of office, home, and country club.

He became disenchanted with this life, but he thought he could stay in business and at the same time find a way to express his dreams and discontents. He evidently would bring his secretary patches of manuscript he scribbled in a study he had constructed in his home and to which no one else was admitted. That study became the center of his life, and, whether from failure or active choice (Anderson's own versions of his past are often unreliable), he gave up business. The decisive break came with his supposed mental breakdown in November of 1912. Shortly thereafter he was back in Chicago, the *Windy* manuscript in hand. He wrote advertising to support himself, but now his attention was on his new life and career. He gradually shed the old one. By 1915 Anderson was divorced; he submitted his last ad copy in 1922.

The story of Sam McPherson shows how much he nurtured the hope during his years in Elyria that he could be a creative businessman *and* a successful artist, but the second half of the novel also reveals that Anderson concluded that business and artistic ambitions were mutually exclusive. Sam left Chicago and Anderson returned to it for the freedom of thought and expression that they thought their commercial careers denied them. Both felt deeply that the spirit of corporate America was opposed to satisfying work, love, and imagination, which Anderson identified with artistry. Having attempted to join that spirit, even to lead it, they decided instead to lick it, Sam by going on his search and Anderson by devoting himself to writing about the modern grotesques he found in both country and city. If neither was entirely successful, Anderson would still call it a victory that they tried to reestablish their lives on a humane basis outside the business world.

A comparison of Sam's and Anderson's life is useful in one other respect. One of the most effective ways in which Anderson expressed the problems of the artist in an urban commercial age was through his treatment of his own and Sam's father. Both Irwin Anderson and Windy McPherson were failures, Sherwood Anderson contended, of a special American kind, and their lives told much about their sons' careers and about America at the end of the nineteenth century. Windy's importance is indicated in part by the fact that it is *his* name, after all, that is in the title of the book about his son. The elder Anderson was, like Windy, a Civil War veteran who was unequipped to deal with practical affairs and so moved gradually down the ladder from small businessman to irregularly employed house painter.

Sam is bitter toward his father, whom he sees as a "blustering, pretending, inefficient old man." Windy blames everyone but himself for his failure, and is always trying to recapture his lost "glory" through some heroic gesture, but he only adds to his family's embarrassment. The most important of such episodes occurs when, as part of an Independence Day celebration, he volunteers to ride through Caxton in a Union uniform blowing a bugle. When the great moment comes and he puts his lips to the horn, what shatters the air is a horrible squawk that is the musical equivalent of all Windy's vainglory. Sam never forgives his father the humiliation he feels at the townspeople's laughter. Anderson's portrait of his father in his *Memoirs* and in *A Story Teller's Story* (1924), his fanciful autobiography, is sufficiently similar—incident for incident—to make the source of Windy unmistakable, though Anderson's feelings for his own father are more affectionate than are Sam's for Windy. The characterization of Windy is not entirely unsympathetic, however. Windy's redeeming feature, and perhaps the source of his failure, is his vivid imagination. In a world of fact he tries to live in his fancy.[69]

Throughout his adult life, Sam attempts to compensate for the shame Windy has caused by becoming everything the father had not been, most notably a worldly success. His drive to be a self-made man is partly motivated by his rejection of his father, his refusal to accept Windy as a force in his life "just because he happens to be my father." His ambitions stem from "the belief within him that to make money and to have money would in some way make up for the old half-forgotten humiliations in the life of the McPherson family and would set it on a more secure foundation than the Wobbly Windy had provided." When he goes back on his promise to Sue and betrays her father, he is still drowning out the town's laughter. "Instead of another Windy McPherson . . . ," Anderson explains, "he was still the man who made good, the man who achieved, the kind of man of whom America boasts before the world,"—a success.[70]

To succeed, Sam must become everything his father was not. Windy was a failure, Anderson explains, because he was "amazed and helpless before facts," so Sam feels he must at times be hard-headed and calculating. Anderson criticizes the way the spirit of the age forces this feeling upon sensitive people. In *A Story Teller's Story,* he sees his father's blighted life as one example of the crushing of the creative spirit by the business mentality. "My father lived in a land and in a time when what one later begins to understand a little as the artist in man could not by any possibility be understood by his fellows," he writes. "Dreams then were to be expressed in building railroads and factories, in boring gas wells, stringing telephone poles. There was room for no other dream and since father could not do any of these things he was an outlaw in his community."[71] But Sam and Sherwood Anderson are finally more like their fathers than they first realize. During his adolescence in Caxton, when Sam energetically hustles after every odd job in town, the Windy in him wanders the country roads with Telfer. Sam the businessman conquers the world that defeated his father so that he can be free to dream as Windy tried to do.

LITERARY AND FINANCIAL AMBITION

Anderson's work is of the literary generation after Norris and Dreiser. His character studies are almost completely free of a Naturalistic obsession with epic forces. His greater concern with language and style is especially important to the transition from the writings of those who proclaimed a new midwestern literature of America in the 1880s and 1890s to Faulkner, Hemingway, and other outstanding authors of international reputation in the postwar period, who learned from Anderson's experiments in developing an authentic and distinctive American literary voice.[72] *Windy* belongs with Norris's and Dreiser's novels of art and business in Chicago, however, because it seconds some of their views, especially on the weakness of art in the city. Anderson did not share the others' contempt for most conventional artists in Chicago,[73] but he did see them as being almost as ineffectual as the cliques of artists in Fuller's *Under the Skylights*. In his *Memoirs* he described even his celebrated Chicago Renaissance group as "the little children of the arts," who naively aspired "to write world shaking novels, become intellectual leaders of a nation, paint a picture that will be at once recognized as a masterpiece, sing a song that will reverberate through the hearts of all men." But their great fear, whatever their accomplishment, was that they would never achieve these goals, and that their ambitions marked them as modern misfits in a society that they were desperate to join.[74]

Like other serious Chicago writers, Anderson longed to get out of this dilemma by turning his creative talents in some direction that affected the commercial world, or at least gave him some sense of confidence that his literary powers could make him self-sufficient. He wanted to be, he confessed in *A Story Teller's Story*, a "famous young prizefighter traveling incognito, not wanting public applause, a young Henry Adams of Boston with the punch of a Bob Fitzsimmons, a Ralph Waldo Emerson with the physical assurance of a railway brakeman." He immediately asked, "[W]hat painter, literary man or scholar has not had moments of indulging in some such dream?" This rhetorical question indicates that he believed that such dreams are born from a feeling of powerlessness. He felt out of touch as a man of imagination and reflection "in a world where only men of action seemed to thrive," in a time when "material and industrial progress" were the "one direction, one channel, into which all such young fellows as myself could pour their energies." He was forced to conclude that the wish to become an artist betrayed some lack of courage. Like Miniver Cheevy, he longed to be a powerful and cunning Renaissance prince, "an Italian desperado of the fifteenth century," but was left to wonder "why had I not the courage to be a desperado of the twentieth? Surely Rome or Naples or Florence, in the days of their glory, never offered any better pickings than the Chicago of my own day."[75]

In *Windy McPherson's Son*, Anderson joined Norris and Dreiser in taking advantage of the "pickings" of Chicago's business life not as a businessman but as a literary artist. By writing about business as they did, all three tried to capture this world through their art and thus empower themselves within it. To do so was not a simple task, but one that required great skill in finding the right words that would grasp what they believed was the truth about Chicago.[76] They began by conceding more to the businessman than perhaps he deserved because it served their artistic purposes to do so. Norris and Dreiser conceived of their protagonists as such dynamic individuals because they believed that this conception was true in some special cases, but also because it enabled them to transform the businessman into a more interesting subject for them as writers. To have pictured Jadwin and Cowperwood as men with a genius for making money—and nothing else—would have run the risk of creating one-dimensional, uninteresting characters.[77] As brooding artists with a special sense of mission that transcends mere wealth, they become men chosen by destiny to play great roles in history. In this sense they are products of wish-fulfillment for Norris and Dreiser, writers fascinated with power but who saw conventional artists as powerless. They did not want to become businessmen but authors who somehow had the power of "captains of industry," and so they portrayed the most extraordinary businessmen of their time as artists to elevate their own calling.

Sam McPherson's story is important, not because Anderson was so fascinated with power but because it suggests that someone with aesthetic sensitivity can succeed in Chicago, and also that even the most successful businessman (perhaps especially the most successful businessman) realizes that ambitions of finding some higher Truth about the sources of peace and harmony in life and effectively expressing this Truth to others are the greatest goals one can have. In *Windy McPherson's Son*, Anderson simultaneously told of his own disaffection from business and tried to convince himself that he was doing the brave and right thing to be so disaffected and to walk out. Writing this novel was a means of convincing himself that his decision was not based in failure, that even if he had succeeded as Sam did he would have given it all up.

All three authors believed that the modern city generally and the activities of the great financier in particular were artistic in that they involved creativity of some sort, but that it took an artist's imagination to perceive them as such. They hoped that in the act of perception the perceiver would become a powerful social figure himself, offering the last word on the great business leaders of the day. They anticipated that by writing their books they would fulfill their own ambitions for artistic power if they would only grasp their subject as boldly as their central characters do their enterprises. None of the three writers was as successful in this task as all hoped they would be. The quality of the writing and the thematic intent of their work are inconsistent and unclear, reflecting perhaps some of the flaws in their authors' talents, but certainly also the problems in their view of business in Chicago.

To see the businessman not merely as the most influential and charismatic figure of his day, but literally as the greatest artist, was a bold way to reconcile art and business and declare that art was supreme in a society which seemed to have rejected it. But this conception could not be pressed too hard. The financier's work could not be readily judged on the same aesthetic terms as a book or painting without obscuring the meaning of both finance and art. Even if Cowperwood can immerse himself in the struggle for control of Chicago's streetcar lines "quite as a poet might have concerned himself with rocks and rills," his (and Jadwin's and McPherson's) business goals are profit and power, and his manipulations, however "artistic" they may seem, are to these ends.[78] The "artistry" the three protagonists practice is a function of business and defined in its terms.

Not only is the business-as-art conceit unconvincing to the reader, but Norris, Dreiser, and Anderson finally do not believe in it themselves. Cowperwood becomes an aesthetic mystic spiritually divorced from business, while Sam McPherson walks out on success. For both, the reflective life their creators associate with the artistic temperament is at last a refuge because it is *not* of the business world, even if it helps them understand and even thrive in this world. Norris clings to his idea of the Pit as epic battlefield (and of himself as the modern Homer) to the end, but once Jadwin loses control of the wheat market the idea of the speculator as urban artist dissolves. By the end of all of these works, each author is back in the middle of the endless debate over whether worldly success and personal happiness are opposed. The difference between their work and that of other writers of Chicago life is that their heroes are people perfectly fitted to win the highest prizes that Chicago offers, so that when even their careers lead to self-destruction and renunciation—with "art" in some sense as a haven—the implicit condemnation of the quality of life in Chicago is stronger than in more overtly critical novels. If even these triumphant men end up unhappy in business, what hope is there for anyone who tries to take materialistic Chicago on its own terms?

GREAT RAILWAY STATION AT CHICAGO—DEPARTURE OF A TRAIN.

Top: Promotional lithograph for the Wabash Route and the new Dearborn Street Station (1885), emphasizing the accessibility of the railroad to the center of the city. (Chicago Historical Society ICHi-05257) *Bottom:* Engraving from *Appleton's Journal,* 1870. By this time, Chicago's railway terminals were already settings of a distinctly modern metropolitan kind, witnessing the arrival and departure of masses of people of every type. (Chicago Historical Society ICHi-05274)

Top: Grand Central Station (1890). Solon S. Beman's design accentuated more sharply than did Dearborn Street Station the contrast between the strong horizontal lines of the terminal and the upward thrust of the clock tower, 222 feet high. (Chicago Historical Society ICHi-17656) *Bottom:* The Loop elevated tracks looking north in Wells Street, about 1900, revealing the unique view of the city available from the train. (Chicago Historical Society ICHi-17655)

Top: Montauk Building (1882), designed by Burnham and Root, a groundbreaking response of modern design ideas and building techniques to the needs of commercial Chicago. As a type, a model for Henry B. Fuller in *The Cliff-Dwellers.* (Chicago Historical Society) *Bottom:* H. H. Richardson's Marshall Field Wholesale Store (1887), which Louis Sullivan praised as "a monument to trade, to the organized commercial spirit, to the power and progress of the age. . . ." (Chicago Historical Society ICHi-01588)

Top: The Chicago Board of Trade, opened in 1885. Frontispiece to volume 3 of A. T. Andreas, *History of Chicago*, 1886. *Bottom:* The Pit, the trading room of the Board of Trade. (Chicago Historical Society ICHi-14783)

Top: Adler and Sullivan's Auditorium Building (1889), now Roosevelt University. Note the influence of Richardson's Marshall Field Wholesale Store. (Chicago Historical Society ICHi-00571) *Bottom:* The stage of the Auditorium Theatre, circa 1895. (Chicago Historical Society, photograph by J. W. Taylor)

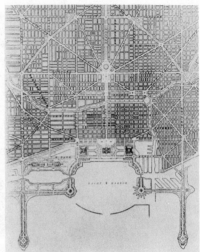

Top left: The central arch of the Peristyle, with the Quadriga on top, at the eastern end of the Court of Honor of the World's Columbian Exposition, 1893. (Chicago Historical Society) *Top right:* Drawing of the proposed central city and lakefront from the Burnham and Bennett *Plan of Chicago,* 1909. *Bottom:* The Court of Honor of the World's Columbian Exposition, looking east toward the Columbian Fountain, the statue of The Republic, and the Peristyle. (Chicago Historical Society ICHi-02526)

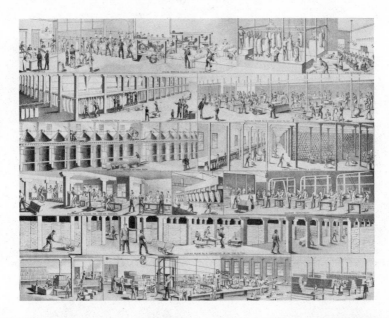

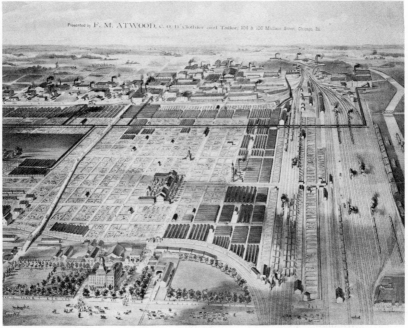

Top: "Interior Views of a Modern First Class Pork Packing & Canning Establishment of the United States of America." Lithograph from about 1880, stressing the scale, order, cleanliness, and scientific efficiency of Chicago meat packing. (Chicago Historical Society ICHi-04064) *Bottom:* View of the Union Stock Yards, about 1885. Note the grid formed by the pens, the stockyard gate in the center foreground, the extent of the railroad service, and the packinghouses on the far side. (Chicago Historical Society ICHi-04070)

Top left: "Trimming," from Adolph Wittemann, *Views in the Chicago Stock Yards and Packing Houses,* 1892. (Chicago Historical Society ICHi-04076) *Top right:* "A half mile of pork, Armour's great packing house, Chicago, Ill." Stereo view by Strohmeyer & Wyman, 1894. (Chicago Historical Society ICHi-17431) *Bottom:* View southwest in the Union Stock Yards toward Swift & Company, about 1910, showing again the close association between the railroad and the livestock and packing industries. (Chicago Historical Society ICHi-04085)

Part Two

The search
for expressive forms

5

The railroad

On October 25, 1848, a secondhand locomotive, the Pioneer, puffed
uncertainly to Oak Park and back with the directors aboard; on
November 20, it brought in a load of wheat from the Des Plaines
River. "Chicago had become Chicago."
       —Harold M. Mayer and Richard C. Wade, Chicago: Growth of a Metropolis

   Mamie beat her head against the bars of a little Indiana
      town and dreamed of romance and big things off somewhere
      the way the railroad trains all ran.
   She could see the smoke of the engines get lost down where
      the streaks of steel flashed in the sun and when the
      newspapers came in on the morning mail she knew there
      was a big Chicago far off, where all the trains ran.
                                    —Carl Sandburg, "Mamie"

The Galena and Chicago Union tracks along which the *Pioneer* made
its way were the first strand in an enormous and tangled network of rails
which by 1860 made Chicago "the greatest railroad center in the
world."[1] When the transcontinental railroad was completed in 1869,
Chicago had become the hub of the national transportation system in
America. By 1910 railroad cars were hauling ninety-five percent of the
freight handled through the city (the rest moved mainly by water), and
some thirteen hundred passenger trains carried 175,000 people in and
out of Chicago every day.

   As Carl Condit observes, "In no city of the world has the railroad
played a more pervasive role, extended its sheer physical presence to a
greater magnitude, offered more possibilities for economic growth, or
created more serious and refractory problems than in Chicago."[2] The
railroad dominated the landscape, redefined property values, and deter-

mined the directions of urban development. The major lines built grand stations in the center of the city and encouraged the construction of enormous industrial zones on the edges of the already settled areas. The Illinois Central ran on a trestle by the lakeshore, blocking off the lake from the center of town (the company acquired this route in exchange for building a breakwater).[3] The train not only brought grain, lumber, coal, machinery, and livestock in and out, but also made the city accessible to hundreds of thousands of new settlers from the farms, villages, and cities of Europe and America. Many of these came for jobs directly created by the railroad in such "cities" within the city as the Union Stockyards and the company town of Pullman.

Chicago's growth was also closely tied to the evolution of an elaborate intraurban transportation system. Horsecars were still in service as late as 1906, but by the last decades of the nineteenth century they had been displaced by modern technologies which, as Condit points out, had the "profound consequence that the modern spread-out metropolis could now evolve."[4] The cable cars which appeared in the 1880s and which ran over almost one hundred miles of track by the mid-1890s were in turn made obsolete by electrical lines. By 1913 these were unified into a single system of almost a thousand miles of track with an annual volume of over six hundred million fares. The first elevated rapid transit line began in 1890, when the South Side Rapid Transit Company started to raise tracks for its steam-powered train south from Twelfth Street. The company completed this link to Jackson Park in 1893 for the opening of the World's Columbian Exposition. An even more significant event of the same year was the ground-breaking for the Union Elevated Railroad, which united the three elevated lines serving the downtown in a large rectangular ring in the commercial district. This most distinctive of all man-made Chicago landmarks was completed by 1897, at roughly the same time the elevated trains switched from steam to electric power. The "Union Loop" not only conveniently combined the various lines that ran south, west, and north, but it also defined Chicago's downtown as the area contained by its tracks.[5]

The railroad peaked in extent and quality of service in the 1920s. Since then the automobile, the truck, and the airplane have undercut the primacy of the train. Within the city, buses have replaced streetcars, while uncertain funding, mismanagement, and decay constantly threaten the elevated system. It is possible, however, to reconstruct the train's importance to Chicago. Though most of the major terminals erected in the years between the Great Chicago Fire and World War I have been razed, the few survivors from this period (whose own future is very much in jeopardy) still retain their aura as great entries to the city. Walking or riding about Chicago today, one sees the pervasiveness of the old railroad network. Landfill has sunk the Illinois Central rails below grade level and reclaimed the lakefront as park land, but from the windows of the Art Institute one can still see the swath of tracks ("the widest railroad main line in the world and as broad as a modern expressway," Condit notes) that once ruled the shoreline. Just south and west of the Loop, behind the Board of Trade and looking out from Canal or Halsted Streets, there are dozens of rail beds hundreds of yards wide that stretch beyond sight. In more outlying areas, near the stockyards district or the southern edge of Chicago, tracks cut over commercial streets at grade like scars and age lines on the face of the city. The elegant retail center of town has edged north across the Chicago River to upper Michigan Avenue, but the financial, cultural, and architectural heart of Chicago is still the Loop. Riding the el as it rattles around the downtown is one of the few experiences that one can share with Chicagoans of eighty years ago.

THE RAILROAD AND THE CITY

Given the historical importance of the railroad to Chicago and its commanding presence in the city, the frequent mention of the train in Chicago literature is highly appropriate. The railroad and Chicago became merged in the popular imagination, especially in smaller communities of the Middle West. For many unsettled souls with some ambition, the train crystallized both their dissatisfactions and their dreams, for it seemed to represent the opportunities and excitement of a new age that was leaving them behind, unless they somehow got on. Chicago was the place where all the trains seemed to go.

The equation of the train with the city appears often in literary works about Chicago. Sandburg's Mamie, for example, who "got tired of the barber shop boys and the post office chatter and the church gossip and the old pieces the band played on the Fourth of July and Decoration Day" in her "little Indiana town," daydreams of "romance and big things" in "a big Chicago far off, where all the trains ran."[6] Floyd Dell, who moved to the city in 1908, described Chicago the railroad nexus as an imaginative promised land in his two autobiographical novels, *Moon-Calf* (1920) and *The Briary-Bush* (1921). At the end of the first book and at the beginning of the second, hero Felix Fay, certain that there is no hope for the fulfillment of his literary ambitions in small-town Iowa (Dell came to Chicago from Davenport), discovers the solution to his dilemma in the local railroad station. There on the wall is the key to his deliverance, a "map with a picture of iron roads from all over the middle west centering in a dark blotch in the corner." That dark cluster is formed by converging railroad routes, and to his mind it represents a mass of power and energy that promises intellectual stimulation. Dell names the blotch in full capitals and an exclamation point: "CHICAGO!"[7]

By the late nineteenth century, of course, the railroad was scarcely a new subject in western art. From its first appearance the locomotive struck observers as the ultimate machine of the machine age. It was the centerpiece (later to be joined by Henry Adams's dynamo) of the new technology, around which a long series of writers and artists had expressed their often ambivalent responses to the Industrial Revolution and its effects on man and the countryside. This tradition flourished well into the twentieth century, though over the last several decades a nostalgia for an earlier America tied to the romance of the rails has almost completely replaced the earlier excitement with the railroad as the objectification of the power of modernity. Chicago writers of the turn of the century could read not only Hawthorne's and Thoreau's reactions to the incursions of the locomotive into modern life but also many contemporary works on the subject, from Zola's sensationally charged story of railroad men and their machines in *La Bête Humaine* (1890) to Henry James's tirades against the train in *The American Scene* (1907).

Those who wrote about Chicago were most innovative in the ways in which they used the railroad to understand and explain the city. One could identify the railroad with any industrial city, but this approach was especially suited to the leading railroad city on Earth, where it took no straining of the metaphor to say that the railroad tracks were the veins and arteries of the metropolis and the railroad terminals and the Loop its heart. The constant movement of trains in, out, and through the city defined Chicago's visual and auditory texture (in some places even its taste and smell), its random yet purposeful activity, and even its time frame.[8]

For the literary tourist eager for some brief impression that he could publish for a reading audience elsewhere, the railroad was a very attractive device by which to talk about Chicago. This visitor would be sure to have come in and out on the train. He would tour places like Pullman, the World's Fair, or the stockyards, where the cars and tracks all clustered. His rides in and out and through the city would take up a relatively large part of his stay, and he would be constantly reminded by acquaintances, guidebooks, and railroad literature that he was in the railroad capital of the world. He had probably gone to Chicago purposely to see the direction of the future and the nature of the brave new industrial age, and the locomotive was the ideal vehicle.

The French author Paul Bourget looked out an office window onto the Chicago of the early 1890s and noted the "mighty murmur" of the cars and the "incessant tinkle" of locomotive bells. "They are every-where," he claimed, "crossing the streets, following the lake shore, passing over the river which rolls its leaden waters under soot-colored bridges, meeting and crossing each other's tracks, pursuing and over-taking one another." He described the shifting vistas in Chicago's to-pography: "Now you distinguish an elevated road, and there, beside the railways on the level of the street, you see other trains on the avenues."

Bourget's account of the incessant comings and goings of locomo-tives was the source of his feeling that the whole city was in violent motion. The locomotive bells that "seem to be sounding in advance the knell of those they are about to crush" expressed the excitement and danger of this movement. The way these engines ran freely everywhere across the city both suggested how industrialism dominated the Chi-cago landscape and set the tone of a competitive society in which every-one was rushing to get ahead of the next fellow.[9]

Other perceptive visitors noted the same details and analyzed their meanings. A year before Bourget, Giuseppe Giacosa, the Italian drama-tist best known for his work on the libretti of *La Bohême, Madam But-terfly,* and *Tosca,* was amazed by the way the train was given the freedom of the city, even at the risk of human life. It rushed along at grade with only a road sign and the train whistle to warn the pedestrian. Giacosa shared Bourget's impression that the train had completely taken over and altered the cityscape. He was told that his hotel room would overlook the lake, but he discovered that "between the hotel and the lake run twenty or thirty railroad tracks." Giacosa tried to count the number of trains that passed his window in an hour. He came up with thirty-eight, almost two every three minutes, "and all of the hours are alike." He compared the sound of the train which filled the ears to "a double hammer: the sound as it fades away on one side is the beginning of what increases on the other; and each bell has its own timbre and each hammer its rhythm."[10] The rhythm of the railroad was that of modern life, of the industrial age that replaced the natural alternation of day and night with the steady cadence of productivity. For travelers and novelists alike, the new rhythm was both exhilarating and exhausting.

Journalist Julian Ralph, touring America for *Harper's* in the early 1890s, claimed that the train not only remade the external world but had been internalized as well by Chicagoans. Ralph described the "clang-clang" of the cable-car gongs and reported, "It seemed to me then (and so it still seems, after many another stay in the city) that the men in the streets leap to the strokes of those bells; there is no escaping their sharp din; it sounds incessantly in the men's ears." The din, which "seems to joy them, to keep them running along," prompted the same ambivalent response in Ralph as did the whole spirit of the city. It struck

him both as a moral guide ("like a sort of Western conscience"), yet also
as something dangerous and threatening ("as if it were a goad or the
perpetual prod of a bayonet"). "It is as if," Ralph continued, the gongs
"might be the voice of the Genius of the West, crying 'Clang-clang
(hustle)—clang-clang (be lively!),' and it needs no wizard sight to note
the effect upon the men as they are kept up to their daily scramble and
forge along the thoroughfares—more often talking to themselves when
you pass them than you have ever noticed that men in other cities are
given to doing."[11] This "Genius of the West" was the muse of commercial Chicago. The clanging of the train bell reminded Giacosa of "a
church on a fête day," a remark which shows that he felt that the sacred
and the profane were combined in Chicago, where every business day
with its full schedule of passenger and freight trains was a fête day.

Ralph's attitude toward Chicago was generally positive, and he effectively expressed this attitude through his treatment of the train. In the
hands of one to whom the commercial culture was deeply suspect,
however, the railroad could be used to depict Chicago as a blighted
world. Bourget's and Giacosa's comments often have a somber tone, as
do Waldo Frank's remarks on Chicago in *Our America* (1919). As Frank
explains, this book was written at the request of the *Nouvelle Revue
Française*, which wanted an unofficial, candid portrait of the United
States by a young American intellectual, and the most revealing approach to Chicago Frank could discover was through its railroads. Observing that "[e]verywhere trains come into Chicago," Frank describes
the city as a cruelly tortured victim of industrialization. Chicago is a
"vast flat city, cut to bits by tracks of steel. A lacerated city. A city
destroyed by the iron flails that beat it into being." There is no peace in
Chicago, he adds, only freight cars unloading on the tracks "along
which the engines scatter their black message over the city."[12] Twenty-five years earlier, journalist and reformer W. T. Stead was horrified
by the "massacre" of citizens by the trains running at grade throughout the city. "This great city with a million and a half of population,"
Stead wrote, "is stretched over a gridiron of rails which cross and re-
cross the city and form a complex network of tracks, every mesh of
which is stained with human blood." The sound of the train bell was a
"solemn weird tolling" of doom, Stead added, remarking, "Sisera with
his 900 chariots of iron never tyrannized more ruthlessly over the
Hebrews than the railroads with their fire chariots of steel have lorded
it over the city of Chicago."[13]

The railroad, especially its tracks, could also strike the uninitiated
newcomer as an objectification of the alienating and ungraspable confusion, disorder, and ambiguity of the city. Theodore Dreiser recalled
that a few days after he first arrived in Chicago on his own, he took a job

washing refrigerator cars in a yard on the South Side. The foreman quickly fired him, and Dreiser confessed that he did the job badly. In retrospect, Dreiser hypothesized that his problem with the job was psychological; he was still disoriented by "the vastness of the city" which, he explained clumsily, "was almost too much for my by now almost rural brain." The railroad yard, which reflected the scale and complexity of all forms of major industry in the city, left him at a loss. The "intricacy and far-flung arrangement of sheds, tracks and cars, confused me not a little," he wrote. "To work here—here and now— seemed to me more like contending with some vast mystery, the details of which could never be mastered, by me or anyone." He then admitted that his problem was that he read the larger incomprehensibility of the city into the task at hand: "Also I believe that what I was really thinking of was the whole city, not any particular part or task, which could not have been so confusing."[14] What Dreiser was doing some forty years after the fact was using the incident of his brief job with the railroad as a way to explain the impact of the city on the imagination.

The View from the Train

Even more distinctive and important than the identification of the train with certain basic features of Chicago was the discovery that the experience of riding the train made the city imaginatively accessible. Travel by railroad coach, cable car, or elevated train in the city involved the passenger in an elaborate combination of actions, including buying tickets, boarding and disembarking, and dealing with other passengers and railroad employees. Of special interest to the writer, however, was the moving panorama of the city that the railroad afforded, especially the train entering Chicago or the elevated moving above street level.

The special heuristic quality of the train ride in the city is apparent even today. In a city without natural elevations, the train (especially the el) and the taller buildings are the only commonly accessible places from which to enjoy a comprehensive look at Chicago. The advantage of the train over the tall building is precisely that it moves, offering the rider an impression of urban variety from a constantly shifting view-point. The train courses through green outlying areas (though they are much further out now and there are fewer trains to take) into a city of stone, steel, asphalt, glass, and concrete. The center of the city looms in the distance well before the passenger's arrival. The elevated moves close enough to the buildings it passes for one to see architectural detail and glimpses of office and domestic life that the walker on the street rarely notices. The alteration of close-up blank walls and then a sudden vista down a long street is an exciting if disjointed experience. In no other way can one see so much of Chicago so quickly and so well, at the same time feeling in one's bones the rumble of the power that built the city.[15]

This experience is not a simple one. In *The Machine in the Garden*, Leo Marx notes, "The sudden appearance of the machine in the garden is an arresting, endlessly evocative image." Marx explains that this image "causes the instantaneous clash of opposed states of mind: a strong urge to believe in the rural myth along with an awareness of industrialization as counterforce to the myth." In its major uses, the motif "is a cardinal metaphor of contradiction, exfoliating, through associated images and ideas, into a design governing the meaning of entire works."[16] The views of the city from the train in Chicago writing are different from the examples Marx explores, for the author or character involved is not in a pastoral setting watching or hearing the machine enter, nor even situated in some stable vantage point in the city; he or she is now *on* the machine as it moves from countryside to metropolis or across the city. The passenger's awareness of the train is not as some counterforce but as part of the development of an urban myth, and it is central to the image of Chicago as the leading railroad city in the age of railroads. For better or for worse, the train and the city are united in the triumph of technology over the natural landscape.

Accounts of the view of Chicago from the train often include a variation on the clash of opposed states of mind that Marx discusses. Two conflicting sorts of recognitions assault the imaginative passenger. The first is positive. The journey is an exciting form of travel, for it is the best way to see the city that the train has helped make and which seems to promise so much. It is as if one is being guided through a great new kingdom by the moving spirit of that realm. For these reasons it is a wonderful thing to be on the train heading through the city, and writers described it as such. At the same time, however, the individual might well feel a deep uneasiness that is rooted in his conscious or unconscious discovery of the conspiracy between train and city that seems to threaten him and others. This uneasiness is increased by his distance from actual control of the train, with which he is allied whether he likes it or not.

Discussions of the expressive qualities of the view from the train, like identifications of the train with the city, are not limited to Chicago writing. As early as 1833, Emerson marveled at the constantly shifting view from the train as he traveled between Manchester and Liverpool (the cars traveling in the opposite direction, he noted, "dart by you like a trout. Every body shrinks back when the engine hisses by him like a squib"). In *The American Scene*, Henry James cast a cold eye on his homeland through the Claude-glass window of the moving Pullman Palace Car, which seemed to him to be "the great symbolic agent" of the mindless "irresponsibility" behind the wholesale destruction of his country.[17]

Chicago writers were no doubt aware of Howells's *A Hazard of New Fortunes* (1890), which describes Basil March's "incomparable perspective" of the view of Manhattan from the el. March claims that the elevated train is "better than the theatre" in offering a view of the spectacle of city life. "What suggestion! what drama! what infinite interest!" The night trains March views from the platform near the Central Depot strike him as "fabled monsters of Arab story ready for the magician's touch, tractable, reckless, will-less—organized lifelessness full of a strange semblance of life." He enjoys riding the train that runs through the lower East Side because the mix of colorful immigrants in this area "offered him continual entertainment." As the mood of the novel becomes darker, however, the "glimpses of material aspects of the city" afforded by the train strike March "as some violent invasion of others' lives." He ceases to see the city as a detached tourist, and he begins to feel "a sense of complicity with it, no matter what whimsical, or alien, or critical attitude he took."[18]

It is hard to determine precisely how much Chicago writers consciously worked in an artistic tradition and how much they independently discovered the train as an excellent means, in turn, to "discover" Chicago.[19] The point here is that those who wrote about Chicago found the train especially useful and appropriate as a way to read and speak about this city because of the omnipresence of the railroad. The imaginative perception of Chicago from the train is one of the major motifs in Chicago literature. The entrance to Chicago by rail was particularly memorable to the generation of artists of the turn of the century who themselves came to Chicago to make a name for themselves. Looking back in their memoirs, they saw the ride in as one of the pivotal acts of their lives. They used their recollections of the event, sometimes written several decades after the fact, to frame their first impressions of Chicago and to explain how much the arrival in the city meant to them.

This motif extends to the memoirs of artists (among others) whose careers were not primarily literary. Both Frank Lloyd Wright's *Autobiography* and Louis Sullivan's *Autobiography of an Idea,* for example, contain animated descriptions of their authors' entry by train and their first reconnoiter of the city in which they were later to triumph. Sullivan's work was published over fifty years after he came to Chicago, but he still remembered vividly the first excitement that he felt as he arrived on the train. His account of his trip mentions the natural landscape more than subsequent accounts, probably because the city was so much less developed in 1873 than it was only a few years later. Sullivan was impressed by the breadth of the prairie ("Here was power—power greater than the mountains"), the lake ("Here again was power, naked power, naked as the prairies, greater than the mountains"), and the midwestern sky. His route passed "miles of shanties disheartening and dirty gray" into a Chicago in the midst of rebuilding. His sense of triumph was unqualified. His narrative ends with an exclamation which reveals that Sullivan saw Chicago as the promised land: "Louis tramped the platfrom [the whole book is told in third person], stopped, looked toward the city, ruins around him; looked at the sky; and as one alone, stamped his foot, raised his hand, and cried in full voice: THIS IS THE PLACE FOR ME!"[20]

Hamlin Garland first visited Chicago a decade after Sullivan, when he was in his early twenties. He passed through en route to his early literary apprenticeship in Boston. Garland's plan was to meet his brother in Chicago before proceeding east. Having never seen a town larger than Rockford, his attitude toward the city was ambivalent—he desired to escape from the cultural restrictions of the country, but he was frightened by the prospect. "I longed to enter the great western metropolis, but dared not do so—yet," he explained three decades later, when he wrote about his experience in *A Son of the Middle Border*. His reaction to his first view of Chicago, which was at this time "only a huge flimsy country town," was shaped by his expectations. What he remembered most of his approach to the city on the train was the "feeling of dismay with which, . . . I perceived from the car window a huge smoke-cloud which embraced the whole eastern horizon, for this, I was told[,] was the soaring banner of the great and gloomy inland metropolis, whose dens of vice and houses of greed had been so often reported to me by wandering hired men." Besieged by the fear that his whole adventure was some great mistake, Garland was helpless to do anything but remain in his seat as he "was carried swiftly on."

Garland's recollection then switches from his troubled response to the special understanding of Chicago the train makes possible. The ride in from country to city is a short lesson in the increasing density of the city as one gets closer to its center: "Soon the straggling farm-houses thickened into groups," he noted, "the villages merged into suburban towns, and the train began to clatter through sooty freight yards filled with box cars and switching engines." It then crawled through "tangled, thickening webs of steel" before plunging "into a huge, dark and noisy shed" where the frightened newcomer faced the piratical hackmen of the city.[21]

Similar scenes appear in Chicago writing both before and after Garland, but none are so rich as those in the work of Theodore Dreiser. Dreiser never forgot his experience of coming into Chicago on the train, nor did he ever tire of writing about it. In his sixtieth year, his best work long behind him, Dreiser published *Dawn*, his autobiography of his early life. This book tells of his boyhood as the ninth surviving child in an unstable family that had lived in some ten different houses throughout Indiana by the time he was twelve. In 1884, the year Theodore turned thirteen, a portion of the family including him lived briefly in Chicago before returning back to Indiana. According to Dreiser, they were in the town of Warsaw three years later when, dissatisfied with life in this city and intrigued by reports of the adventures of friends and relatives in Chicago, he was finally spurred by a Sunday newspaper feature telling of life on Halsted Street to decide that he was going back to Chicago alone. His mother loaned him six dollars, which included $1.75 for his fare, and he boarded the three o'clock train. "That ride to Chicago was one of the most intense and wonderful of my life," Dreiser recalled.

This spur-of-the moment afternoon's trip was a significant journey both for Dreiser and American letters. He returned to his home state in 1889 for a brief year at Indiana University but he would remain a city dweller for much of the rest of his life, and he would soon become America's outstanding urban writer. The little episode from *Dawn* does several significant things. First, Dreiser explains the lure of the city. His journey begins even before he steps on the car in Warsaw, when he first responds to the sound of the locomotive, which seems to accentuate the limitations of small-town life. Dreiser's boarding the train is a major demographic shift in microcosm, one tiny part of the movement of America from a rural to an urban nation. Dreiser's conscious rejection of the past in taking this trip underlines this aspect: he leaves his mother, and, as he tells it, he avoids for a time seeing his elder siblings already settled in Chicago in order to discover the promise of the city for himself. "Rather, and most determinedly," he writes, "I wanted to reconnoiter this fairly and alone, to wander about and get work."

Dreiser's description of what he saw as the train neared the city is a more elaborately detailed version of Garland's account. At South Chicago a "sudden smudge" of factory life appears against the surrounding "great green plains." Here "a crowd of Italians, Huns, Poles, Czechs" boarded the train, joining this Indiana greenhorn in their common journey into the prodigious city of immigrants. Next, the cars rattled by primitive roads, "strung with telephone and telegraph poles and dotted with wagons." Then the train took him by other railway lines running parallel to his own, past "immense car yards packed with thousands of cars, and street crossings outside the gates of which waited shabby cars and a congestion of traffic." Finally, he reached the dark heart of the city, "the long, low sheds of the then Pennsylvania Depot," whose "hurly-burly of trunks and porters and bags, lines of cabs and busses outside" belonged to the city as the center of frenetic movement.

Dreiser's eager anticipation of what lies ahead as he courses toward Chicago contrasts with Garland's dread. The landscape looks wholly new to him, though he had been this way three years before. His trip in, like Sister Carrie's, is inextricably tied to a dream of triumph. "Besides," he explains, "never before had I made a railroad journey alone, and here now I was, bag in hand, going to Chicago and wondering what I should do and where I should stay once I was there and for how long." He seems to absorb the confidence the railroad exudes as he arrives at his destination. "Stepping out of the train," he concludes his memory of the trip, "it was as though I were ready to conquer the world."[22]

This description of Chicago through and from the train was most adaptable to an author's purposes. In *Our America*, Waldo Frank's survey of Chicago from the train is very ominous. He emphasizes more than any other writer the brutality of the industrial technology that now dominates the scene. As the train moves over the "flat land" toward Chicago, the green farms and the "warm, brown lurch of country roads wither away" under a "sooty sky hanging forever lower," in which the sun is "a red ball retreating" over "grimed horizons." The buildings the train passes are "gray, drab, dry"—a "litter of broken steel, clutter of timber, heapings of brick" amid "this fall of filth, like black snow—a storm that does not stop." The city at the end of the journey is a black hell:

The train glides farther in toward the storm's center. Chimneys stand over the world, and belch blackness upon it. There is no sky now. Above the bosom of the prairie, the spread of iron and wooden refuse takes on form. It huddles into rows: it rises and stampedes and points like a layer of metal splinters over a magnet. This chaos is polarized. Energy makes it rigid and direct. Behold the roads without eyes wrench into line: straighten and parallel. The endless litter of wood is standing up into wooden shanties. The endless shanties of wood assemble to streets. Iron and smoke and brick converge and are mills and yards. The shallow streets mount like long waves into a sea of habitations. And all this tide is thick above the prairie. Dirt, drab houses, dominant chimneys. A sky of soot under the earth of flaming ovens. Rising into a black crescendo as the train cuts underneath high buildings, shrieking freight-cars, to a halt. . . .

You have come in on a train.[23]

Imaginative accounts of the entry to Chicago by train were a staple in Chicago novels before any of these nonfiction passages appeared. By placing a central character on a train heading into Chicago, writers found a concise and compelling way to introduce this character and his or her setting. In many novels there is some scene, frequently at the very beginning, that involves the approach or arrival of a character on a train. As in the autobiographies, this trip is momentous because it offers some important insight into Chicago and the passenger. As early as 1898, Robert Herrick introduced Chicago to readers of *The Gospel of Freedom* by observing ironically, "The complex quality of this wonderful city is best seen as the stranger shoots across the prairie in a railroad train, penetrating layer after layer of the folds." Through the "manifold strands" of the "huge spider's web" of railroad lines, Chicago, "a stupendous piece of blasphemy against nature" which gets "hotter and fiercer" as the train enters its core, "touches the world." Herrick's description anticipates Frank's nightmare view of Chicago: "Once within its circle," he writes, "the heart must forget that the earth is beautiful."[24]

The most effective uses of the rail journey into Chicago are those which, like *A Son of the Middle Border* and *Dawn,* move back and forth between a description of the city as seen from the moving train and an account of the experiences of the individual passenger. Garland and Dreiser, who adopted this strategy in their autobiographies, employed it more fully in their fiction long before they used it to talk about their own lives. The analogous passages are so similar that one suspects that in their recollections they made their lives imitate their art, even if their fiction in turn was at least loosely based in personal experience.

Garland's Rose Dutcher of *Rose of Dutcher's Coolly* (1895) is one of the earliest Chicago novels that center around a woman who comes to Chicago to fulfill specifically artistic ambitions (she wishes to be a writer), and she is initiated into the city on the train. The novel actually has two important train episodes, the first being her trip from her home in rural Wisconsin to the state university in Madison, the second her journey to Chicago.

The first ride is decidedly unsettling, as Rose's hopes and fears about her future battle within her. At first she is very excited by what this simple train trip means to her. "The speed of the train, which seemed to her very great," Garland writes, "aided her to realize how swiftly she was getting into the world." As the landscape "whirled by in dizzying fashion" and the engine whistles furiously, Rose believes that this adventure is "all on a scale more splendid than her dreams." Then she gets a foretaste of the unpleasant aspects of her new urban independence, in which she is no longer protected by the gentle intimacy and concern of her family and hometown. Rose is unnerved by the rude attentions of several of the male passengers, and she soon finds herself clinging to her seat in terror every time the train passes through a tunnel, fearful of what liberties they might take in the darkness. Instead of aiding Rose, the brakeman and conductor also pester her "with their low presences." At last she is comforted by a self-assured female traveler. The end of the journey sums up the two-sided nature of the whole trip. Rose sees the dome of the state capitol looming up, "and the romance and terror of her entry into the world came back to her."[25]

Her subsequent entry into Chicago is much more detailed. As the train nears its destination and Rose's dream of going to Chicago is rapidly turning into fact, the city becomes more formidable to her. Rose thinks back to the simpler, safer farm world she and so many others like her have left. Like Robin Molineux recalling his family during his bewilderment in Hawthorne's "My Kinsman, Major Molineux," Rose pictures her kindly father rising from the farmhouse table as "here she sat, rushing toward that appalling and unimaginable presence—Chicago." But this homesickness is only temporary; it is no match for the eagerness that drives her and others toward Chicago and the future. She pursues a vision of success which she identifies with entering the city on the train. Garland, using figurative language that suggests that her journey is natural and inevitable, explains how broadly representative an action it is. "It was this wonderful thing again," he writes, "a fresh, young and powerful soul rushing to a great city, a shining atom of steel obeying the magnet, a clear rivulet from the hills hurrying to the sea." He observes further, "On every train at that same hour, from every direction, others, like her, were entering on the same search to the same end."

Someone on the train then informs Rose that what appears to be a cloud in the distance is Chicago. As Garland describes it, this cloud looms ahead like the presence of God leading the Children of Israel out of bondage. It is "in shape like an eagle, whose hovering wings extended from south to east, trailing mysterious shadows upon the earth." The scene then starts to resemble the approach of a wandering knight to some mysterious chapel, which may contain either the Holy Grail or some grim beast—or both. As Rose's train rushes toward "this portentous presence," Garland's account next switches to a description of Chicago as a netherworld in a spiderweb of tracks:

> *The brazen bell upon the engine began to clang and clang; small towns of scattered wooden houses came into view and were left behind. Huge, misshapen buildings appeared in flat spaces, amid hundreds of cars. Webs of railway tracks spread out dangerously in acres of marvelous intricacy, amid which men moved, sooty, grimy, sullen, and sickly.*

Rose sniffs "incomprehensible and horrible odors" as the train takes her past sprawling slums: "Streets began to stretch away on either side, interminable, squalid, filled with scowling, squaw-like women and elfish children. The darkness grew, making the tangle and tumult a deadly struggle."

The bell of the train raises her hopes again, even if it does not entirely ease her mind, and the cityscape becomes more promising: "The engine's bell seemed to call back *'Good cheer! Good cheer!'* The buildings grew mightier but not less gloomy; the freight cars grew fewer, and the coaches more numerous. It was an illimitable jungle filled with unrecognizable forms, over which night was falling." A baggageman calms Rose somewhat by helping her gather up her things at the end of this momentous journey. She has arrived: "'Chicago, *She-caw-go!*' called the brakeman, and her heart for a moment stood still, and a smothering sensation came upon her. She was at the gate of the city, and life with all its terrors and triumphs seemed just before her."[26] The train has been both the means of her deliverance into this world and the foreshadowing of all its threats and possibilities. Garland's dramatization of her trip in establishes a whole state of mind that runs through this and other novels which try to reveal the "feel" of urban experience in Chicago, particularly the mixture of hope and fear, expectation and dread, clarity and confusion, power and helplessness, that many individuals share.

Garland's depiction of Rose Dutcher's arrival in Chicago is more extensive than most of the several similar passages in Chicago writing, but it was Dreiser who best and most frequently translated his own experience of coming into the city into fiction. All of Dreiser's Chicago fiction includes scenes in which the central character approaches Chicago in a train. His description in *The "Genius"* of the journey into Chicago of aspiring painter Eugene Witla, who is more directly modeled after Dreiser than any other character in his fiction, predicts detail-for-detail and sometimes word-for-word the corresponding section from *Dawn.*

Dreiser's first use of this motif, in *Sister Carrie,* was his finest. Dreiser's prose has drawn justifiably sharp criticism, but such gracefully orchestrated writing as the opening chapter of *Sister Carrie* demonstrates his literary skills. It is difficult to find a more incisive statement of what turn-of-the-century Chicago signified to the newcomer than this chapter, which begins one August day in 1889 when Carrie boards the train for Chicago. It ends eight or nine pages later when she is met by her sister Minnie in a downtown terminal.

The chapter also contains many of the same elements as the passage from *Dawn,* as this ambitious soul from the small-town Midwest encounters Chicago. With her small trunk, cheap imitation alligator satchel, box lunch, and snap purse containing four dollars, Carrie is on a one-way ride from the past into the future. After a tearful kiss of farewell from her mother, she boards the coach, "bright, timid and full of the illusions of ignorance and youth." The first phase of this trip reviews for her and the reader just what she is leaving behind. The train passes the flour mill where her father works, and Carrie emits "a pathetic sigh" as she takes a last look at her green little village. Carrie finds some comfort (as did Dreiser himself) that she is not going very far. The hurtling train then distracts her and prompts her to "swifter thoughts" and "vague conjectures of what Chicago might be."

Carrie then makes the chance encounter that determines the subsequent course of her life. She meets Charles Drouet, the slickly handsome salesman who will later keep her as his mistress. (Dreiser met his first wife, Sara White, on the train to Chicago in 1893 when, as a St. Louis newspaperman, he was assigned to cover the visit of a group of Missouri schoolteachers to the World's Columbian Exposition.) The meeting of Carrie and Drouet seems perfectly natural in the open society of the train, so different from that of Columbia City and so like Chicago. He makes some small talk, then gives her his card. After some hesitation, she gives him her sister's address. Dreiser then turns their attention to the passing landscape. "Already vast net-works of tracks—the sign and insignia of Chicago—stretched on either hand." "[A]ffected by her wonder," Drouet notes various landmarks, fueling Carrie's excitement as the train measures out the city. He identifies the Chicago River, and "[w]ith a puff, a clang and a clatter of rails it was gone."

Pulled along by the locomotive, Carrie senses—as did Rose—that her excitement is edging into terror, but she is again distracted by the colorfulness of the city, where they presently arrive. Unwilling to let Drouet meet her sister Minnie, Carrie bids him goodbye in the crowded train shed. Her sister spots her, and their embrace takes Carrie from Drouet's sparkling company into another side of Chicago, "the grimness of shift and toil" that her sister "carried with her." Minnie asks about their parents and "all the folks at home." A few hours before, Carrie could not think about leaving them without feeling "a touch in the throat." Now she does not even answer but looks away toward Drouet, the swain of the parlor car, and "felt his absence thoroughly."

Sister Carrie owes a good deal to *Rose of Dutcher's Coolly*, which preceded it by five years and which was probably known by Dreiser.[27] The two scenes describing a heroine's arrival in Chicago are very much alike in several small and large ways. Like Rose, Carrie was drawn to Chicago by what Dreiser describes as invisible lines of attractive force. While Garland compared his heroine to "a shining atom of steel obeying the magnet" of Chicago, in his revised manuscript Dreiser titled his first

116

chapter (the original text has no chapter titles) "The Magnet Attracting: A Waif amid Forces." Even the wording of some passages from this chapter is uncannily like *Rose*. Compare the arrival of Carrie's train with the parallel passage, cited earlier, from Garland:

Her heart was troubled with a kind of terror. The fact that she was alone, away from home, rushing into a great sea of life and endeavor, began to tell. She could not help but feel a little choked for breath—a little sick as her heart beat so fast. She half closed her eyes and tried to think it was nothing, that Columbia City was only a little way off.

"Chicago!—Chicago!" called the brakeman, slamming open the door. They were rushing into a more crowded yard, alive with the clatter and clang of life. She began to gather up her poor little grip and closed her hand firmly upon her purse.

In Garland's novel, Rose's experiences on the train are important but still relatively minor incidents in her career, but in *Sister Carrie* the afternoon rail journey is a major structural device. Placed at the very beginning of the book, it provides an overture for the entire plot. Dreiser immediately informs the reader more fully than did Garland that this little trip is no casual adventure but an illustration that life—particularly modern urban life—is defined by constant movement and change, and that what the reader is witnessing as this country girl enters the city on the train is a drama encompassing a national as well as an individual loss of innocence. Her arrival in Chicago on that evening in 1889 is also evidence of the city's imaginative appeal. That Carrie, possessed only of the vaguest thoughts of what she wants in life, disembarks in the expectation that this place will somehow fulfill her dreams indicates how potent an attraction Chicago had become by this time.

Lest the reader miss the significance of Carrie's train ride, Dreiser interprets it as he presents it. He turns his realistic depiction of this young woman riding the train into Chicago into a moral tale that applies well beyond the case at hand, combining his pseudoscientific interest in human action with his novelist's desire to tell a story effectively. As the train pulls out of Columbia City in the very first paragraph, Dreiser reflects on how "the threads which bound her so lightly to girlhood and home were irretrievably broken." "When a girl leaves her home at eighteen . . . ," he states a few sentences later, "she falls into saving hands and becomes better, or she rapidly assumes the cosmopolitan standard of virtue and becomes worse." There is no alternative to this movement, and it is more likely that she will become worse than better since "[t]he city has its cunning wiles" and whispers its temptations "into the unguarded ear" of the "half-equipped little knight."

No sooner has Dreiser made this observation than Drouet appears. He is an ambiguous figure in this scene, a good-willed charmer whose intentions are not clear, a perfect master-of-ceremonies of the city-bound train. She first apprehends his presence as "a voice in her ear," like the serpent enticing Eve. As he points out what it is she sees through the window, his voice picks up the steady rumble of the train that speaks now as a powerful seducer. Carrie awkwardly tries "to forestall and deny this familiarity," but his "daring and magnetism," his confident air of comfort and luxury, are disarming. In his presence, Carrie's yearnings become more focused and acute: "There was a little ache in her fancy of all he described. Her insignificance in the presence of so much magnificence faintly affected her." She instinctively feels that "there was something promising in all the material prospect he set forth. There was something satisfactory in the attention of this individual with his good clothes."

Drouet's advances arouse the same ambivalent responses in Carrie that the city will. When she first turns to look at him, "the instincts of self-protection and coquetry" are "mingling confusedly in her brain." The future actress does not know whether to follow her "maidenly reserve" or her "wild dreams of some vague, far-off supremacy," whether she should play the modest virgin or the woman-about-town. In responding to his advances, she chooses the latter and half-consciously enters into his world and his "insatiable love of variable pleasure—woman—pleasure." Her subsequent rejection of her sister's lean and narrow life to become Drouet's mistress is thus foreshadowed in her awkwardly bandying words with this well-dressed and self-assured "drummer" and "masher" as they travel together toward the downtown.

Dreiser uses the trip into the city to adumbrate other aspects of Carrie's experiences once she reaches Chicago. Drouet's fashionable and tight-fitting brown wool business suit, his pink-and-white striped shirt, his cat's-eye cuff links, and his broad-soled tan shoes activate material desires in Carrie that the town soon will incite further. His mention of his dealings with the clothier and the dry goods merchant of Columbia City reminds her of "memories of longings the displays in the latter's establishment had cost her," and looks ahead to her eager window-shopping in Chicago and Drouet's giving her the money to buy the clothes on display behind the glass. Above all, "the air" with which Drouet does things introduces her to the whole idea of urban style, of the ways one can consciously shape the way one looks, talks, and acts.

He has won her over. Her seduction is further foretold when she gives him her sister's address: "Now she felt that she had yielded something—he, that he had gained a victory." Dreiser continues in the same vein: "Already they felt that they were somehow associated. Already he took control in directing the conversation. His words were easy. Her manner was relaxed." The casual seriousness of their affair, the way urban relationships are rooted in such chance meetings by strangers on their way to or from somewhere in an endless number of such comings and goings, rises and falls, is summarized in this young girl's apparently trivial conversation with a salesman on a train.[28]

Dreiser realized how effective an opening for a book was this extended entrance into Chicago by train, for he used it again at the outset of *The Titan*. The novel opens with Cowperwood leaving Philadelphia for a business trip to the West that will take him to Chicago. His train ride, like Sister Carrie's, is another journey from past to future, but what is involved here is not the movement from country to the city, but from an old established city to a new one. Cowperwood is weary of "the dull, staid world of Philadelphia, with its sweet refinement in sections, its pretensions to American social supremacy, its cool arrogation of traditional leadership in commercial life, its history, conservative wealth, unctuous respectability, and all the tastes and avocations which these imply." He seeks "some of the boundless opportunities of the far West." He kisses his Aileen and gets on board. His first impression of Chicago as he sees it in the distance from the train has an aesthetic quality that appeals to his sensibility: "For some reason a crystalline atmosphere enfolded the distant hazy outlines of the city, holding the latter like a fly in amber and giving it an artistic subtlety which touched him.[29]

Since Cowperwood at this point is a mature man whose past includes a wife, a mistress, and a prison term, his entry can hardly be construed as a journey from innocence to experience. In his plush car, Cowperwood is a powerful presence quite different from Carrie uncertainly holding up her end of the conversation with Drouet. Now the train is not so much the engine of yearning as it is the driving force of capital, regally bearing the financier into the rising center of competition.[30] Cowperwood's "gaudy Pullman," which tries "to make up for some of the inconveniences of its arrangements by an over-elaboration of plush and tortured glass," is a proper vehicle for this city that is yet more show than substance (Cowperwood's arrival in the early 1870s precedes Carrie's by some fifteen years).

Dreiser makes much of the fact that Cowperwood's primary business is street railways, and he specifically links the financier's growing transportation empire with the idea of the city as a center of power. At the end of the chapter, Cowperwood sizes up the flimsy streetcars he sees in Chicago. Already he is considering how he might become the titan of Chicago's financial world. Streetcars are the "natural vocation" of this ambitious businessman precisely because they satisfy his desire for some objective sign of his control over the world. As Dreiser observes,

"Even more than stock-brokerage, even more than banking, even more than stock-organization he loved the thought of street-cars and the vast manipulative life it suggested." He soon enters into this "vast manipulative life." His acquisition of the street railway system on the North Side of the city inspires him to take over the entire system, a feat which is presented as being tantamount to ruling the whole city: "He might readily become the sole master of street-railway traffic in Chicago! He might readily become the most princely financial figure in the city— and one of the few great financial magnates of the nation."[31]

A little later he successfully executes his plan for using the tunnels under the Chicago River, and his crews go to work. The scale of this undertaking further reflects the financier's strength and the titanic ambitions that drive him to shape his empire. Dreiser obviously wants the reader to accept Cowperwood's achievements as epic, and to conceive of his hero in mythic terms. His men work "day and night in the business heart of the city, their flaring torches and resounding hammers making a fitful bedlamic world of that region." The "large, shining powerhouses" he erects to drive his cars further symbolize his dominant presence in the business affairs of Chicago. The whole city is a modern train of which he is the merciless engineer.[32]

Cowperwood's control of Chicago traction is almost complete near the close of *The Titan*, when he has accomplished his plan of constructing the Union Loop at the center of the city. His lines form a diagram of his dominance. One major advantage in choosing a financier whose business was urban transportation as a central character was that his power was so visible. When Dreiser describes Cowperwood's manipulations of banks and stock certificates the action becomes hard to follow, but in those scenes in which he uses the railways to show Cowperwood's influence in Chicago, he vividly demonstrates how finance capital on such a scale shapes the modern world.

Dreiser was working on *The "Genius"* at about the same time he was writing *The Titan,* and when it appeared in 1915 it included his third major use of a scene in which his main character comes into Chicago on the train to start a new life in the city. *Dawn* would make the fourth. Together this group of books form a composite portrait of the city as Dreiser saw it. What is Chicago, Dreiser appeared to be asking, but a series of trains coming ceaselessly in, bearing bold yet timid girls from small-town Wisconsin, ambitious young artists from downstate Illinois, ruthless financiers from Philadelphia, and a future novelist who saw himself in all of them as he told their stories?

6

Chicago building

Come, let us build ourselves a city, and a tower with its top in the heavens, and let us make a name for ourselves, lest we be scattered abroad upon the face of the whole earth.

—Genesis 11.4

It demands of us, what is the chief characteristic of the tall office building? And at once we answer, it is lofty. This loftiness is to the artist-nature its thrilling aspect. It is the very open organ-tone in its appeal. It must be in turn the dominant chord in his expression of it, the true excitant of his imagination. It must be tall, every inch of it tall. The force and power of altitude must be in it, the glory and pride of exaltation must be in it. It must be every inch a proud and soaring thing, rising in sheer exultation that from bottom to top it is a unit without a single dissenting line—that it is the new, the unexpected, the eloquent peroration of most bald, most sinister, most forbidding conditions.

—Louis H. Sullivan, "The Tall Office Building Artistically Considered"

From the beginning of its modern settlement in the 1830s, Chicago has been known for ambition and innovation in construction. Chicago's sudden growth in the decades before the Civil War spurred the development of cheap and convenient balloon-frame structures, which were easily assembled out of light boards that could be cut in sawmills and hammered into place with machine-made nails. This method replaced the slower if more substantial technique of framing with large beams held together by carefully fashioned mortise-and-tenon joints. Siegfried Giedion maintains that the balloon frame "practically converted building in wood from a complicated craft, practiced by skilled labor, into an industry."[1] It required raw materials that Chicago had in good supply, and it met the housing needs of the quickly expanding town. If the results were sometimes flimsy, they merely pointed out the makeshift nature of early Chicago society and the willingness of newcomers to put up with such conditions in pursuit of the golden future.

By the time Chicago had evolved from a promising village to a prospering city in the latter decades of the nineteenth century, more substantial and pretentious forms of building appeared. An eclectic hodgepodge of derivative styles dominated the private mansions and the new commercial and public buildings of the postwar years, reflecting a mixture of civic pride and aesthetic uncertainty. The Great Chicago Fire of 1871 was a critical event in the history of Chicago architecture. Although many structures were rebuilt in the image of the old, the almost total destruction of the downtown created opportunities that attracted an outstanding group of architects to Chicago. Their work collectively formed one of the great artistic achievements of the era and completely changed the physical appearance of the central city.

The key technological breakthrough that made their new buildings possible was the development of iron and steel framing in the early 1880s. The height and design of earlier structures were restricted by the fact that these buildings were supported by their masonry walls. Metal framing, along with the invention of the electric light, the telephone, and the elevator (the first in Chicago was in 1864), as well as rising land values and the impatience of Chicago capital, spurred architects to build taller and more simply than before. The centerpiece of their achievement was the modern skyscraper. The skyscraper both rose higher and allowed more window space than masonry-supported buildings, which were usually limited to around ten stories. Carl Condit, the leading historian of the Chicago School, has noted the two-sided character of the new architecture. On the one hand, he explains, it was utilitarian, "marked by a strict adherence to function and structure" and aware of precedents in urban vernacular construction in Europe and the eastern United States. On the other, it was "formal and plastic, the product of a new theoretical spirit and the conscious determination to create rich symbolic forms—to create, in short, a new style expressive of contemporary American culture."[2]

The mass and height of these new buildings insisted that Chicago be taken seriously, that here people and resources from all over the world had gathered to make a great city. The skyscraper seemed to suggest that all those people coming into Chicago on the train transferred the direction of their hopes directly upward. In one continuous movement, it appeared, they got off the train and onto the elevator. The design of the massive downtown railroad stations further emphasized this fact. Like Solon Beman's Grand Central Station (1890), several of Chicago's train terminals were great horizontal structures (that included the train shed and the waiting rooms and ticket offices) to which were attached tall vertical office towers. These towers, including the one on Grand Central Station, were sometimes topped with a four-sided clock, reminding passersby that they must keep up with the pace set by the railroad and the office building.[3]

All of these large buildings were expressions of primordial power in this city which honored power so highly. The lofty upward thrust that Louis Sullivan exhorted his fellow architects to emphasize was the assertion of man's will over the pull of the earth's gravity, another triumph of his technology over the natural world. With good reason Chicago repeatedly evoked the legends of Babel in the minds of visitors. This gathering of immigrants from all over the earth, who built a city full of towers with their summits in the sky, seemed to be a second and more successful attempt to assault the heavens.

While the symbolic connection between height and aspiration was immediately manifest, Chicago's large commercial buildings also embodied the city in ways of which even their architects and developers were less aware. The face of the new office building was a map of the urban grid—a flat surface laid out into regular rectangles of windows. The building itself was a vertical structure divided into public and private areas, and the private areas included places of special privilege such as meeting rooms and the offices of corporate executives. They expressed simultaneously the mobility and hierarchy that coexist in a democratic urban society. Any individual can get into the building and ride the elevator, but few can reach the places of highest power. The tall office building, with its elevators and multiple stories, was thus the field against which a career could be charted in an age of opportunity. Where one stood or was headed *within* the building, as well as where and what the building was, indicated one's place in Chicago.

Viewed from the street, from some remote point on the lake or the prairie, or, best of all, from the top of one of the skyscrapers, the progress of construction told also of the malleability of Chicago. Entrepreneurs continually cleared space in the precious downtown land; buildings were put up, torn down, and new ones were erected in their places with remarkable, and, to some eyes, alarming speed. This was happening in other cities, as James complained in his observations on New York and Boston in *The American Scene*, but travelers noted that such constant alterations seemed particularly characteristic of Chicago.[4] The creative energy of building in Chicago asserted that experience is never final, that even a city of a million or more could be made and repeatedly remade so that, as seemed to be the case in the late nineteenth century, each generation would have a new Chicago to inhabit. The hand was equal to anything the mind and will would direct.

How would the mind and will of Chicago direct? The architecture of Chicago, and particularly the city's larger buildings, prompted sharp responses which contradicted each other. Chicago writers were interested in aesthetic issues that centered around whether the great buildings of the Chicago School were, as most critics today believe, better aesthetically as well as functionally than those they replaced or those that continued to be built in derivative styles (sometimes with metal frames behind their Gothic or Renaissance facades). But they were more concerned with the symbolic dimensions of these buildings. Some read them as the dramatic expressions of controlled power, but others saw them as monuments to greed, ruthless competition, and egotism, and thus finally as signs of terrible disunity and deep-seated social chaos. What sort of Babel was this? A race of bold heroes nobly reaching for the stars, or a fractious gang of overreachers screaming at each other in incomprehensible languages?

POEMS IN STONE

The architects of the Chicago school were convinced that the significance of their work reached beyond the details of this or that building to the social conditions of the whole city. Several of them spoke to their colleagues and to the general public about the importance of sound design to the well-being of the entire community. Some of their writings were intended to publicize and popularize their work, but a few leading architects offered an elaborate social and aesthetic rationale for what they believed was a new and responsible urban architecture.

Louis H. Sullivan and John Wellborn Root were most eloquent in this regard. Influenced by Taine and theorists of organic architecture, Sullivan and Root consciously promoted building forms that reflected their time, place, and function. The observations of both men were intensely "literary" because the two architects explicitly "read" buildings as texts that expressed certain ideas to those who saw and used them, and, more directly, because they conceived of themselves as poets who worked in steel and stone. Sullivan, who worshipped Whitman and wrote poetry himself, asserted that the architect was "not a merchant, broker, manufacturer, business man, or anything of that sort, but *a poet who uses not words but building materials as a medium of expression*" (the emphasis is Sullivan's).[5] The writings of Root and Sullivan, and the buildings they designed, related closely to the call of many authors and critics for a new literary form that realistically reflected life in Chicago. As practicing architects, however, they had the advantage over writers in that their work incontrovertibly became part of the world of which it spoke, and so its meaning could not but be heeded.

Root, who was born in Georgia and educated in England and New York, was twenty-one when he arrived in Chicago in 1871, the year of the Fire. While working for the firm of Carter, Drake, and Wight, he met Daniel Burnham, and the two young architects opened their own office in 1873. Until Root's untimely death in 1891 during the preliminary planning of the World's Columbian Exposition, the partnership was unquestionably one of the most important in American architectural history.[6] Root conceived of the great architect as a uniquely gifted person whose task was to integrate the contemporary spirit into his designs in a way that would be faithful to that spirit and which at the same time would instruct and improve it. Architecture to Root was thus a thoroughly moral occupation. In determining what kinds of buildings Chicago or any other place had to have, the architect was deciding what virtues should be championed.

Root's description of the virtues of a good building sounds like a prescription for what makes a good man. This is because he believed that a fine urban building possessed the best human qualities and civilized all who saw it with its very presence. A sound style, he argued, would have such qualities as repose, refinement, self-containment, sympathy, discretion, knowledge, and modesty, not to mention urbanity. A building with these attributes would elevate the tone of the city in which it was situated. Its "expression" would be "well adjusted to the mood of the spectator; not lowered down to his plane, but, although above the sordidness of his daily thought, sufficiently in recognition of it to escape total neglect."[7]

On another occasion Root was more explicit about just what large commercial buildings must say and why. He argued that the conditions of climate, atmosphere, trade, and society "demand . . . the simplest and most straightforward expression" made in enduring and simple materials. He maintained that a large office building, "standing in the midst of hurrying, busy thousands of men," could not hope to appeal to them "through the more subtle means of architectural expression." Instead, commercial buildings "should . . . by their mass and proportion convey in some large elemental sense an idea of the great, stable, conserving forces of modern civilization." Architectural art, Root believed, served the city by using its authority as an expression of disciplined power that resisted the potentially debilitating effects of ambitious go-getting. It would be a source of stability in a city characterized by motion and change. The building would house and facilitate the activities of the "hurrying, busy thousands of men," but it would somehow uplift them with its commanding form.[8] The commercial building thus offered a promising means by which an art form might refine the business world.

Louis Sullivan was the most outspoken architect of the Chicago School. Sullivan was born in Boston in 1856 and trained at M.I.T., where he rejected the academic style that dominated the architectural curriculum. After a brief stay in Philadelphia that was followed by an apprenticeship in Chicago in the office of William LeBaron Jenney, the pioneer of metal framing, he studied briefly at the Ecole des Beaux Arts before returning to Chicago. Sullivan enjoyed his greatest success from the early 1880s to the late 1890s in partnership with the more stable and businesslike Dankmar Adler. Together they designed such master-pieces as the Chicago Stock Exchange (1895) and the Auditorium Building (1889), the latter of which successfully reconciled commerce and art by combining in one magnificent building a hotel, offices, and a stunning theater.[9]

Sullivan's famous dictum that form must always follow function was but one aspect of an often hazy visionary aesthetic. Sullivan shared Root's belief in the instructive value of great architecture. Note, for example, his praise for H. H. Richardson's Marshall Field Wholesale Store, which was the most important source of ideas for his own design of the Auditorium. "Four-square and brown, it stands," Sullivan wrote, "in physical fact, a monument to trade, to the organized commercial spirit, to the power and progress of the age, to the strength and resource of individuality and force of character." In spiritual terms, Sullivan continued, it stood for intelligent control over these forces, "as the index of a mind, large enough, courageous enough to cope with these things, master them, absorb them and give them forth again, impressed with the stamp of large and forceful personality." The artist who could achieve this was "one who knows well how to choose his words, who has somewhat [sic] to say and says it—and says it as the outpouring of a copious, direct, large and simple mind."[10] Sullivan here specifically linked architecture to literature by calling the Field Wholesale Store an "oration," arguing that Richardson was one artist at least who had solved the problem of finding the right "words" for Chicago by speaking in stone.

In *The Autobiography of an Idea,* Sullivan explained that he was originally drawn to architecture because building seemed to him to be at once the most exciting and important outlet for the creative spirit of man, whose highest attribute was his ability to redeem experience by making the external world follow the dreams of his imagination. He called this capability "a portentous power—the power to change situations; he [man] can make *new situations.*"[11] No wonder Sullivan loved postfire Chicago, which so urgently demanded that "new situations" be made. The main problem with Chicago (and Sullivan here again conf-lated literature and architecture) was the "illiteracy" of its builders.

Instead of erecting the functional buildings that he and Root championed, others had followed false, dead dreams. The derivative schools, Sullivan argued, sounding very much like Hamlin Garland and Stanley Waterloo, paid homage to corrupt, plutocratic power. The American architect was woefully out of touch with the democratic spirit. There was no better example of this problem than New York: "For art is not in the hearts of men here. Gold is in the hearts of men here and fills arteries, capillaries, veins, with its maddening stream."[12] Chicago was a Caliban, ugly and twisted by false ideas, but still not beyond salvation. If a good architecture could be established here (as it no longer could be, in Sullivan's estimation, in New York), Chicago building would be the expression of the virtues of democracy.

In a speech before the Western Association of Architects in 1885, Sullivan told his audience that even if they were harassed by the pressures of daily life, there still lived within them "an insuppressible yearning toward ideals" which must be "protected and nourished" for the good of all humanity. If the commercial conditions of the time demanded that a building be tall, he argued a decade later in "The Tall Office Building Artistically Considered," then it is the duty of the architect to use that height in a way that is imaginatively thrilling and which both reflects and transcends the economic conditions that brought the building into being. Sullivan thus reaffirmed Root's idea that commercial architecture must express the explosive, driving energy of business in a powerful form that controls that energy. When his ideas were accepted, Sullivan claimed, now invoking Lincoln as well as Whitman, "then it may be proclaimed that we are on the high-road to a natural and satisfying art, an architecture that will soon become a fine art in the true, the best sense of the word, an art that will live because it will be of the people, for the people, and by the people."[13]

THE TALES OF THE CLIFF-DWELLERS

Of all Chicago writers, Carl Sandburg was closest in spirit to Sullivan. Sandburg, of course, shared Sullivan's devotion to Lincoln and Whitman and his reverence of democracy. More sympathetic with the common laborer than Sullivan was, Sandburg in several poems depicted the large buildings of the commercial downtown as vainglorious displays of private wealth. In some of his work, however, he celebrated the skyscraper's contribution to the colorful vitality of the city, and he marveled at it as proof of what man, "the little two-legged joker," could accomplish.[14] As collector of democratic wisdom and folktales in *The People, Yes*, he began his book by retelling the story of the tower of Babel in terms of a modern construction job in which God is an "understanding Boss" who "shuffled the languages"

And the material-and-supply men started disputes
With the hauling gangs and the building trades
And the architects tore their hair over the blueprints
And the brickmakers and the mule skinners talked back
To the straw bosses who talked back to the superintendents
And the signals got mixed; the men who shovelled the bucket
Hooted the hoisting men—and the job was wrecked.

Later in the same book, the skyscraper is an objectification of American aspiration and ingenuity, as Sandburg speaks of "yarns / Of a skyscraper so tall they had to put hinges / On the two top stories so to let the moon by."[15]

Sandburg had asserted two decades earlier that the skyscraper could even be perceived as the fulfillment of urban democratic community. In "Skyscraper," Sandburg stated that the huge building "has a soul" which is given life by the ordinary men and women who build and work within it, not by those who legally own it.[16] He saw the skyscraper as the urban community in microcosm and pointed out that its highest purpose was to serve and express the spirit of the people who inhabited it. By the democratic logic Sandburg inherited from Whitman, the individual was most creatively and spiritually alive when he was fully integrated into the life of the skyscraper. In this view, the tall building is potentially one of the most striking illustrations of the right relations between the individual and the community in urban society.

Sandburg made this point most effectively in one of his finest early poems, "Prayers of Steel," which was published in the collection *Cornhuskers* in 1918:

Lay me on an anvil, O God.
Beat me and hammer me into a crowbar.
Let me pry loose old walls.
Let me lift and loosen old foundations.

Lay me on an anvil, O God.
Beat me and hammer me into a steel spike.
Drive me into the girders that hold a skyscraper together.
Take red-hot rivets and fasten me into the central
*   girders.*
Let me be the great nail holding a skyscraper through blue
*   nights into white stars.*[17]

The poem recalls John Donne's "Batter My Heart" and, even more, Edward Taylor's "Huswifery," in which the Puritan poet asked his God to make him "thy spinning wheel complete" so that he might better serve the Lord. Sandburg's poem is also full of sacred passion, combining democratic and Christian idealism in a vision of a secular crucifixion. If the skyscraper is to be the great urban democratic institution, the individual must be willing to devote himself utterly to its highest possibilities. In so doing, he most fully realizes what he as an individual can achieve.

The main thing to note about these poems, besides their parallels with some of Sullivan's writings, is that their sentiments are comparatively rare in the serious literary response to Chicago's large buildings. Other writers were eager to discuss Chicago's skyscrapers and other ambitious construction projects as reflections of the condition of the urban community, but it is hard to find similar treatments of them as affirmations of the promise of democracy. The discussion of large buildings in Chicago literature, particularly fiction, breaks down along the general lines of the major responses to the city as a whole. Depending on their point of view, novelists effectively used Chicago's commanding architecture both to demonstrate the pervasiveness and destructive tendencies of commercial culture and to celebrate the city's uncontrolled vitality and power without reference to social ideals.

Henry Blake Fuller prefaces the complicated plot of *The Cliff-Dwellers* with an "Introduction" that sets the stage for what is to follow. In the space of five pages he develops a conceit which attempts to summarize the contradictions that make up Chicago. At the heart of this conceit is a conception of the downtown buildings as immense cliffs, and of the "large and rather heterogeneous" group of people who populate these structures as modern and yet still primitive "tribes" of cliff-dwellers. Their world is "a restricted yet tumultuous territory," which Fuller ironically describes in natural images to emphasize as others had how much the man-made landscape has displaced and blighted nature. By Fuller's conceit the buildings have not risen, but the streams of commerce, rushing faster and faster, have worn the land around the buildings away, so the streets are "cañons" along the sides of which the "soaring walls of brick and limestone and granite rise higher and higher with each succeeding year." The "seething flood" of commerce that causes the erosion "surges with increasing violence for every passing day."[18]

Fuller's choice of metaphor was not unique. The buildings that began to crowd the downtown in the decades after the Fire, rising so dramatically out of the flat terrain, suggested a man-made mountain range to many people. George Steevens advised readers to take an elevator to the top of the Auditorium Building and look out on the lake. "Then," he continued, "turn round and look at Chicago. You might be on a central peak of the high Alps. All about you they rise, the mountains of building—not in the broken line of New York, but thick together, side by side, one behind the other." He joked that the viewer would be surprised to see no snow on these "peaks," adding that the steam "that gushes perpetually" from the chimneys of these "mountains" "might well be clouds with the summits rising above them to the sun."[19] Paul Bourget, writing at almost the same time as Fuller, also spoke of the skyscrapers as modern communities of cliff-dwellers. "The portals of the basements," he commented, "usually arched as if crushed beneath the weight of the mountains which they support, look like dens of a primitive race, continually receiving and pouring forth a stream of people."[20]

Fuller's most original achievement was that he shaped a whole novel around this landscape which he found so appalling. Among the "great host of other modern monsters," he placed a fictive building he called the Clifton, which extends eighteen stories from its basement beer hall to its top-story barbershop. Its hundreds of windows glitter with gold and silver letters that proclaim the names of its fortunate tenants, and its awnings flutter in the lake breezes. The Clifton has all the comforts and conveniences of central heating and modern communications. It contains both a ground-floor lunch counter and a fancy restaurant upstairs, so no one ever need leave the building during the working day. In fact, the very comprehensiveness of the bulding is the key to its usefulness to Fuller, as the author explains in the last paragraph of the Introduction: "In a word, the Clifton aims to be complete within itself, and it will be unnecessary for us to go afield either far or frequently during the present simple succession of brief episodes in the lives of the Cliff-dwellers."[21]

Fuller's decision to make the Clifton the center stage of his book freed him to present coherently several different plots simultaneously and to dramatize the special quality of the city as a locus of both accidental and organized activity.[22] While all the figures in an English country novel might be found in the village church on a Sunday morning, Fuller demonstrated that in writing a Chicago book an author would do well to look for his characters in the offices and elevators of a downtown commercial building during working hours. He argued that such buildings shaped and reflected human action within and around them, and whether the writer approved of these buildings or not—and Fuller certainly did not—he would do well to study these Cliftons from beer hall to barbershop.

Fuller carefully charts where each of his dozen or so leading characters are placed throughout the Clifton, but his main interest is not so much in the daily operations of the building as in how the business values it embodies distort the personal relations of his characters. Virtually all these characters lead unhappy and misguided lives, Fuller implies, because the materialistic and success-crazed culture that has built the Clifton dictates the standards by which they live. The unctuous and corrupt real estate man McDowell, for example, "looked on domestic arrangements as a mere incident in business life," and without a second thought he embezzles money from his wife's family.

The banker Erastus Brainard is worse off. Once an honest farmer and an earnest preacher at Methodist camp meetings downstate, he became rich in railroad dealings and has since become even wealthier in other scandal-tainted ventures. His business consumes him so completely that he is little more than a mechanical fixture in the money-making machine called "The Clifton." As Fuller presents him, Brainard is "merely a financial appliance—one of the tools of the trade," with "no friends—none even of the poor sort known as 'business' friends. He had no social relations of any kind. He had no sense of any right relation to the community in which he lived. He had next to no family life." When George Ogden hears Brainard arguing in his office with his daughter Mary about her engagement, Ogden feels "a disgust for the man who would arrange the most sacred and confidential affairs of his family circle in the same general fashion that he would use for dealing with the concerns of an ordinary business acquaintance; a disgust for the family life in which such a state of things was possible." Fuller implies that the spirit of the Clifton enforces this state of things, so infecting Brainard's consciousness that he even writes notes to his family on business letterhead addressing them as "Dear Sir" and signing "Yours truly."[23]

Fuller skillfully uses the Clifton as the objectification of the field of social movement and aspiration in Chicago. McDowell purposely rents an office next to Arthur Ingles, the owner of the building, in the hope of getting an accidental introduction and then the favor of the great man. Fuller handles especially well the movement of characters up and down in the building as their careers rise and ebb, particularly in the case of a minor character named Cornelia McNabb. Fuller has much affection for Cornelia, as he does for Sue Bates in *With the Procession*. He admires her independence, energy, and cheerful candor, as well as her ability to make her own way without hurting or exploiting anyone. When she first appears early in the novel, she is working in the ground-floor eatery in the Clifton, which is called, in this world of overblown names, the Acme Lunch Room. ("[P]erhaps," Fuller comments, "with a lower ceiling and situation on a level lower still, it would have been called the Zenith.") She strikes up a conversation with George Ogden and tells him that she left a job as a schoolteacher in Pewaukee, Wisconsin. In the spirit of self-help that made Chicago, she is learning typing and shorthand so that she can crash the business world. She expresses her determination in no uncertain terms: "And I'm going to get along, let me tell you; I haven't jumped on to this hobby-horse of a town just to stay still."[24]

Cornelia wants to ride that hobby-horse up the Chicago social ladder, and she knows that the Clifton is the best place for a woman like her to meet a promising husband. At the top of the ladder is Ingles, whom she calls, in a telling phrase, "Mr. High-and-Mighty." In Chicago, height is the index of might. Her social ideal is Ingles's wife Cecilia, whom Cornelia has never seen but whose doings she follows religiously in the society columns of the newspapers. News of Mrs. Ingles is, of course, at the *top* of these columns. Leaning over the lunch counter, Cornelia confesses to George her envy of Mrs. Ingles: "Now there's a woman who interests me. She is in the papers every day; she goes everywhere. She's 'way up, I guess; I'd be wild if she wasn't." She pulls a paper from under the counter to prove her point to Ogden: "Yes, here she is, first pop. *Mr. and Mrs.*—Cluett, Parker, Ingles. My sakes, how I envy that woman! Course I don't want that she should come down here and wash my dishes, but wouldn't I like to go up there and eat off hers!"[25]

With such spunk and determination, Cornelia cannot help but penetrate into the exclusive chambers of the Clifton. One day Ogden spots her busily engaged in his own office. She times her lunch hour to coincide with his, and they scorn the Acme for the elevator ride *up* to the more elegant restaurant many floors above the street.[26] Cornelia tells George that she is taking only piecework in different offices so that she can have more variety, make more money, and meet more people. In a short time, her strategy pays off: she catches the eye and then the heart of Brainard's son Burton, who works in the bank. In a very charming scene, Cornelia later entrusts George with the care of her parents when they come down from Pewaukee for the wedding. She urges him, fittingly, to take them to the top of the Clifton, where they can look down upon the world their daughter has conquered.

This happy moment contrasts sharply with the action that follows, as the novel moves with terrible violence toward the undoing of many of its characters. Ogden, ruined by McDowell's double-dealing and his wife's expensive social climbing (which *she* hopes will get *her* in Cecilia Ingles's charmed circle), steals from Brainard and is discovered. This gentle man goes directly from Brainard's threats that he will prosecute him to McDowell's office and smashes him to the floor with a chair. "There fell away from him [Ogden] all the fetters that shackle the super-civilized man who is habitually conscious of his civilization," Fuller comments, sounding for the moment like a Naturalist.[27] Brainard does not live to press charges. His son Marcus, who has become dissolute and unhinged from failure and rejection, stabs the old banker and then hangs himself in remorse. The news of Marcus's death is the last thing Brainard learns before he succumbs, and he dies with a horrifying vision of his dead boy's grotesquely distended face. Even Cornelia McNabb does not fare well. Three months after she and Burton move into their French Renaissance chateau on Lake Shore Drive, they must move out, for Burton is not the businessman his father was. Undaunted by the sudden fall that followed so quickly upon her rise, however, the plucky Cornelia vows that she will soon rise again.

At the close of the book, George Ogden is living comfortably in the city, but his ambition and optimism are long gone. After the death of his flighty first wife, he has married Abbie Brainard, the level-headed and long-suffering older daughter of his former employer (George's two marriages in many respects recall those of David Copperfield). One evening at the theater, he has a final insight into the damage the spirit of the Clifton has caused. He sees Ingles and an attractive woman entering a prominent box. He suddenly realizes that this woman is Cecilia Ingles, and "his heart was constricted by the sight of her." The novel ends: "It is for such a woman that one man builds a Clifton and that a hundred others are martyred in it."[28]

A prolific essayist and reviewer, Fuller published an article in the *Atlantic Monthly* in 1897 in which he again cited the architecture of Chicago while analyzing life in the city. The purpose of "The Upward Movement in Chicago" was mainly to survey a number of civic-minded organizations that were trying to improve Chicago's social, political, and cultural affairs. Fuller praised the Civic Federation, the Woman's Club, the Municipal Voter's League, and Hull-House, but he was still skeptical that there could be any sweeping alteration of the conditions these organizations were trying to reform. Fuller pointed to the chaotic jumble of buildings in the city as a sign of an irretrievably fallen world. "Life in Chicago continues to be," he wrote, "—too largely, too markedly—a struggle for the bare decencies." In direct contradiction to Sullivan and writers like Garland, he attributed the city's problems in part to the fact that Chicagoans adhered too little, not too much, to cultural forms developed in Europe. Sounding like James complaining about the "thinness" of America, Fuller coveted "those desirable, those indispensable things that older, more fortunate, more practiced communities possess and enjoy as a matter of course."

Fuller did not specifically name these things, but they evidently included what he believed were more coherent and traditional buildings than were evident in Chicago. Fuller thought that a sound and coordinated architecture could foster a sense of community that benefited everyone, but this was not to be the case in Chicago. Speaking of building in the city, he observed with bitterness, "Possessed of a single sheet of paper, we have set down our crude, hasty, mistaken sketch upon it, and we shall have the odds decidedly against us in any attempt to work over this sketch, made on the one surface at our disposal, into the tasteful and finished picture that we may be hoping finally to produce." In Fuller's opinion, "The associated architecture of the city becomes more hideous and more preposterous with every year, as we continue to straggle farther and farther from anything like the slightest artistic understanding." The source of the problem was the unbridled individualism which built Chicago. "Nowhere is the naïf belief that a man may do as he likes with his own held more contentiously than in our astounding and repelling region of 'skyscrapers,'" Fuller complained, "where the abuse of private initiative, the peculiar evil of the place and time, has reached its monumental development."

Chicago's public buildings in particular, Fuller believed, were constructed with "haste and incompetence, and executed with haste and dishonesty," which was the way public life in the city was managed. He followed this observation with his most direct attack on the city's architecture as a sign of the failure of both economic freedom and urban democracy. In Chicago, Fuller claimed, "for the first time in the rearing of a vast city, the high and low have met together, the rich and the poor have *built* together: each with an astonishing freedom as to choice, taste, expenditure; each with an extreme, even an undue liberty to indulge in whatever independences or idiosyncrasies might be suggested by pride, greed, carelessness, or the exigency of the passing moment,—democracy absolute manifested in brick, stone, timber." Fuller's outrage fully surfaced as he concluded, "The sociological interest of such an exhibit is necessarily great; its artistic value is *nil*." Not only was the "picturesque flagrancy" of Chicago's municipal affairs "amply figured in the associated effect of Chicago's architecture," but "the extent of our failure in the art of living together is fully typified by our obvious failure in the art of building together."[29]

Robert Herrick agreed with Fuller's "reading" of Chicago's buildings, criticizing America's "intensely modern cities" for being "at least externally and in mass, undeniably ugly—sprawling, uncomposed, dirty, and noisy." The aesthetic failure of America's cities revealed deeper social problems, Herrick believed. "With their slovenly approaches, their needless crowding," he wrote, "they express the industrial greed and uncoördinated social necessities of a rapidly multiplying and heterogenous people." He further attacked these cities for being little more than "huge industrial camps, with all their massive buildings, rather than agreeable homes of human beings," calling them "convincing proofs of the terrible power of an uncontrolled selfishness." Herrick specifically denied that the skyscraper had any imaginative or spiritual value.[30]

Architecture is naturally a major topic in Herrick's *The Common Lot,* whose central character is the architect Jackson Hart. Helen Hart sounds like Louis Sullivan when she reminds her husband that he has tremendous power to make society better with his work, urging him to keep in mind the masses of people who live in Chicago but who have no power to shape it. Until he is brought back to his senses (both social and aesthetic) by the terrible fire in the hotel he designs, Hart worships not at Helen's altar but at that of a wealthy social climber named Mrs. Phillips. Her selfishness and insincerity are on prominent display in the world she constructs around herself. She is described as being of "the modern barbarian type that admires hungrily and ravishes greedily from the treasure house of the Old World what it can get, what is left to get, piling the spoil helter-skelter into an up-to-date American house." Her home, which she calls Forest Manor, reflects all her predatory tastelessness. What is this house that Hart designs for her? Root and Sullivan be damned: "Mediaeval, Renaissance, Italian, French, Flemish—it was all one! Between them [Hart and Mrs. Phillips] they would turn Forest Manor into one of those bizarre, corrupt, baroque museums that our lavish plunderers love,—electric-lighted and tele-phoned, with gilded marble fire-places, massive bronze candelabras, Persian rugs, Gothic choir stalls, French bronzes—a house of barbarian spoil!"[31] Soon there is nothing "honest" in Hart's work, only "clever contrivance."

Fuller and Herrick condemned the architecture of Chicago as a way of attacking the irresponsibility of the commercial culture, but to a novelist like Frank Norris, determined to celebrate economic competi-tion, the large commercial building was a symbol of the crude energy of the city as a dramatic setting for this heroic struggle. Norris makes this point in the opening chapter of *The Pit,* as Laura and her party drive home from Sullivan's Auditorium. Their carriage rolls through the fi-nancial district, the site of "that other tragedy," the Helmick failure, which distracted Laura's attention from the opera. Here is the theater on whose stage is played the "drama of the 'Provision Pits,' where the rush of millions of bushels of grain, and the clatter of millions of dollars, and the tramping and wild shouting of thousands of men filled all the air with the noise of battle!"

Laura's sister Page points out Burnham and Root's Rookery Building (which still stands on the southeast corner of Adams and LaSalle Streets) and several other commercial structures before finally direct-ing Laura's attention to the Chicago Board of Trade, "a sombre mass"

135

with "a black and formidable facade" that sits rooted at the base of LaSalle Street. This facade is Laura's "last impression of the evening," and Norris invests it with great significance. It seems to express all the attractive mystery, power, and danger of heroic capitalism. Amidst the other lighted buildings still bustling with people working late in the aftermath of the Helmick failure, the Board of Trade sits "black, grave, monolithic, crouching on its foundations, like a monstrous sphinx with blind eyes, silent, grave,—crouching there without a sound, without a sign of life under the night and the drifting veil of rain."

This impassive monster is much more striking than the luminous Auditorium full of its fancy crowd and foolish opera. Norris again stresses how imposing a presence the Board of Trade is at the close of the book, when it reappears as the last impression of Laura's entire life in Chicago. Now her carriage is taking her and Jadwin, a defeated man, to the railroad station and their new life somewhere in the unspecified West. Norris repeats his description of the Board of Trade word-for-word as it appears at the close of the first chapter.[32]

Norris further dramatizes the power of the business world for which the Board of Trade Building stands by juxtaposing it with a series of other settings in the city besides the Auditorium. These settings include the Dearborns' comfortable house near State and Huron, the Jadwin mansion fronting Lincoln Park, and Corthell's exquisitely appointed studio in the Fine Arts Building next to the Auditorium on Michigan Avenue. The unpretentious social intercourse of Laura's home, the empty staginess of the ornate mansion, and the delicacy of the artist's rooms are all overshadowed by the "crouching monolith" at the foot of LaSalle Street. The Pit invades all of these settings and greatly alters everyone's life in one way or another.

As both an actual place and a symbol, the Board of Trade Building served Norris very well in his effort to present the energy of Chicago business life. The very name the Pit has so many vivid associations suitable to his purposes. It suggests the cockpit and impresses the reader with Norris's image of speculation in wheat as a battle, a combination of gambling and blood sport. The grain exchange is a world of unmistakably male conflict, housed in this immense structure which rises out of the main junction of the business district of this business city. It is also the bull and bear pit, where men become brutish, temperamental beasts in their desire for wealth and power. At the same time, the Pit is Chicago as inferno, as pit of hell. In all cases, the immediate association is with destruction and violent, chaotic action.

Several other accounts of Chicago as a collective entity cited the special importance of the Board of Trade and the action in the Pit as essential to understanding the city. "Upon the broad floor . . . ," the

London *Times* reported in 1887, "assemble the wheat and corn and pork and lard and railway kings of the town, in a typical American life scene of concentrated and boiling energy, feeding the furnace in which Chicago's high-pressure enterprise glows and roars." The use of the term "furnace" suggests that the Pit is simultaneously a primordial forge and living hell. The *Times*, again anticipating Norris, called the traders "gladiators" who "with their calls and shouting make a deafening uproar" that remind one of Bedlam. There was no question that this building was the heart of Chicago, for "here in fitful fever beats the pulse of the great city whose exalted province it is to feed the world."[33]

As a work of architecture, the Board of Trade was just the kind of monument to undisciplined greed that Sullivan and Root detested. Nineteenth-century Chicago historian A. T. Andreas proudly praised the structure's Fox Island granite and mahogany-paneled offices with their "artistic wood mantels" in claiming that "it far exceeds any other building of the kind ever erected,"[34] and he used an engraving of it as a frontispiece to the last tome of his vast three-volume *History of Chicago,* but W. W. Boyington's design was a structural and aesthetic disaster. Thomas E. Tallmadge, historian of early Chicago architecture and an architect himself, belittled the Board of Trade's clumsy combination of "Eastlake" chamfers, mansard roofs, and what he called "bedstead motives," all improbably topped with a Victorian Gothic tower.[35] The tower was over three hundred feet high, the tallest in Chicago, when it was erected in the early 1880s. Unfortunately, its weight caused the building to settle so badly that the tower lasted only a decade before it had to be removed. Frank Lloyd Wright, fresh from Wisconsin in 1887 and seeking work in Chicago, took one look at this "thin-chested, hard-faced, chamfered monstrosity" and decided to pass by Boyington's office.[36] Montgomery Schuyler, perhaps the finest architecture critic of the turn of the century, declared that the building lacked any style or merit. "And, indeed," he added, "there are not many other structures in the United States, of equal cost and pretension, which equally with this combine the dignity of a commercial traveller with the repose of St. Vitus."[37]

Norris, however, did not want a well-proportioned and unified building. The more primitive, the more out-of-control, the more useful was the Board of Trade for his purposes of viewing it as a crouching monster. Never mind Root's call for dignity, repose, and discretion. Here was a *real* Chicago building more honest to the spirit of the town than any graceful edifice could be precisely because it was so monstrous and forbidding. Norris would not have changed one stone. He agreed with the wisdom of those who thoughtfully built a visitors' gallery that overlooked the trading floor. From this perch several characters in *The Pit* watch the frantic action. The directors of the Board of Trade evidently felt that here, not over at the Auditorium, was the best show in Chicago.

Although his response to Chicago's downtown buildings was more mixed than was Norris's, Theodore Dreiser was also impressed with the forcefulness of their presence, and he devoted several important passages in *Sister Carrie* to showing how they shaped the individual's sense of the city. Chicago's assembled architecture both excites and daunts Carrie. It holds so many of the city's attractions, but at the same time it seems to have been built to exclude her. As Carrie makes her way through the "walled city," Dreiser describes her journey in terms of her progress in getting into certain buildings, until by the end of the novel she is dining in fancy restaurants and living in lofty hotel suites.

When Carrie is looking for work shortly after her arrival in Chicago, the immense commercial buildings, with their large windows and polished brass signs, discourage her and make her feel unworthy. "The entire metropolitan centre possessed a high and mighty air calculated to overawe and abash the common applicant," Dreiser explains, "and to make the gulf between poverty and success seem both wide and deep." She feels desperately that she must find a way to fit in one of these buildings if she is to survive, but she wonders how she can possibly penetrate them successfully. The enormous office buildings strike her as "strange mazes which concerned far-off individuals of importance," and she does not know how she can solve them. Depressed by her early job-hunting failures, she perceives the commercial section of the downtown as growing "larger, harder, more stolid in its indifference." Her impression of the city at this point is of a large building that slams its door in her face: "It seemed as if it was all closed to her, that the struggle was too fierce for her to hope to do anything at all."[38]

Once she finds work on an assembly line making shoes, even her factory building seems to radiate the city's promise. Now that she is placed, she immediately seeks to identify herself with the establishment's solidity to bolster her own self-esteem. Carrie reflects, "This was a great, pleasing metropolis after all. Her new firm was a goodly institution. Its windows were of huge plate glass." When asked by her sister and brother-in-law about her job, she tells them simply that she is with a company that has "[g]reat big plate glass windows and lots of clerks."[39] She sees it as a triumph that she has gotten behind those windows and into that building, and thus joined the city.

The meaning of certain other buildings is all too clear to Carrie. The department stores fascinate and captivate her as she is searching for employment, making the threat of poverty all the more painful. Wandering past the clerks and patrons, she is dazzled by the displays. She feels that there "was nothing there which she could not have used—nothing which she did not long to own." These stores make her realize "in a dim way how much the city held—wealth, fashion, ease—every adornment for women, and she longed for dress and beauty with a whole and fulsome heart."[40] It comes as no surprise that Drouet's taking her shopping later is one of the key steps in his seduction of Carrie.

In his steady decline, Hurstwood also conceives of the city as a large fortification that shuts him out. He begins to view the world he left behind in Chicago "as one sees a city with a wall about it. Men were posted at the gates. You could not get in. Those inside did not care to come out to see who you were." He makes a painful pretense at getting in when he becomes the kind of figure he once despised, a "chair-warmer," finding refuge in the lobby of the elegant Broadway Central Hotel in order to shield himself from "the weariness of the streets" while he is job hunting. Later, things get far worse and he finds himself sitting now in a dingy "third-rate" hotel, reading in the paper of Carrie's success on Broadway. He thinks back on the "old shiny, plush-covered world, . . . with its lights, its ornaments, its carriages and flowers," and of Carrie's position in the city: "Ah, she was in the walled city now. Its splendid gates had opened, admitting her from a cold, dreary outside. She seemed a creature afar off—like every other celebrity he had known.[41]

There are related scenes in other novels. In *The Common Lot*, Helen Hart is horrified by what most of the buildings of contemporary Chicago signify. After attending a concert and eating an expensive meal with other well-to-do women, she understands with sudden clarity the human cost of the showy downtown, including the hotel in which she dines. "It seemed to her plain nature simply wicked to pay so much money—the blood of human beings—merely to eat," Herrick explains. "They paid, she knew, for the tarnished ceilings, the heavy carpets, the service—all the infinite tawdry *luxe* of modern life."[42] In Upton Sinclair's *The Jungle*, Jurgis Rudkus is, like Carrie, very pleased when he finds his first job in the stockyards, for he takes it to mean that he has been successfully assimilated into the prosperity of Chicago. He soon realizes how short a distance he has been admitted and how much is forbidden to him: "Everything was built to express it to him: the residences, with their heavy walls and bolted doors, and basement-windows barred with iron; the great warehouses filled with the products of the whole world, and guarded by iron shutters and heavy gates; the banks with their unthinkable billions of wealth, all buried in safes and vaults of steel." Sinclair adds later, "There is one kind of prison where the man is behind bars, and everything that he desires is outside; and there is another kind where the things are behind the bars and the man is outside."[43]

Norris's *The Pit* opens with such an image of exclusion. As Laura, her sister, and their aunt await the rest of their party in the vestibule outside the resplendent lobby of the Auditorium, Norris turns his attention to those who are watching all the wealthy ticket holders pushing into the glittering building. Shut out of this bright temple of wealth and culture, "a crowd of miserables, shivering in rags and tattered comforters," gather around the theater awning and across the street. These unfortunates find "an unexplainable satisfaction in watching this prolonged defile of millionaires."[44] Despite Sullivan's democratic sympathies, his greatest architectural achievement is an institution of the city of privilege: the strong and favored march in, while the poor and powerless find their entertainment in their envy of the grand parade.

Dream Cities

Two unique projects in Chicago building of the turn of the century also had significant literary dimensions. The first was the construction of the World's Columbian Exposition, which ran from the beginning of May to the end of October 1893 on a site in Jackson Park that was completely relandscaped under the direction of Frederick Law Olmsted. The Fair was a triumph for the city's civic and commercial leaders, who had won in national competition the right to celebrate in Chicago the four-hundredth anniversary of the discovery of America. The heart of the Fair was the heroic Beaux Arts Court of Honor, in which colossal buildings designed by the nation's leading architects and devoted to exhibitions of international achievements in mining, electricity, manufactures, machinery, and agriculture ringed a central Grand Basin. Surrounding the Court of Honor were several additional exhibition halls, such as the Fine Arts Building. Several states and countries also erected their own individual buildings, and these were interspersed with various restaurants and other sources of relaxation, refreshment, and amusement. The various parts of the White City were connected by an attractive system of sidewalks and waterways.

The second project was not a building or group of buildings, but a comprehensive plan for reconstructing Chicago. The *Plan of Chicago*, as it was officially called, was published in 1909. In terms of the future development of the central city, it was even more influential than the Fair. The most important single figure in both events was Daniel Burnham, who was the director of works of the Columbian Exposition and coauthor (with Edward H. Bennett) of the *Plan of Chicago*.

The World's Columbian Exposition appeared to demonstrate that Chicago's obsession with great individual commercial achievement could be directed toward the creation of a beautiful and conveniently ordered city, that business and art could be combined. The Grand Basin was the ultimate proof of this. It was surrounded by some of the largest structures ever built. The Manufactures and Liberal Arts Building designed by George B. Post was, in fact, the biggest roofed building ever constructed. Its forty-four acres of floor space were covered with an enormous glass skylight supported by the most extensive steel-frame construction of the age. It was reported that it could readily contain the United States Capitol, the Great Pyramid, Winchester Cathedral, Madison Square Garden, and St. Paul's Cathedral.[45] The design of the buildings in the Court of Honor, large as they were, was subordinated to the idea of a unified whole. The architects built in related neoclassical modes of a uniform cornice height and colored their creations snowy white—hence the popular name, White City. Augustus Saint-Gaudens oversaw the sculpture that adorned the Fair, and his own *Diana* graced the dome of the Agricultural Building. In the Grand Basin itself was Frederick MacMonnies's fountain depicting Columbia atop her barge (with Father Time at the rudder, Fame in the prow, and eight allegorical goddesses at the oars), and Daniel Chester French's sixty-five-foot gilded statue of the Republic, a first cousin to Miss Liberty. At the east end of the basin was the Peristyle, five hundred feet long and one hundred and fifty feet high, supported by forty-eight Corinthian columns. At its center was an arched portal opening to Lake Michigan, and over the arch was a statue of Columbus called the Quadriga, depicting the great explorer in a chariot pulled by four horses, which in turn were led by two maidens.

The Fair inspired a literary response big enough to have provided an exhibit in itself. This response included every manner of official and unofficial guide to the Exposition, not to mention more detailed volumes covering the work of special committees, the proceedings of various ceremonies, and the contents of individual buildings. Then there was a secondary range of books of photographic views with gushing captions, plus specialized vademecums with strategies on how to see it all—and Chicago as well—in a short visit. Beyond this were the ponderous multi-volume histories of the Fair, many commemorative issues of newspapers and magazines, and countless impressions of famous and lesser known visitors. Finally, there was the poetry and fiction of the Fair, including even a small body of dime novels and children's stories, such as *Two Little Pilgrims' Progress* by Frances Hodgson Burnett, author of *Little Lord Fauntleroy*.

Much of the literature of the Fair discussed the Columbian Exposition's relationship to the city that built it. The official language of the Fair—and that of most guidebooks, history, poetry, and fiction—claimed in no uncertain terms that what all these splendid buildings signified was that Chicago, built on the cultural heritage of Europe and the democratic freedom of the North American continent, marked the culmination of all history. Two decades before she became the champion of modern poetry, Harriet Monroe won the competition for the official poem of the Fair with her highly conventional "Columbian Ode," which was read and sung to orchestral accompaniment at the dedication ceremonies in October, 1892. The "Ode" proclaimed that the Exposition was part of the working out of God's millennial purpose. "To this proud day have led the steadfast hours;" Monroe's poem declared, "Now to thy [America's] hope the world its beaker fills."[46] Chicago, Monroe argued, showed that America was ready to lead the world to a tomorrow as free and bright as the sun and sky reflected on a breeze-blown Lake Michigan.

This viewpoint extended to the unofficial and more imaginative responses to Chicago and the World's Columbian Exposition. In "The White City," one of the early poems of Edgar Lee Masters, the buildings of the Fair are symbols of freedom and progress. Steam and electricity, which the Fair celebrates and which have made the rise of Chicago possible, are handmaidens of "Justice," who "shook to earth her chains / Unfettered now to do her will."[47] Henry Van Brunt, architect of the Electricity Building in the Court of Honor, described the Fair as one of those rare moments in history when one could see the movement of civilization to a higher plane, as an event comparable in its significance to the Age of Pericles, the Italian fifteenth century, the defection of Luther, and the reign of Queen Elizabeth.[48] Even Hamlin Garland, who in 1893 was no spokesman for the classical splendor of the Court of Honor, recalled writing to his parents in Dakota, "Sell the cook stove if necessary and come. You *must* see this fair."[49]

Theodore Dreiser was likewise impressed with the architecture of the Fair. "[T]his vast and harmonious collection of perfectly constructed and snowy buildings," he recalled, "containing in their delightful interiors the artistic, mechanical, and scientific achievements of the world," seemed to have been created "[a]ll at once and out of nothing in this dingy city." He stated that even those who had previously thought that "nothing of any artistic or scientific import could possibly be brought to fruition in America, especially in the Middle West, must have opened their eyes as I did mine at the sight of this realized dream of beauty, this splendid picture of the world's own hope for itself."[50]

Dreiser's remarks, however, also hinted that the most striking thing about the Fair in relation to Chicago was that it was so different from the city. He said that the Fair struck him not as the carefully organized work of many minds, "but rather as though some brooding spirit of beauty, inherent possibly in some directing oversoul, had waved a magic wand quite as might have Prospero in *The Tempest* or Queen Mab in *A Midsummer Night's Dream,* and lo, this fairyland." Dreiser thus described the White City as a separate, unreal kingdom, a magic island or an enchanted forest, where anything could happen because some special spell was at work which did not reach beyond its gates. This view implicitly questioned whether the Fair was any more than an escapist fantasy, a fanciful utopia born and gone in the space of six summer months. The Fair was instructive, but it was a symbol of what the city was not rather than what it was.

Dreiser's comment was in agreement with a widespread belief that the Fair displayed a potential for coordinated creative achievement never before realized, but it also unintentionally suggested that the grand show had no vital link with Chicago. This was the basis of the sharpest criticism of the Fair, which came from Louis Sullivan. Sullivan attacked Burnham for betraying Chicago's innovations in democratic architecture by giving in to the "feudal" taste of leading eastern architects, such as Richard Morris Hunt, whose domed Administration Building presided over the Court of Honor. Burnham is the villain of Sullivan's *Autobiography of an Idea,* and the Exposition is his great crime. He is depicted as a fraud who sold Chicago's aesthetic future out to plutocratic business interests, a merchandiser of the "bogus antique." The Fair itself is "a naked exhibitionism of charlatanry in the higher and domineering culture, enjoined with expert salesmanship of the materials of decay."[51]

The embittered Sullivan overstated the case when he asserted that the fair set back American architecture fifty years, but not when he argued that most of the Exposition's major architects relied on borrowed forms that differed considerably from the functionalist design of Chicago's best buildings. Several contemporary critics who praised the Fair as a temporary showcase were quick to point out in gentler terms than Sullivan used that it had little application to the world beyond its gates. Montgomery Schuyler observed that the buildings in Jackson Park represented the triumph of illusion, not reality. "Arcadian architecture is one thing," he wrote, "and American architecture is another."[52] William Dean Howells, speaking through his Altrurian traveler, noted how "so little American in the accepted sense" was the Fair's disciplined order.[53] The more accurate reflection of Chicago seemed to be just outside the Exposition on the mile-long Midway, a strange grab-bag of culture and carnival where a visitor could get a tour of a mock-up Javanese Village, a ride on the first Ferris Wheel, a gander

Chapter Six

at the dwarf elephant Lily in Hagenbeck's Animal Show, or even a peep
at the provocative *danse du ventre* in the "Streets of Cairo."

The contrasts between the White City, with its rippling pennants and
its daily garbage pick-up, and the dirty city outside Jackson Park that
was suffering through the effects of the depression of 1893 simply
astounded some visitors. Henry Adams sat on the steps of Hunt's Administration Building at the west end of the Grand Basin to ponder what
it all meant. He concluded that the biggest surprise of the Fair as a
scenic display "consisted in its being there at all—more surprising, as it
was, than anything else on the continent, Niagara Falls, the Yellow-
stone Geysers, and the whole railway system thrown in, since these
were all natural products in their place; while, since Noah's ark, no
such Babel of loose and ill-joined, such vague and ill-defined and unre-
lated thoughts and experimental outcries as the Exposition, had ever
ruffled the surface of the lakes."[54] Only in its incomprehensibility did
the Fair seem to offer some key to Chicago.

The fiction of the Fair generally praises it as a creative achievement,
but even those works which celebrate it at least imply that its appeal
rested in its differences from Chicago. One of the most favorable imaginative treatments is *Sweet Clover: A Romance of the White City*, which
was published in 1894 by Clara Louise Burnham (not a relation of
Daniel Burnham), a long-time Chicago resident and author of some two
dozen works of popular fiction. Title character Clover Bryant, a young
woman as sweet and natural as her name, is one of four confused lovers
who weave their way through the enchanted kingdom on the lake
before they finally pair off happily. Clover's sister Mildred marries handsome and wealthy Jack Van Tassel, while Clover herself weds Jack's
cousin Gorham Page.

Burnham intends to applaud the Fair as a credit to Chicago, but her
book implicitly rejects the modern city almost as much as does the work
of another "old settler," Henry Blake Fuller, although her light romance
has none of his irony. *Sweet Clover* is full of nostalgia for the time when
Hyde Park, where Clover lives, was a friendly village of decent, middle-
class people like the Bryants and the Van Tassels. The Fair is so attractive because it is a magic place, not only unlike Chicago but even not of
this earth. Going to the Exposition is a holy experience in which the
visitor worships the spirit of Republic in her sacred shrine of purity,
order, and beauty. At the opening ceremonies, when the machinery
that drives the exhibitions is about to be put in motion, Clover and
Mildred, their breath coming fast as they stand by the Peristyle, instinctively clasp hands, and Jack stands beside them, "his head bared before
this beginning of a new era." As the veil drops from the statue of the
Republic, water spurts from jets on the fountains, flags unfurl, and

144

artillery thunders, "the multitude, swayed by mighty feeling, rent the air with cheers," and "the sun burst from a cloud and blessed the scene with new splendor."[55]

Soon the Fair is explicitly described not as the image of the promise of this world, but of the next one. Adrift on the Grand Basin by the Columbian fountain at sunset in one of the gondolas used to navigate the lagoons, Jack Van Tassel looks up at the statues on the Court of Honor, which strike him in his rarefied mood as angels. Glad that "no mortal friend" is with him, he thinks of his dear departed father, one of the wealthy men who helped plan the Fair. Jack for the first time is reconciled to his father's death by this "realization of the possibilities of the Celestial City" that the Court of Honor (elsewhere called "the Mecca of all Exposition pilgrims") suggests. Another visitor to the Fair confesses, "I never expected to go to heaven till I died; but I've been there."[56]

Jack's spinster aunt, who comes from rural Massachusetts to visit Chicago, develops this idea of the Fair as heavenly city to its farthest limits. The Midway, which she calls "just a representation of matter," is the more accurate image of Chicago. It is, in her words, "some dirty and all barbaric. It deafens you with noise; the worst folks in there are avaricious and bad, and the best are just children in their ignorance." Moving from the Midway to the Fair proper is a magic transformation, for "when you come out o' that mile-long babel where you've been elbowed and cheated, you pass under a bridge—and all of a sudden you are in a great beautiful silence. The angels on the Woman's Buildin' smile down and bless you, and you know that in what seemed like one step, you've passed out o' darkness into light." Lest the reader miss the point, she tells her nephew that "perhaps dyin' is goin' to be somethin' like crossin' the dividin' line that separates the Midway from the White City." She thinks that the reason for this is "just the fact that the makers o' the Fair believed in God and put Him and their enlightenment from Him into what they did; and we feel it some like we'd feel an electric shock."[57] The great comfort of this heaven on earth is that it is assuredly not like Chicago.

The image of the White City as spiritual world continues. Alone beneath the arch of the Peristyle one evening, Clover and Gorham confess their everlasting love for one another. They gaze across the Grand Basin to the illuminated Administration Building, which looks like "an aerial castle, with no affinity for earth; an exalting vision such as visited the prophets of old." The transcendent beauty of the Fair strangely impedes the progress of the other pair of lovers. Although she is very fond of Jack, Mildred feels that she cannot fully respond to his affection because of her devotion to the ideal of eternal beauty that the Peristyle symbolizes. Fortunately, fate intervenes to resolve this peculiar dilemma. The book ends dramatically with the destruction of the Peristyle by fire after the official close of the Fair, and Mildred and Jack are in the crowd that watch it burn. As the Quadriga falls, Jack puts his arms around Mildred. Her voice chokes as she concludes that the Peristyle has "gone back—to heaven," and she tells her grateful suitor, "Your rivals are all gone, Jack. . . ."[58]

The burning of the Peristyle and Quadriga (as well as the opening ceremonies) did in fact take place as Burnham described it, and was an important scene in two other novels which used the buildings of the Fair much more pointedly to criticize contemporary Chicago. After the Exposition closed at the end of October, officials were undecided about what to do with the grounds. They did not intend the plaster structures of the Court of Honor to last beyond the summer, but the Fair was such an inspiring success that it seemed a shame to many that it would not continue in some form. A series of unexpected events settled the matter. The grounds were pillaged first by souvenir hunters, who in the depression winter came back to grasp some relic of the Fair's enchantment. On the first Sunday of 1894, the *Chicago Tribune* reported, several thousand souvenir seekers vandalized the grounds. Except for the police and Fair guards, the paper's observer noted, they "would have pulled the plaster figures off the Administration Building." As it was, these human locusts tore the arms off statues and even picked up bits of glass and tin cans in their eagerness for spoil. The scene must have been bizarre and unnerving. In the Midway's Java Village, two "stylishly-dressed" women ripped the wickerwork from a coffee hut, and a man and his wife hauled away a log of bamboo six inches in diameter while their children followed with sections of roof.[59]

The real disaster occurred the next day. At about four in the afternoon a guard told a group of tramps to move out of the empty Music Hall. These members of the city's army of unemployed had been "swarming" into the area in recent days. Whether by accident or intent, soon after this incident a fire started that quickly spread as the evening wore on, and which attracted an estimated twenty thousand spectators. This was the fire by whose light Mildred declared her love for Jack. It began in the Casino south of the Peristyle and moved north toward the Manufactures Building. It was, the *Tribune* said, "the greatest pyrotechnic display of the Fair," lighting up the area "like a midsummer's day at noon." The spectators who gathered appreciated the show immensely, cheering as statury fell off the cornices into the icy lagoon. Viewed from the Administration Building, the spectacle of this "solid wall of smoke and flame 500 yards long" was sublime, "showing a lurid hue over the adjacent building and in the reflections from the ice on Grand Basin." The statue of the Republic "seemed to stand in the midst of it all like a giant silhouette, with uplifted arms as if appealing for help. The wind blew furiously, and now and then made great rifts in the smoky wall, revealing the blood-red skeleton of arch and column."[60]

After the flames were doused, the Fair was turned over to a salvage company, but another fire beat the wreckers to what was left of the Court of Honor. On the evening of July 5, during the climax of the Pullman Strike, flames consumed the Terminal Station and the Mines and Manufactures buildings. The last group of statuary that collapsed before the Administration Building itself fell was the one depicting "Fire Uncontrolled."[61]

For Robert Herrick, the burning Court of Honor was a more salient reflection of Chicago than the White City had ever been, even though he earlier viewed the efforts of the builders and planners of the Exposition as a sign of hope for the future. He wrote that the Columbian Exposition "in a way was Chicago, its dream, its ideal, its noblest self incarnated in magnificent building, in splendor of size and pomp and beauty," and he called it "the fête day of our new world." Herrick agreed with Dreiser's comment that the Fair was very important for America's reputation and the country's own opinion of itself, since it showed that American life need not be unsightly and chaotic. The Fair "proclaimed to everybody that in spite of all the haste and ugliness and makeshift character of its civilization," America "had preserved its love of the ideal, of beauty and could accomplish it too—could achieve anything."

After the Fair closed, however, its promise was forgotten. The area surrounding Jackson Park, which had been built up quickly and haphazardly in anticipation of the business the visitors would bring, was suddenly deserted. What remained, Herrick recalled, was an unsightly landscape that spoke eloquently not only of its "makeshift character" but of the generally unhappy economic conditions of the time. "The skeleton that had been heroically shoved into the closet all that summer," Herrick wrote, "the skeleton of financial panic, now stalked forth. There were unemployed men by the hundreds of thousands in the cold streets that cold winter, and even the prosperous citizens were quaking in the throes of 'hard times.'"[62]

In their decay and ruin, the Fair and its related buildings seemed to Herrick to provide a better metaphor for modern urban life than they had in all their glory. He used the abandoned Exposition grounds as a setting in *The Web of Life* (1900), which takes place shortly after the Fair closed. He describes the area as spreading out on the lakefront like a dead civilization. The "rotting buildings of the play-city" are an ironic symbol of Chicago. They remind the hero of the novel, Dr. Howard Sommers, that in the actual city there is no evidence of any plan or continuity in building, only "sporadic eruptions of dwellings, mere heaps of brick and mortar dumped at random over the cheerless soil." The sky above Chicago strikes him as a "dome of vitrified glass" which "shut down the illimitable, tawdry sweep of defaced earth." The ruins of the Fair are more like the real Chicago than the ethereal White City ever was.

Later Herrick describes the second burning of the Fair buildings at length ("The Court of Honor with its empty lagoon and broken bridges," Herrick writes, "was more beautiful in the savage glow of the ravaging fire than even on the gala nights of the exposition").[63] Elsewhere in the city, angry members of the striking American Railway Union are overturning and torching cars managed by scabs, and federal troops are about to move in. Sommers is at this point highly agitated by his uncertainty over what is the right course of action to take in a society that is metaphorically on fire with social unrest. The scene in which he watches the Court of Honor collapse is a masterful stroke by Herrick that dramatizes the fact that the individual of deep social sympathies in Chicago of 1894 is a burning man in a blazing building.

Fred Haward of Will Payne's *Mr. Salt* is a figure much like Sommers. He leaves his job as a bank clerk halfway through the book and becomes for a while a labor organizer in a factory town outside the city that is owned by the industrialist Mr. Salt. Fred had earlier attended the Fair and was impressed by its scale and harmony, which to one "coming abruptly from the cluttered ugliness of the city itself, . . . was like a dream." The colossal facades of the Court of Honor had "the air of something ancient, august, haunting the mind with an idea of power." To Fred and his friends, the presence of the Fair in Chicago promised "something richer and finer than had ever been known." They felt that "[l]ife itself was lifted to a higher power." Fred's subsequent radicalization takes place during the violence surrounding the Pullman strike. As in *The Web of Life,* the Fair on fire matches the state of mind of the hero and the time and place in which he lives, as it casts its "fiery glow" on "wrecked railroad yards and sullen mobs confronting armed men. It was fitting, the proper setting of a scene in which the great smash-up was to be enacted." The fire "burned" Fred's blood, as this "picture of destruction, colossal and superb, keyed up his mind."

Payne recalls at this point that Fred had watched the Fair go up, "and had seen it in its glory, when it had seemed serenely to affirm the immortality of the system which produced it." But the view of this blaze "was the greatest of all." Payne continues, "The triumph of Salt and his kind was succeeded by this triumph of mere destruction. This fire was the end of the old order, a sign of the dissolution of the hard frame of things which held him prisoner."[64] Compared with scenes like this one, which depict the failure of the urban industrial order to satisfy the human spirit, *Sweet Clover*'s love plot seems especially frivolous. Payne and Herrick, more skillful writers than Burnham and dedicated to a realistic portrayal of the modern world, indicate forcefully that the most dramatic and important statement the Fair had to make was not of a snowy wonderland but of a fiery apocalypse.

In the text of their *Plan of Chicago,* Daniel Burnham and Edward Bennett argued that the Fair need not be merely a passing dream, that its principles of order and beauty could be applied to the real city. The Exposition was one of the most important catalysts of the City Beautiful movement, inspiring several comprehensive efforts to redesign Chicago and other cities in the image of the Fair. Burnham himself was principally involved in efforts of beautify and improve Washington, Cleveland, San Francisco, and Manila, as well as Chicago.[65] The *Plan of Chicago* was the culmination of fifteen years of ferment. Prepared under the auspices of the Commercial Club and published in 1909, the *Plan* was one of the major documents of Progressive urban reform, a remarkable testimony to a faith in rational professionalism no matter what the problem at hand. It was issued as a large and handsome book full of pastel-shaded diagrams, maps, and illustrations by Jules Guerin, presenting images of a city as different in its own serene grandeur from the actual Chicago as was the White City. This vision of a better Chicago became the unofficial guide for major civic construction projects until 1917, when it was officially adopted by the city government.

Though many of Burnham and Bennett's suggestions remain unfulfilled, several of the most successful planned reconstructions of the cityscape—including the use of landfill to turn most of the lakefront into a public park, the building of Lake Shore Drive, the development of the Forest Preserve, and the elevation of Michigan Avenue—were outgrowths of their recommendations. The Plan has had its detractors, especially those made uneasy by its elitism, its concentration on commercial building and the downtown, and its obsession with monumental order, but it is still widely praised as one of the best responses of its time to both the aesthetic and functional problems of the city.

The *Plan of Chicago* is impressive partly because it was realistic as well as visionary. "The plan frankly takes into consideration," its authors wrote, "the fact that the American city, and Chicago preeminently, is a center of industry and traffic." Their aim was to turn this chaotic center into "a well-ordered, convenient, and unified city," which would meet the practical requirements of commerce and at the same time make the physical appearance of Chicago more attractive. Burnham and Bennett argued along with Root and Sullivan that it was up to professional architects such as themselves to take this sprawling city into their capable hands and remake it for the good of those less able to see Chicago's needs. Their confidence in themselves and their faith in Chicago are present in every page. "The complicated problems which the great city develops are now seen not to be beyond the control of aroused public sentiment;" they asserted, "and practical men of affairs are turning their attention to working out the means whereby the city may be made an efficient instrument for providing all its people with the best possible conditions of living."[66]

The *Plan* called for a system of lagoons along the lakefront, which, the authors asserted (momentarily ignoring Chicago's climate in their enthusiasm), would compete as a vacation spot with the Riviera. Much impressed with the rebuilding of Paris, they suggested that major downtown boulevards could be altered and the banks of the Chicago River might be made to look like those of the Seine. With the rational reorganization of the railroad passenger terminals, the placement of major cultural institutions in an expanded downtown lakefront park, and the construction of a central civic center, the disjointed city might be reformed into a unified whole—a real community. The new Chicago would be more breathtaking than the Fair.

Burnham and Bennett argued that the size of the undertaking should not discourage Chicagoans. Burnham's most famous statement was, "Make no Little Plans; They have no magic to stir men's blood and probably themselves will not be realized," and he put some of this inspirational rhetoric into the *Plan* itself. "The mind of man," the *Plan of Chicago* observes, "at least as expressed in works he actually undertakes, finds itself unable to rise to the full comprehension of the needs of a city growing at the rate now assured for Chicago." The proper response to this set of circumstances was clear: "Therefore, no one should hesitate to commit himself to the largest and most comprehensive undertaking; because before any particular plan can be carried out, a still larger conception will begin to dawn, and even greater necessities will develop."[67]

The *Plan of Chicago* declared that Chicago might be Jerusalem and not Babylon if its citizens would only have the courage and vision to make it so. The *Plan* does not speak directly to the deeper problems of personal dissatisfaction and social unrest in urban life, but, along with the Fair, it is as significant an attempt as exists in turn-of-the-century Chicago to show that, in city planning at least, the requirements of business need not conflict with the standards of art. A beautiful city might be built that would work efficiently and serve the spiritual needs of the individual citizen. The rhetoric of the *Plan* is overly optimistic, but to the extent that its ideas have been enacted, Chicago has been made a more attractive and smoothly functioning city.

To the degree that it can be compared to literary works, the *Plan* is a unique document in Chicago literature of its time. Most traveler's reports, journalist's accounts, poems, and novels were based in their author's responses to the city, but here was a case where Chicago itself was expected to respond and conform to the descriptions and images in a book. It was a singular linking of text and city in which the latter was to take its lead from the former. In this one case, the right words were to be found first, and then made fact.

7

The stockyards

A trip through the big slaughtering-houses is very interesting. The wonderful dexterity of the butchers, the mechanical inventions to help the work, the methodical system employed, the extreme cleanliness, and, above all, the rapidity and silence with which everything is done, strike a stranger very forcibly, and an impartial person who visits those great meat manufactories comes away convinced that American ingenuity in this respect "beats creation."
—*John J. Flinn*, Chicago: The Marvelous City of the West. A History, an Encyclopedia, and a Guide

. . . all distinguished strangers, upon arrival in the city, at once were taken to the Stock Yards . . . to view with salutary wonder the prodigious goings on, and to be crammed with statistics and oratory concerning how Chicago feeds the world; . . . the reporter's first query would be: "How do you like Chicago?" Next, invariably: "Have you seen the Stock Yards."
—*Louis Sullivan*, The Autobiography of an Idea

One could not stand and watch very long without becoming philosophical, without beginning to deal in symbols and similes, and to hear the hog-squeal of the universe.
—*Upton Sinclair*, The Jungle

Chicago was an important meat-marketing center before it was a major city. In the late 1820s, Archibald Clybourne provisioned the small settlement from his slaughterhouse on the Chicago River. Over the next few decades a number of livestock yards were established in scattered locations, mostly on the South Side, the most noted being the pens of John B. Sherman (later the father-in-law of Daniel Burnham), which

152

were constructed in 1848. As was the case with most Chicago businesses, it was the railroad that enabled livestock selling and meat packing to become major enterprises by making both suppliers and customers more accessible. Other developments, such as the demand of the Union army for portable supplies of prepared meat, further spurred Chicago's growth as a livestock conversion center, so that even before the famed Union Stock Yards opened on Christmas of 1865, the city had become the meat-packing leader of the nation.

The Union Stock Yards introduced unprecedented volume and efficiency to the industry. A four-hundred-acre marsh about four miles south and west of the downtown was drained and then subdivided into animal pens that were arranged along a rectangular grid of service streets. All major railroads in the city ran their freight cars to this area. To serve those who worked and traded in meat, the Union Stock Yards eventually included an Exchange Building, restaurants, a bank, a hotel, and a branch of the fire department. At the main entrance to the yards was a gabled limestone gateway in the gingerbread style of the post–Civil War period, fifty feet wide and over thirty feet high, complete with a bull's head gargoyle that surveyed the bovine parade below. The gateway is now a lonely national landmark, for the yards went into complete decline after the Second World War and closed in 1971. The vast expanse of pens and livestock behind the bull's head became a surreal landscape of tall prairie grass and wildflowers criss-crossed by untraveled streets and rusty railway tracks and bordered by turn-of-the-century red-brick factory buildings, all waiting for redevelopment.

These few buildings are the remnants of Packingtown, the area adjacent to the Union Stock Yards where the meat-processing plants were located. During the 1870s and 1880s the Chicago meat trade diversified and expanded considerably. The city remained the central market for livestock that was butchered elsewhere, but the stockyards area also developed into a processing empire where animals were slaughtered and converted into food and other by-products. Packers including Nelson Morris, Philip Armour, Gustavus Swift, and several others here assembled the largest industry in this industrial city. Their technology and scientific management were impressive. Here was the first major use of the modern assembly line, in which the product moves by a series of workers, each with a specific task. By the 1890s it took only minutes for a cow to pass several dozen workers as it went from meat on the hoof to butchered beef hanging in the cooling rooms. With the expanded application of the new railroad refrigerator car in the 1870s and 1880s, the packers could supply a world-wide demand for dressed meat. At the same time, they further increased their profitability by finding every manner of new use for portions of the carcasses that were formerly discarded. "Everything but the squeal" was the byword of Pack-ingtown.

Even by the standards of this city obsessed with quantity, the numbers were awesome. The stockyards and packinghouses represented, as Upton Sinclair stated, "the greatest aggregation of capital and labor ever gathered in one place." By one careful count, almost two-and-a-half million cattle and close to five million hogs were slaughtered in Chicago in 1892. At the turn of the century the capacity of the pens was seventy-five thousand cattle, fifty-thousand sheep, three hundred thousand hogs, and five thousand horses. The value of the products of the packinghouses grew from just over nineteen million dollars in 1870 to close to two hundred million in 1890. At the turn of the century, some one hundred packing companies in the stockyards district directly employed thirty thousand people.

The dominion of the Chicago packers was impressive. By the mid-1880s almost ninety percent of the dressed beef shipped to Boston, New York, and Philadelphia came from Chicago, and at this same time the British government purchased packed meat from Chicago for its Nile expedition. The livestock and meat-packing trade, Chicago historian Bessie Louise Pierce observes, "tapped deeply the fount of Chicago's expanding empire as probably no other single business venture did."[1] She might have said "America's expanding empire," for in these few hundred acres was located what Siegfried Giedion calls "the most important link between the raisers and consumers in a vast country." "In Chicago," Giedion adds, "we are dealing with dimensions for which there is, even today, no yardstick. A spontaneously growing center of force, it embodies, as few other places do, that brutal and inventive vitality of the nineteenth century."[2]

Hog Butcher for the World

Sometimes to the embarrassment of Chicago residents, "Porkopolis" was a common turn-of-the-century nickname for their city. Despite its museums, expositions, and other more seemly industries, Chicago could not escape its close identification in people's minds and, when the wind was right, in their noses, with the stockyards. The guidebooks that described the stockyards in detail, such as John J. Flinn's 1892 all-purpose *Chicago: The Marvelous City of the West*, were meeting rather than creating a demand for information. Every newcomer would be sure to have heard of the stockyards ahead of any other feature of Chicago, and would be eager to visit them. This was easily understandable. The enormous numbers of cattle and sheep and pigs, the mass slaughter, and the ingenuity of the mechanized preparation of the daily diet of the world could not but be fascinating.

The traders and the packers were proud of the world they made, and they were ready to show it off to these visitors. The *Baedeker Handbook to the United States*, first published in 1893, carefully instructed the traveler to take the South Halsted tramway or the State Street line (with a transfer) to the gateway, where one could then hire a stockyards guide for twenty-five cents before proceeding to the tours of the packing-houses. "The guide should be asked," the *Baedeker* soberly advised, "to point out 'Old Bill,' the 'bunko steer,' who acts as a decoy for his mates." Flinn stressed the scientific efficiency, economy, and hygiene of the packers. All the guidebooks recognized, however, that the most profound attraction of the yards was the bloody spectacle of life and death. "The processes of killing the cattle and hogs are extremely ingenious and expeditious," commented the *Baedeker*, "andwill interest those whose nerves are strong enough to contemplate with equanimity wholesale slaughter and oceans of blood."[3]

The *Baedeker* implied that a tour of the stockyards was perhaps not for everyone; but there were even more dismaying, if less dramatic, aspects of the slaughteryards and packinghouses than the killing, and these aspects the management did its best to keep from view. The giants of the meat industry argued that the scale and streamlined methods of their operations meant better and cheaper products for the customer, but there was strong evidence that parts of the gigantic operation were unethical and unclean. The stockyards managers were attacked for inflated space and feed charges, dishonest weighing and docking procedures, and cruelty to the animals. The packers threatened to break the control of the managers by setting up their own yards, but in 1892 they settled with the company in return for financial compensation and a voice in running the operation.

Public criticism centered on the packers themselves. Muckraker Charles Edward Russell, author of *Lawless Wealth,* exposed the abuses of Packingtown in *The Greatest Trust in the World,* which was published in 1905 after serialization in *Everybody's Magazine.* Russell's main target was the greedy arrogance of the larger converters, whose collaboration led, he claimed, to such abuses as price fixing, railroad rebates, overcharges for the use of refrigerator cars, and even the theft of city water through secret pipes. To Russell, the stockyards revealed neither the industrial might or efficiency of Chicago, but its corruption. He contended that Swift, Armour, and Morris combined to drive down the cost of beef on the hoof and push up the price of meat on the table— thereby robbing both producers and consumers—and that their quality control was a sham. Contemptuous of the well-being of their customers in their hunger for higher profits, the packers processed inferior or even diseased beef and pork, covering their tracks with dangerous chemicals.

Russell ridiculed the Packingtown tours, with their "neatly uniformed attendants." These guides, he contended, lead the visitors past butchers "in immaculate attire," who "perform for the delectation of the grand stand," so that "you marvel at the exceeding neatness and cleanness of everything." This was just a "show," a "play" put on to fool the public. "The real work is done where no outsider can see it; attempt at any point to wander from the beaten path and see how swiftly you will be driven back," Russell claimed. "You shall see nothing but what the Company is willing to show you, the play-actors with their white aprons, the girls in neat dress."[4]

In Russell's opinion, the secret operations of the packinghouses made inspection laws a jest. Such laws had been in effect since the early nineties when, in the face of numerous scandals, the Board of Trade called on the government to pass statutes to regulate this important industry and restore the public's trust. These laws did not prove to be effective, however, and allegations concerning unsanitary conditions continued to elude the packers' attempts to dismiss them. Russell mentioned the horrifying findings of scientific examinations of the packinghouses that were undertaken by the British medical journal *Lancet*, and the public outrage over the "embalmed beef" sent to American troops during the Spanish-American War. According to Upton Sinclair, the latter scandal was the reason why he found a sympathetic audience in Theodore Roosevelt, who supposedly told him, "Mr. Sinclair, I bear no love for those gentlemen [the packers], for I ate the meat they canned for the army in Cuba."[5]

The tours sought to hide not only the manufacturing abuses of the meat packers, but also the miserable state of labor in Packingtown. The terrible working conditions were no secret to settlement workers and sociologists, however, who saw in the stockyards the widespread plight of urban industrial labor in Chicago and elsewhere. In 1902, Charles J. Bushnell published his University of Chicago doctoral thesis, *The Social Problem at the Chicago Stock Yards*. In the course of this study, he spoke of the high child-mortality rate in the stockyards area, the lack of basic public services such as street paving and sewers, the abundance of saloons, the scarcity of more constructive social centers, and the absence of ventilation, light, and safety devices in the packinghouses. Bushnell explained that he chose the stockyards for study "because the vast aggregation of business at this place affords an unusual opportunity to observe in strikingly typical forms the special characteristics of modern industry." The consolidation of industry had begun to jeopardize human freedom, Bushnell argued, and perhaps created the necessity for some form of socialism. In his introduction he argued that "American national life, and especially the cause of universal democracy, has, within the last few years, come to be seriously threatened by social conditions in the large American cities." He explained that he chose to study this large urban industry "because it is believed that therein today is to be found, in its most acute stage, the central problem of democracy: the physical, economic, and cultural advancement of the whole people as an organic body, rather than as a wasteful collection of warring groups."[6]

In starting from the premise that the stockyards displayed the general problems of urban industrialism, Bushnell was treating them as a symbol as well as a discrete social and economic fact. So did many others, including Flinn and Russell, though they disagreed on what this symbol represented. The stockyards came to be synecdochically interchangeable with Chicago as a collection of such titanic industries. The yards *did* seem to be a gloss on Chicago. With their own rail service, their rectangular grid of avenues and alleys forming "blocks" of pens, and their bank, hotel, and other amenities, they were often described as a city in themselves. For those impressed or repelled by Chicago's crudeness and vitality, the stockyards were a perfect objectification of the spirit of the place. They were awesome and unnerving, a stark expression of the industrial age and the highly organized transformation of raw material into product.

Since the yards were so richly symbolic and expressive, literary visitors were especially eager to see the operation, even if they were careful to keep their distance. Paul Bourget, for example, commented on the usefulness of the stockyards as a way of learning about Chicago, asserting that "these abattoirs furnish materials most precious to the foreigner who desires to understand the spirit in which Americans undertake great enterprises." He was put off by the slaughtering just as he was distressed by the city itself, but the yards won from him the same grudging praise and wonder as did the whole town. "A colossal effort of imagination on the one hand," he reflected after his tour, "and, on the other, at the service of the imagination, a clear and carefully estimated understanding of the encompassing reality,—these are the two features everywhere stamped upon the unparalleled establishment we have just visited."[7] Other visitors more sharply critical of Chicago made fuller figurative use of the yards in discussing the entire city. Max Weber passed through Chicago on a lecture tour in 1904 and found "incredible" the complexity, contradictions, and violence of what he saw, including the "steam, dirt, blood, and hides" of the stockyards. The imagery of Packingtown permeated his impression of "the whole gigantic city." He likened Chicago to "a man whose skin has been peeled off and whose entrails one sees at work."[8]

Rudyard Kipling disliked several of the American cities he visited after he arrived from India late in 1889, but he despised Chicago most of all. "Having seen it," he wrote, "I urgently desire never to see it again. It is inhabited by savages." He mercilessly attacked Chicago's unrelieved flatness, its boorish business culture, and its worship of production for its own sake. As part of his visit, he made the obligatory trip to the yards and described the killing in harrowing detail ("The blood ran in muttering gutters," he wrote. "There was no place for hand or foot that was not coated with thicknesses of dried blood, and the stench of it in the nostrils bred fear"). But he ironically confessed that he was grateful that he had taken his stockyards tour. He thanked "the same merciful Providence that has showered good things on my path" for sending him "an embodiment of the City of Chicago, so that I might remember it for ever." All the brazen, anarchic savagery of this place where every activity, even murder, could be turned into a big business and managed with high efficiency for profit, converged in his view of other tourists in the yards.

One fellow visitor particularly caught Kipling's eye. He was struck that women sometimes take the tours, "as they would come to see the slaughter of men," and he noticed that "there entered that vermilion hall a young woman of large mould, with brilliantly scarlet lips, and heavy eyebrows, and dark hair that came in a 'widow's peak' on the forehead." Attired in "flaming red and black," with "the red blood under her shoes, the vivid carcasses packed round her, a bullock bleeding its life away not six feet from her, and the death factory roaring all round her," she seemed to personify the brutal spirit of Chicago. As a human being, he was appalled: "She looked curiously, with hard, bold eyes, and was not ashamed." As an inquiring tourist, however, he was satisfied: "Then said I: 'This is a special Sending. I have seen the City of Chicago!' And I went away to get peace and rest."[9]

Those who were attracted and even charmed by the general "savagery" that offended Kipling, however, could read even the slaughterhouses in a positive light. The common defense of Chicago's crudity was that if it was true that the city was not appealing by the "civilized" standards according to which a Kipling judged it, these standards were outdated in an industrial age. To ignore the stockyards and Chicago was to ignore reality. This is part of the point of Sandburg's incantation in the opening lines of "Chicago" and of his description of the city as a "tall bold slugger" so different from "the little soft cities." H. L. Mencken later rousingly praised Chicago as the true capital of America because it was more vital and creative than more "refined" places. He saw nothing but positive connotations in the identification of Chicago with the stockyards. "I give you Chicago," Mencken told the world. "It is not London-and-Harvard. It is not Paris-and-Buttermilk. It is American in every chitling and sparerib, and it is alive from snout to tail."[10]

More than any other feature, the stockyards continued to be the most salient landmark of the city in the eyes of those who tried to capture its essential spirit. When British journalist W. L. George came to Chicago in 1920, he visited the Armour plant and was astounded by "the quiet officialdom of this murder." Like Kipling, he feared that this process seemed to desensitize and thus dehumanize all those involved in it. George wrote, "Death is so swift, the evidence of tragedy so soon gone, that one feels no shock that flesh loses its character. Cattle are being handled like brass, so swiftly that life becomes merely a raw material." It was a perfect expression of the city, he noted, concluding, "That is Chicago." He wondered what it all boded for the future of the city: "A superior force, which is called organized industry, has cut up the cattle on a traveling belt and carried them away. For a moment I have a vision of Chicago carried away on its own traveling belt. Carried away . . . where to?"[11]

More recently, Norman Mailer used the stockyards in *Miami and the Siege of Chicago*, his account of the Republican and Democratic national conventions of 1968, to characterize Chicago as a brutally "honest" town whose admirable, no-nonsense quality was exemplified by the slaughterhouses. Like Mencken, he criticized those who would try to ignore or hide "reality," and he saw something earthy and appealing in the yards. "But in Chicago," Mailer observed, "they did it straight, they cut the animals right out of their hearts—which is why it was the last of the great American cities, and people had great faces, carnal as blood, greedy, direct, too impatient for hypocrisy, in love with honest plunder."[12]

The yards were all but gone by 1968, and the passage tells more about Mailer perhaps than it does about Chicago; but it reveals above all how strong a symbol the slaughterhouses were to authors trying to write about the city. Those who might dispute just what the stockyards and Chicago said about the conditions of contemporary life still agreed that, if one wanted to find the right words for Chicago, one need only pay a nickel to the South Halsted tram and get off at the bull's-head gate.

HORRORS AND HOMILIES

The stockyards are the principal setting of much of the action in several turn-of-the-century works of fiction which vary a great deal in the way they use Packingtown to talk about Chicago. One of the best is Herrick's *Memoirs of an American Citizen,* the "autobiography" of meatpacker Van Harrington. Van responds to those who criticize his questionable tactics by explaining that he is no better and no worse than his context, which is literally and figuratively a slaughtering operation. If the competitive business world of Chicago forces one to choose between being the butcher or the lamb, Harrington argues, he will always pick up the knife. He fully accepts the stockyards as a reflection of the "real" world. In spite of their "filth" and "ugly look," "it fired [Van's] blood" to be a part of the yards. He sees them as "a stout, hearty place to fight in," one that fairly rewards the hardy and ambitious individual. [13] He also argues, as the packers did, that people like him are needed to stay the appetite of a growing country. There is something appealing in Harrington's impatience with pretentiousness and propriety, but the corruption of such a capable and open-spirited man is very sobering. Although Chicago and the stockyards make Van wealthy and powerful, they have demanded all his energy and intelligence and have thrown his conscience out with the squeal.

John Ganton, of Arthur Jerome Eddy's *Ganton & Company: A Story of Chicago Commercial and Social Life* (1908), is another self-made Chicago millionaire in the meat-packing business. His men kill over sixty thousand animals a day and ship his dressed beef around the world, so that the sign "Ganton & Company" is "almost as familiar in Hong Kong as in Omaha," and his name means "more to the millions who ate his foods and consumed his products than that of any monarch." Atop the corporate world, he is still ambitious, determined "to double the output of his company, to make it greater than that of all other packing companies taken together, to extend his control over the slaughtering and packing industry until the world depended upon him for meat." [14]

The novel offers a sweeping, if confused, picture of a city that is without saving graces. It specifically singles out for attack labor unions and big businessmen, high society, and social reformers. One of the central tensions in this book is the conflict between Ganton and his son John, who has been determined to avoid going into the meat-packing industry from the time he first visited the stockyards and was profoundly shocked by this hell-on-earth. Ganton grudgingly concedes that his empire must be left to his other son, Will, and he lets John go away to college. He refuses to allow him to go into professional school, however, and his stockyards thinking determines him in this as in every other matter. His response to his son's possibly becoming a lawyer is, "I buy my pettifoggers as I do my cattle; it don't pay to raise 'em." [15] He finally agrees to grant the boy an independent income on the one condition that John work for a year in the company after he completes college.

Contrary to both his and his father's expectations, John proves to be a chip off the old block. By the end of the novel, the company becomes his by the terms of the old man's will. The son turns out to have all the shrewdness and daring of the father, and these attributes are only enhanced by his greater cultivation and humanity. Eddy implies that John's move into the stockyards is somehow fated and, to a degree, fortunate, for the stockyards are once again the "real world" where the great events of life take place. Here, amid all the bloody activity, the latent virtues of this supposedly effete boy can be developed and given a field of important creative action.

Eddy may have believed that the stockyards, and Chicago generally, are the kind of place one must confront if one is to live the fullest and most significant life that contemporary conditions make available, but this still does not necessarily mean that he found the stockyards-city attractive in absolute terms. Even the elder Ganton, whose irresistible will to dominate is the result of a deep-seated bitterness toward life, finally sees the stockyards as a horrible place. Mortally ill with cancer, he delays surgery because he associates knives only with killing. In his sickroom, Ganton hallucinates about the agony of all the slaughtered beasts. When he closes his weary eyes he sees all the terrors of the stockyards, "the great steam-filled rooms, the bubbling vats, the men barefooted and sweaty moving about amidst slime and offal, the sheep and the hogs and the cattle in the long narrow runways moving in an endless stream on to the killing-rooms."[16]

Eddy restates his idea of the world as stockyards in another of the several dream passages that recur in the novel. As Ganton goes under the ether on the operating table, he beholds a vision of the "bright, happy days" of his youth. He recalls how he drove cows to the meadow rather than to the slaughter in a pastoral setting that knew nothing of the killing-beds which have consumed his energies in Chicago. In his dying reverie he envisions another city, the heavenly one his saintly mother described to him. Its beauty and wonder make the ugliness of the stockyards-city all the more apparent. The world of which he dreams in his deepest hopes of release sounds remarkably like the World's Columbian Exposition. It is "a beautiful city of light" that is accessible by a broad white stairway and gates of pearl. He sees himself mounting the stair and taking a last, backward glance at the hellish world which he has made and which has totally consumed him, and he envisions it as one big stockyards, "hidden and lost in darkness, shrouded in smoke and bathed in steam and noisome vapors,—a place of slaughter and offal."[17]

Two other books that center around a leading meat packer offer a far more benign view of the city as stockyards. In 1901, George Horace Lorimer, then in the early years of his nearly four-decade tenure as editor of the *Saturday Evening Post*, began a series of "Letters from a Self-Made Merchant to His Son." These letters proved to be very popular, prompting Lorimer to collect twenty of them into a book he called *Letters from a Self-Made Merchant to His Son*, subtitled, *Being the Letters written by John Graham, Head of the House of Graham & Company, Pork-packers in Chicago, familiarly Known on 'Change as "Old Gorgon Graham," to his Son, Pierrepont, facetiously known to his intimates as "Piggy."* The wide appeal of the book—it was available for forty years and appeared in translation abroad—encouraged Lorimer to collect more letters into a second volume that was more humbly titled *Old Gorgon Graham: More Letters from a Self-made Merchant to His Son*.[18]

Lorimer's "letters" drew on personal experience. His father was a prominent Baptist minister in Chicago whose parishioners included Philip Armour. Armour supposedly encouraged young Lorimer to drop out of Yale and make his fortune in the yards. Lorimer accepted the offer and in eight years moved up from mailroom clerk to head of the canning department before leaving the company. Armour's total dedication to his work impressed Lorimer. He recalled that when he got married his boss allowed him time off for a honeymoon but advised him (in a remark that found its way into the *Letters*), "You might as well call on the trade as long as you're travelling."

The voices of Armour and of Lorimer's minister father merge in the letters, which are little homespun homilies on the importance of hard work, common sense, and pragmatism. Over and over the lesson is the same: success is won by initiative, honesty, good judgment, and, above all, single-mindedness. "You've got to eat hog, think hog, dream hog—" Graham tells his son, evidently blissfully free of John Ganton's hog nightmares.[19] This lesson, he implies, applies to the conduct of all one's affairs. To the elder Graham, the world is just the pork-packing business writ large.

Gorgon Graham's words of advice follow his son from the time of his departure for Harvard (a luxury which his father, of course, never had) through his early career in the business. After Pierrepont proves his worth, he is finally made a partner. Together these letters are a benign variation on *Ganton & Company*, particularly as they treat the relationship between the self-made man and his son. They also owe a great deal to the conventions of standard success literature. Graham seems very strict in his conviction that Pierrepont must work his way through the various departments of the business, but he is a proud father who loves his boy and wishes to reward him without spoiling him. He fears that his son's character will be ruined if he tastes the finer things in life without first facing hard personal challenges.

"Character" is the key term of the book. As in *Ganton & Company,*
the stockyards are the place where character is forged. Harvard, to be
sure, will educate Pierrepont, but Chicago will make him a man. In an
odd way, Graham gives Pierrepont the same "loving" treatment he gives
his livestock. Graham the elder brags, "I found the American hog in a
mud-puddle, without a beauty spot on him except the curl in his tail,
and I'm leaving him packed in fancy cans and cases, with gold medals
hung all over him."[20] He might say a like thing about his son. Pierrepont is a fine young man, but he needs to be tested and "processed" by
the yards. Lorimer's handling of Pierrepont's rise through merit reveals
his belief in the dream of success and his admiration for American
entrepreneurial capitalism, of which he was, through the *Post,* the
leading popularizer of the day. Indeed, the "letters" appeared in some of
the same issues in which Lorimer serialized *The Pit.* The meaning of
Pierrepont's career is that the stockyards-as-city is a rugged but fair
place where the truly talented and ambitious will make the prime grade.

Lorimer's view of the stockyards as symbol of the urban commercial
and industrial world is reassuring, for in his eyes Packingtown and
Chicago are where human worth is honestly weighed and tested. As
Lorimer sees them, the stockyards are not an inferno but a source of
wisdom. Graham is always drawing out moral truisms from his work.
For example, he tells Pierrepont, "You can cure a ham in dry salt and
you can cure it in sweet pickle, and when you're through you've got
pretty good eating either way, provided you started in with a sound
ham." Then he explicates the lesson: "And it doesn't make any difference how much sugar and fancy pickle you soak into a fellow, he's no
good unless he's sound and sweet at the core."[21]

While other writers used the stockyards to show the human costs of
the selfish pursuit of private wealth, Lorimer depicted the packing-
house in terms of sound personal relationships. He had little trouble
translating even the most precious and intimate family experiences into
stockyards terms. Graham responds to the news that his grandson is a
hefty twelve pounds by bragging that the baby keeps up the family
reputation "for giving good weight" and praising the infant for being "a
credit to the brand."[22] Whether consciously or not, Lorimer was obviously not interested in a realistic treatment of the stockyards or of
Chicago the industrial city. He conveniently omitted any mention of the
blood and violence of the yards. Although he would proudly brag of the
time he rode a supply train through pickets to strikebreakers, he offered
only the briefest glimpse of the unskilled laborers who do the dirty work
Pierrepont never touches.

By casting his meat packer as Lord Chesterfield, Lorimer was trying
to show that industrial capitalism was a form of benevolent paternalism

and not cutthroat war. Lorimer took great pains to domesticate the stockyards, to show that big business and modern urban life are not dehumanizing. He tried to prove that large industries were not disruptive of the cherished ideal of the simple social harmony of the small town of the early republic, a point that Herrick and Eddy directly refuted in their tales of the corruption of the good-hearted village boy who makes it in the stockyards. The elder Graham's major formative experience besides the yards is his boyhood in rural Missouri, a world whose values he keeps intact in Chicago. In this respect the two books of letters are nostalgic for a way of life that Lorimer himself knew was no longer possible.

INTO THE JUNGLE

Although Upton Sinclair was not the first nor by any means the only writer to examine the stockyards as an expressive symbol of Chicago and the modern city, he succeeded better than anyone before or since the publication of *The Jungle* in 1906 in exploiting their many meanings. Work on the book began in 1904, when Fred D. Warren, editor of the socialist journal *Appeal to Reason,* suggested that Sinclair write something to expose the evils of wage slavery. Sinclair later dedicated *The Jungle* to "the Workingmen of America." He decided to focus on the Chicago stockyards because he was aware of the troubles of organized labor in the meat-packing industry, notably an unsuccessful strike earlier in the year. He also knew that the high visibility of the packers' products and the lingering scandal of the tainted meat they provided during the Spanish-American War assured a wide public interest. So he left his home in Princeton, New Jersey, to take advantage of what Charles Bushnell called "the unusual opportunity" the stockyards afforded to examine "the special characteristics of modern industry."

Sinclair spent seven weeks wandering about Packingtown, which he described in his autobiography as a "fortress of oppression." As he recalled it, during the day he would pick up a dinner pail, and, dressed as a worker, ferret past the watchmen Russell mentioned and through the secret operations of the yards that the tours did not reveal. In the evenings he would speak to workers and other residents in the district. He claimed that he checked his findings by talking to the staff of the University Settlement nearby and with other investigators. Sinclair's hunch that the stockyards would provide a dramatic means to explore wage slavery in the industrial city was richly confirmed, and he returned to Princeton to write his book. The resulting novel is an odd and sometimes uncertain mixture of muckraking and melodrama that transcends the conventions and intentions of both genres to form, despite flaws that Sinclair himself recognized, one of the most powerful books in American literature.[23] What makes *The Jungle* so forceful and distinguishes it from other novels of exposé and reform is the remarkable effectiveness with which he traces the breakdown in the stockyards of the family of Jurgis Rudkus after their immigration from Lithuania.

From the very beginning of their adventures in America, Chicago and the stockyards mean virtually the same thing to Jurgis and his relatives. "Chicago" is the only English word they know when they set out, and they keep repeating it to officials and ticket agents along their journey so that the way to it may be pointed out to them. When they finally arrive in Chicago, however, like many other immigrants they wander about "in the midst of deafening confusion, utterly lost." They are fortunate to find temporary shelter in a police station, where they are furnished with an interpreter and "taught a new word—'stockyards.'" This new word displaces and subsumes the old one, so that "America," which once meant "Chicago," now means "stockyards."

Their trip into Chicago is another instance of the view of the city from the train. "Every minute, as the train sped on," Sinclair writes, "the colors of things became dingier; the fields were grown parched and yellow, the landscape hideous and bare." The streetcar ride Jurgis's family takes the next day to the stockyards is a condensed version of their trip into Chicago itself. On the train they had distinguished in "the thickening smoke" of the city "another circumstance, a strange, pungent odor." As they ride the trolley, "they realized that they were on their way to the home of it—that they had travelled all the way from Lithuania to it." The new arrivals are "still tasting it, lost in wonder, when suddenly the car came to a halt, and the door was flung open, and a voice shouted—'Stockyards!'"[24]

As Sinclair then describes them, the stockyards are the city as a fearsome combination of Babel, bedlam, and hell. The immigrants' first visual impression of Packingtown is of a group of buildings from which emanate "half a dozen columns of smoke, thick, oily, and black as night." This smoke "might have come from the centre of the world, . . . where the fires of the ages still smoulder. It came as if self-impelled, driving all before it, a perpetual explosion. It was inexhaustible; one stared, waiting to see it stop, but still the great streams rolled out." The noises the newcomers hear are as elemental as the sight and smell of the smoke, suggesting "endless activity, the rumblings of a world in motion." It takes them some time to realize that this sound is made by the animals, "that it was the distant lowing of ten thousand cattle, the distant grunting of ten thousand swine." The collective cry of the condemned beasts in their pens reverberates like "all the barnyards in the universe." Likewise, the "uproar" in the killing-beds is "appalling, per-

165

ilous to the ear-drums; one feared there was too much sound for the room to hold—that the walls must give way or the ceiling crack."[25]

Sinclair concedes that the display of controlled power in the stock-yards is fascinating. The trains move ceaselessly in and out, the great pulleys that control the lines on which the carcasses hang never stop. The endless activity of this world in motion is one of carefully directed processes, "a picture of human power wonderful to watch." The form that this power takes is mythic: the "alchemists" of Packingtown use their gathered machinery to turn life into death and then convert the dead flesh immediately into things whose source is scarcely recognizable. But this place is also horrifying. Sinclair's strongest image of the stockyards-city as inferno is that isolated section of the works where the blood, bones, and excrement of the stock are made into fertilizer. Few tourists ever view this section, he notes, "and the few who did would come out looking like Dante, of whom the peasants declared that he had been to hell." Here, "in suffocating cellars where the daylight never came," is best illustrated the condition of industrial labor. In this awful place one might see "men and women and children bending over whirling machines and sawing bits of bone into all sorts of shapes, breathing their lungs full of the fine dust, and doomed to die, every one of them, within a certain definite time."[26]

As this passage indicates, Sinclair uses the stockyards to show how much unnatural and malignant elements have replaced the natural landscape in the modern city. Along with Henry B. Fuller and others, Sinclair argues that the builders of Chicago have made a perverse world in nature's own image that denies nature and life itself. In the stock-yards area there is no green at all except a tiny plot of grass in front of one of the office buildings. Instead of normal vegetation, there is "a forest of freezing hogs" in the chilling rooms. Sinclair also speaks of the factory chimney smoke forming "one giant river" and flowing above the "river of hogs" that moves on its way up the slaughterhouse chute, which is called "a very river of death." The "sea of pens" is the source of the noise which sounds like "a far-off ocean calling." Together these "forests" and "rivers" form "a thing as tremendous as the universe—the laws and ways of its working no more than the universe to be questioned or understood." In his naivete Jurgis at first accepts this inversion of the natural world. He feels that "to be given a place in it and a share in its wonderful activities was a blessing to be grateful for, as one was grateful for the sunshine and the rain."[27]

Sinclair's handling of Packingtown is more detailed and impassioned than that of any other writer, but the differences between his descriptions of the district and those of most other observers are ones of degree rather than of kind. Like the remarks of Kipling, most of the passages from *The Jungle* that have been cited are placed within the context of a tour of the yards, the one that Jurgis and his family take when they first arrive. Sinclair's more original technique of examining the yards and explaining their relationship to the contemporary city was to view them from the inside by making Jurgis the center of the book. By showing what happens to this one worker, he analyzed conditions in Chicago with pointed force. Jurgis's career presents the horrors of the yards as a felt process, especially as the Lithuanian and his fellow workers inevitably become indistinguishable from the livestock they slaughter and process. Sinclair convinces the reader that the best way to see the stockyards—and the city—is not from the tourist walks, but from the conveyor hoists and steam vats, and even through the eyes of one of Phil Armour's hogs.

Sinclair first makes this point with a somewhat forced personification of the beasts that pass before Jurgis when he takes his tour. "Each one of these hogs was a separate creature, . . . " he writes, "[a]nd each one of them had an individuality of his own, a will of his own, a hope and a heart's desire; each was full of self-confidence, of self-importance, and a sense of dignity." Then a "horrid Fate" grabs each hog by the hind legs and drags him away: "[A]ll his protests, his screams, were nothing to it—it did its cruel will with him, as if his wishes, his feelings, had simply no existence at all; it cut his throat and watched him gasp out his life." Shaken by what he sees in the killing beds, Jurgis mutters, "Dieve—but I'm glad I'm not a hog!"[28]

Once he begins to work in the stockyards, Jurgis finds that he is treated like the dumb beast he pities. The packers are, if anything, less humane to him than they are to their stock in extracting all they can out of him while ignoring his rage and torment. On his first day of job hunting they pick him out of the hiring line because he is young and strong—a good bull—but his working and living conditions eventually weaken him until he is forced into the fertilizer factory if he wants a job at all. He is relatively fortunate. His father, who works in a pickling vat, has his legs and lungs literally eaten away by chemicals. Jurgis's young brother-in-law loses his mind in his terror of working in the yards and is later devoured alive by rats. A work boss forces Ona, Jurgis's innocent young bride, into prostitution, and she later dies in childbirth when her family cannot get her adequate medical help. After Jurgis attacks the foreman responsible for exploiting Ona, he is thrown into jail like a pig in a stockyard pen.

At every stage the packingmachine crushes the spirits of the Lithuanians, but they keep trying to assert their humanity. The novel begins with the wedding feast of Jurgis and Ona (it then moves back to the time of their arrival in Chicago), which they try to celebrate according to Old

World customs. The meal costs the family a year's earnings, but they are determined to preserve the ethnic rituals which give their life some joy and meaning. Despite Lorimer's assurances that traditional values are not threatened in the new industrial order, the newcomers discover that they cannot preserve the old ways in Chicago. The ethos of the yards invades even this ceremony. The guests, conscious of the horrors of the world outside the feast, dance and drink themselves senseless to block out the hardships of their daily life. Having learned to prey on others in this "jungle," many eat heartily and then disappear before the hat is passed. The saloon keeper who caters the wedding overcharges the family. As Ona is carried to her marriage bed, she is fearful that she will lose her job if she does not show up on time the next morning.

When Jurgis gets out of jail, his education in the realities of Chicago and Packingtown continues. Blacklisted for his attack on a boss, he manages to get a job in the reaper works. Here the conditions are more healthy, but he loses his position as soon as business slackens. Next, a settlement worker learns with dismay what has happened to the family and gets Jurgis a job in a steel mill, but this is another false lead. The steel works are just another industrial hell where workers are sacrificed and tortured for simply trying to earn enough to feed their families. Jurgis burns himself badly while saving the life of another man and then is docked for lost time. He has not yet learned the law of the jungle, that he would have done better to let the other man perish. Then he comes home to find that his baby boy, the one source of joy in his life, has drowned after falling off the sidewalk into a puddle in the unpaved street. This is his breaking point. He deserts the remnants of his family, hops a freight out of Chicago, and supports himself in the countryside with odd jobs and thievery.

Like other Chicago writers, Sinclair believed that this kind of escape could only be temporary, since the general conditions of urban life could not be avoided. The oncoming winter and the shortage of work in the country drive Jurgis back. Desperate to land a job, he cannot even make his way through a mob of unemployed trying to find overnight shelter in a police station. He soon is back in prison. On his release, he progresses from petty crime into strong-arm politics and union busting. This leads him finally—it seems inevitably—back to the stockyards, where the bosses make him a foreman so that they can better control the workers' votes. He meets and again attacks his wife's seducer, who has since become a political power, and Jurgis suddenly finds himself stripped of all his advantages.

At this point Sinclair once more describes Jurgis's condition in the language of the yards. Jurgis "could no longer command a job when he wanted it; he could not steal with impunity—he must take his chances with the common herd."[29] His situation becomes increasingly difficult. After he loses a job he desperately needs because he is too weak to do the work, he is reduced to begging. The revival of his fortunes begins when he accidentally wanders into a socialist meeting in search of a warm place to sleep. He dozes, but awakes as to a revelation: the words he hears inspire him in the new social and political faith, and the novel ends with Jurgis's individual concerns lost in Sinclair's political pamphleteering.

What the socialists teach Jurgis is the relevance of the metaphor that shapes the whole book. Ostrinski, Jurgis's socialist friend, explains to him that the power of the yards is *not* that of fate, but of capital, which preys on "the People." This condition holds everywhere in the world, but, as Ostrinski explains, nowhere does it seem so strikingly clear as in Packingtown, for "there seemed to be something about the work of slaughtering that tended to ruthlessness and ferocity." The Beef Trust is the symbol of all that is wrong in Chicago and every other industrial city. The packers are "the incarnation of blind and insensate Greed." The trust is "a monster devouring with a thousand mouths, trampling with a thousand hoofs; it was the Great Butcher—it was the spirit of Capitalism made flesh. Upon the ocean of commerce it sailed as a pirate ship; it had hoisted the black flag and declared war upon civilization." The stockyards, Sinclair concludes, is the ultimate factory, the apotheosis of capitalism and wage slavery; and the city, whose government he calls one of the "branch-offices" of the Beef Trust, is the ultimate stockyards since it is a collection of such sophisticated killing operations where workers in all industries are slaughtered to feed the owners' greed. The great industrial process which private enterprise—best symbolized by the meat packers—has mastered is the conversion of the worker's blood into money.[30]

Sinclair's exposure of the secret world of Packingtown in such graphic detail and his dramatization of its deeper abuses through the story of Jurgis Rudkus remain powerful to this day. Indeed, *The Jungle* itself is probably largely responsible for the perpetuation of the continuing association of the stockyards with Chicago in the popular mind well after the stockyards closed. At the time the book was written, however, Sinclair was concerned that he could not deal with his subject as effectively as he wished. He was caught in a dilemma that faced other Chicago realists. He feared that he might not be equal as a writer to depicting the horrors that he witnessed, but at the same time he was worried that he might lose his audience if he were too accurate. No words, he claims in *The Jungle*, could communicate what goes on in the yards. Speaking of the fertilizer works, he states, "For the odors in these ghastly charnel-houses there may be words in Lithuanian, but there are none in English." The suffering of his characters, Sinclair maintained, was "unredeemed by the slightest touch of dignity or even of pathos." It was "a kind of anguish that poets have not commonly dealt with; its very words are not admitted to the vocabulary of poets."[31] But he would try his best. Chicago was a shocking place, and if his readers were to know it rather than be misled by the likes of Lorimer, neither he nor they could be squeamish. Pooled capital was feeding the nation something it labeled free enterprise, but this was a pig-in-a-poke that the muckraking novelist felt that he had to dissect if any change for the better was to occur.[32]

Sinclair succeeded far beyond his expectations, but not without some initial difficulties in getting his shocking book published. According to Sinclair, George P. Brett of Macmillan advanced him five hundred dollars, but dropped the project when Sinclair refused to follow the suggestion that some of the "blood and guts" be removed from the text. After other rejections, Sinclair decided to issue the novel himself through a mail-order "Sustainer's Edition." When this project was near completion, a friend advised him to try another commercial publisher, this time Walter Hines Page of Doubleday, Page, and Company. After verifying the accuracy of the book, Page agreed to print it.

Jack London, rallying to Sinclair's cause in the midst of the publishing difficulties, compared *The Jungle* to *Uncle Tom's Cabin*. His comment proved prophetic. The book was a controversial best-seller, outraging the packers as Mrs. Stowe's work had antagonized the slaveholders, winning Sinclair a long-standing international renown and the immediate attention of Congress and President Roosevelt. Despite the success of his novel, Sinclair probably envied Mrs. Stowe a bit. She had effectively linked a documentary study to a melodramatic plot aimed at an evangelical call for spiritual and political reform. Sinclair tried to do the same thing, but he missed the mark slightly. His primary intention was to reveal the bondage of the industrial worker (as Stowe had struck at slavery), not the unsanitary aspects of meat packing. His readership, however, was more immediately concerned with what reached their dinner tables than with the inhuman working and living conditions of workers. Assessing his achievement, Sinclair commented, "I aimed at the public's heart, but by accident I hit it in the stomach."[33] Regardless of these remarks on the "failure" of *The Jungle*, Sinclair perhaps knew that the most direct route to the nation's heart was through its stomach, just as he sensed that one of the best ways to understand Chicago was by investigating the meaning of the stockyards.

8

Conclusion:
Chicago and the American
literary imagination

In 1913, the same year he left Chi-
cago for Greenwich Village, Floyd Dell surveyed the accomplishments
of Chicago novelists for the *Bookman*. Dell, one of the most perceptive
critics among Chicago writers, was concerned with why authors who
approached the subject of Chicago with such eagerness produced such
uneven results. Speaking of Herrick in particular, Dell said that Chicago writers were unable to develop and convey a sense of place in their
writing, and he claimed that a source of this failure was their tendency
to treat the city "as a pervasive influence—a condition and not a place."
Eager to understand in the broadest terms what the city "meant," they
overlooked some of the richest aspects of the subject that originally
engaged them. These writers were "obsessed with Chicago," Dell contended. "It has appealed to them as a problem rather than as a vast and
splendid collection of fictional materials."[1] Dell's point is well taken, but
it is not entirely fair or accurate. As Blake Nevius has observed, Chicago
writers *were* dealing with a condition as well as a place, a problem as
well as a collection of literary materials.[2] The condition was the state of
modern urban life; the problem was how to write about this condition.
The deeper question inherent in the literary problem, and one which
writers were trying to answer, was how does one live in this city.

The matter of how one might best write about and live in the city was
by no means restricted to Chicago literature. Those who wrote about
Chicago were influenced by Zola and Dickens, Howells and James and
Crane, and by a tradition of urban literature that went back at least as far
as the beginning of the Industrial Revolution.[3] Their efforts were also

171

part of a broad contemporary context of cultural change that constituted what John Higham has called the "reorientation" of American life at the end of the nineteenth century.[4] The emergence of new social and intellectual patterns along with the rise of the modern American city pervaded not only literature, but also manners, politics, philosophy and social thought, and new institutions of high and popular culture. The issue of the importance of art in industrial and commercial life was frequently raised in other places besides literature—whether explicitly in the writings of Dewey and Veblen, or implicitly by the new museums, concert halls, and universities endowed by Chicago's business elite and by the theaters and department stores that entranced Sister Carrie.[5]

But in the literary response to Chicago, the question of what the city "meant" came into particularly sharp focus, since Chicago seemed to press this question very hard upon writers. The authors examined here generally agreed that whatever Chicago meant, it demanded of them that they reject or at least rework inherited aesthetic forms and ideas. Some, such as Dreiser, were delighted with the prospect and embraced the city as subject; others, including Fuller, accepted Chicago with regret and defended the value of older and more settled civilizations which, he felt, set a standard to which his native city should aspire.

For all the eagerness of writers like Garland or Anderson to strike out against the inadequacy of certain traditions, however, many of them found this task more difficult than they anticipated. Some underestimated how pervasive an influence were the conventions that they associated with Europe, the East, and the literature of gentility. Innovation is never simple, but is itself a slowly evolving process that relies on an awareness of tradition and convention. More than they admitted or perhaps even realized, the most ardently realistic and innovative writers employed genteel conventions to make their meanings. This is true not only in the work of Lovett and Payne, but also in that of more outspoken critics of the old literary order such as Garland and Norris. Fuller and Herrick wished to make an original statement about their city, but they were predisposed to see Chicago through the eyes of Howells and James. Anderson and Dreiser wanted to reject the writing they associated with New England and Victorian England and forge a new and native literary art, but they still wanted to be considered part of a great tradition that included much of western literature.

In addition, several of these writers brought an excessively romanticized sense of calling and very imprecise notions of art to their work. They seemed to be defining their critical and aesthetic ideas in, rather than prior to, the act of writing, and so their use of the central and much-invoked term "art" is often nebulous and contradictory. In some cases, their conceptions are not at all fully worked out, and "art" is diffused into the vaguest of ideals, a mystical faith amid the world's troubles.[6] This general tendency worked against their realistic ambitions to tell the truth about life, and it sometimes made their writing groping and uneven. Nowhere was this more apparent than in the case of Dreiser. He could talk about art in the *Trilogy of Desire* as "the first faint radiance of a rosy dawn," which was something that Henry Blake Fuller, who criticized the "verities" of Chicago and writers who tried to capture them, would never do without intended irony. Perhaps Dreiser, Norris, and Anderson could only maintain their faith in the power of art because their definitions were so vague and mystical. Were they as precise in their thinking as was Fuller, they could never have written their business novels, for they would never have conceived of the "artists" of capital who were their heroes.

Largely untrained and uneducated in a formal sense, confronted by cultural conditions that inspired them to write and yet challenged them as much as any artist has been challenged, writers like Dreiser and Anderson were both free to say something new and forced to wander over what was to them and others an uncharted literary ground. There was difficulty enough with critics who attacked their work as crude, pessimistic, or immoral. There was also the problem of how to shape the new materials they discovered. In seeking what struck them as suitable themes and expressive forms, they were trying to report the actualities of Chicago faithfully yet also put the mark of their imagination on their subject. They wished to find ways to make the meaning, not just the facts, of Chicago dramatically clear and display their literary power as something more than reporters or tourists. This would demonstrate the primacy of imagination and art as independent forces, not just servants of commercialism and industrialism, and their own importance as interpreters of modernity. To do so they would have to find the right words—conventions, images, ways of seeing—through which they could comprehend their subject.

Even the best means they found were full of problems. To dramatize the urban condition through the plight of art in the city was discouraging, while to see the businessman as artist could debase rather than elevate the value of art and imagination. The most resourceful writers found that they could use elements of the city such as the railroad, urban architecture, and the stockyards as a way of getting to the heart of the subject of Chicago, but each of these was itself a relatively new subject for the writer, and not easily captured.

All three elements were sometimes *too* rich as subjects since their explicit meaning as displays of the power of the modern city challenged the importance of the writer as mediator. The impact of all three was so primordial that it threatened to exclude any would-be interpreters.

173

Each of these elaborate technologies made its own order, like the dynamo to which Henry Adams prayed. The direct witnessing of them was an imaginative experience of such immediacy of effect that it could seem to make literature obsolete except for the kind of limited descriptions that appear in unreflective works like Sandburg's "Chicago." Once a writer posited Chicago as the embodiment of reality, he had partly conceded that the city expressed its meaning more effectively than he ever could. It spoke a poetry beside which poetry paled. It is not surprising that some writers wondered if their art had any relevant purpose in Chicago. Could it be a bearer of value as well as of fact, or must it simply give in to Chicago, concentrating on description and dramatic action that might celebrate or condemn the city without ever understanding or transcending it?

The problems those who wrote about Chicago encountered and the shortcomings of their work must be understood, however, in light of their very real achievements. They discovered in Chicago a vital subject for literature, and they successfully demonstrated its importance and made it come alive in the pages of their books. Through their discussions of the condition of the artist, of the place of women, and of the relationship of business and art in Chicago, they did explore with creativity and intelligence the essential tensions and difficulties of modern life as they affected all citizens and not just writers. They perceived that among these difficulties was the fact that in important ways the city denied the individual a real understanding of urban experience and of his or her own place within it. They argued for the necessity of art in attaining this understanding and putting life on a humane basis, and they dedicated their search for expressive forms and their work in general to this purpose.

The social and literary significance of their work was considerable. Speaking at the Chicago Public Library in 1972, Saul Bellow emphasized the challenges Chicago writers faced in finding forms and themes appropriate to their subject. Bellow agreed with those who felt that there was a fundamental opposition between the spirit of the city ("This furious spirit," he called it, "the transforming power of the modern") and traditional high literary culture. "With us," Bellow said, "there has always been a wild discrepancy between the thing of the book and that of the street, between the poem and the poolroom, between the plaster bust of Pericles gathering lovely dust in the assembly hall and the real nose of Big Bill under his campaign hat."[7]

Bellow claimed that there were in Chicago "two sets of facts, two languages, two codes," the "*beau ideal*" and "the hustle," the "sacred teachings" and the "secular deeds." The "great and triumphant reality of American society," he contended, "was and is the public one, the industrial, capitalistic, political, democratic, noisy, hustling, real reality." He argued that the importance of a group of writers of the first decades of the century (he included Dreiser, Anderson, Cather, and Sinclair Lewis), most of whom were from or who wrote about Chicago, was that they demonstrated "that what we knew best was filled with the highest meaning." Through the "transforming touch of art" they showed that "this common life, our life, our very common selves, astonishingly enough, contained important meanings, that we belonged to that same human species which had supplied Sophocles with his Oedipus, Shakespeare with his Lear."[8]

Writing with care, courage, and compassion about the "important meanings" of life in the city has been the major heritage of Chicago literature. Characters as diverse as Richard Wright's Bigger Thomas and James T. Farrell's Studs Lonigan belong to a line of Chicago protagonists who are eager to be part of a world that satisfies them, that does not deny their personal value and exclude them. They read in the physical face of the city the forces that crush their spirits and turn them away. Perceptive enough to know that something important is lacking in their lives, and that the problem dwells outside themselves and in the city where they live, they try to find some meaningful form of action even if they are at last unable either to articulate the nature of their distress or overcome it.

Bellow's own fiction provides the best illustration of the continued presence of Chicago writing of the turn of the century. From Augie March to Moses Herzog to Charles Citrine, his Chicago heroes are sensitive men trying to feel physically, intellectually, and spiritually at home in Chicago and the modern world. Bellow's *The Dean's December* (1982) reads like an anthology of major themes that Chicago writers have been grappling with for a hundred years. Albert Corde is a writer—a journalist—who accepts his deanship partly in order to return to his native city, which has continued to obsess him. He hates it, but he cannot shake its grip on his imagination. Corde sounds like Fuller and Herrick when he talks about Chicago's "curious lack of final coherence, an environment not chosen to suit human needs . . . favorable to manufacture, shipping, construction." There is also something familiar, something reminiscent of Dreiser or Anderson, in Corde's observation, "That was always one of the peculiarities of Chicago. Where could you take your most passionate feelings?" Bellow even describes the dilemma in terms of art. Corde is convinced that there is "[s]omething very wrong here," and he reflects, "To belong fully to the life of the country gave one strength, but why should these others, in their strength, demand that one's own sense of existence (poetry, if you like) be dismissed with contempt?"[9]

Like earlier writers, Bellow is ambivalent toward the Chicago businessman and his culture. And, again like his predecessors, he makes this very ambivalence a thematic center of his art. Corde feels odd being a dean, "for wasn't a college dean a kind of executive?" He cannot stand the businessmen who have made Chicago what it is, but he envies their ability to feel comfortable in Chicago and admires their power and practicality: "In realism and cunning these LaSalle Street characters were impressive because they had the backing of the pragmatic culture of the city, the state, the region, the country." In the opinion of his sister's husband, a businessman, "the Dean had given up the real world to take refuge in philosophy and art." Corde even concedes that his brother-in-law's type "belonged fully to the life of the country, spoke its language, thought its thoughts, did its work. If he, Corde, was different, the difference wasn't altogether to his credit."[10]

Corde has painstakingly studied his city and written two essays in *Harper's* on the dissolution of any decent, civilized life in Chicago. Through all his anger and his outrage at what has happened, he continues to have a faith in the importance of saying what he has to say. As Fuller, Herrick, Anderson, and Dreiser did, the Dean "had taken it upon himself to pass Chicago through his soul." Corde thinks to himself near the end of the novel, "A mass of data, terrible, murderous. It was no easy matter to put such things through. But there was no other way for reality to happen. Reality didn't exist 'out there.' It began to be real only when the soul found its underlying truth." Looking back on his effort, which has puzzled and angered friends and colleagues, Corde concludes that his purpose was to try "to find out what Chicago, U.S.A., was built with. His motive—to follow this through—came out of what was eternal in man. What mood was this city? The experience, puzzle, and torment of a lifetime demanded interpretation."[11]

Responding to this demand for interpretation by passing Chicago through one's soul was, as Bellow notes, "no easy matter." It did not make it any simpler to do it, as Chicago writers tried to do, with the "transforming touch of art." They were determined to confront the issues Chicago raised, as Corde does, and make their writing a significant personal and cultural statement. Most of the texts examined here are to some degree polemical; but behind any specific arguments in these works are assertions about what is important in life, what is right and wrong about Chicago, and what can, should, and must be done about it. Implicit in all of their efforts is the belief that what one can and should do is write about the city seriously and directly. The belief that something important was at stake in the opposition of life and art in Chicago, along with the desire for artistic independence, fueled frustration and impatience with traditional forms and fired the call for innovation. Chicago writers, individually and collectively, were convinced that they had an important mission, and by fits and starts they led American letters into the twentieth century.

Appendix

The Lake and the River, the Fort and the Fire,
the Streets of the Town:
Notes and Afterthoughts on Chicago Images

The railroad, the large building, and the stockyards were not the only distinctive features of the Chicago cityscape at the turn of the century, nor were they in any sense the sole ones discussed by those seeking the "right words" with which to talk about Chicago. Several other elements of lesser scale and impact appear in Chicago literature of the period, and a few deserve at least brief attention. Although they are less significant as sources of expressive images and dramatic motifs than the three features discussed in Part Two, their use (and nonuse) is important to a fuller understanding of the imaginative literary response to the rise of modern Chicago.

It has always been impossible to think of Chicago without thinking immediately of Lake Michigan. As Kevin Lynch and others have observed, the lakefront is the city's most outstanding and attractive physical feature. The lakefront includes not only the water itself, but also several parks and beaches, pleasure-boat harbors, the exceptionally scenic Lake Shore Drive, the spine of elegant residential buildings that follow the shoreline, the commercial buildings along Michigan Avenue, and most of the city's major cultural institutions. But in Chicago literature there is relatively little use of the lake as a means of seeing and understanding modern Chicago as a whole.

To be sure, travel writers, publicists, novelists, and poets have sung of the watery jewel glistening under the rising sun, and of the shifting moods of this inland sea. Harriet Monroe dedicated a sonnet to the lake, which she described as "Blue as eternity, bright as God's smile, / Pure as the folded wings of seraphim." But though Chicago has called itself the Queen City of the Lake, and has depended on Lake Michigan for trade, transportation, and its water supply, by the end of the nineteenth century the city had become a railroad, office, and factory city whose daily life was oriented away from the lake either as a center of commerce or as a place of special natural beauty. The recreational possibilities of the shoreline, while certainly used to great advantage in Lincoln Park and by the World's Columbian Exposition, were not extensively exploited until after the Chicago Plan of 1909, when the area was enlarged with fill and developed. Characters in Chicago fiction commonly find themselves too concerned with their careers, with urban fashion, or with simple survival to wander by the lake. Sister Carrie does her main sightseeing in department store windows in the Loop or along the fancy residential blocks that lead to Evanston. Jurgis Rudkus and his family live and work in what could be described as an open sewer a short way from "the blue waters of Lake Michigan," but, as Sinclair explains, "for all the good it did them it might have been as far away as the Pacific Ocean."

The lake frequently figures in Chicago writing as an escape or relief from the city. In Monroe's sonnet, the lake seems to "flow . . . at the rim / Of paradise," a place of eternal love and youth and truth. She hopes that her soul "might sail into your blue" and be "purged of earthly dross and stain. . . ." In some major examples of Chicago fiction, the lake is a refuge for individuals who confront certain urban dilemmas. Abandoned by her husband, Laura Jadwin finds some solace meditating on the shore that is a block or two from their mansion. (The Pit, however, which is described not only as a whirlpool but also as a troubled sea where the wheat comes in waves, is a more compelling water image than the lake itself.) When Sam McPherson ponders the meaning of his life, he takes walks away from the downtown and toward the lake. It is here that he decides to break his promise to his wife that he will not vote against her father in the fight for control of the arms trust. In the moment that he resolves to forsake her and master the Chicago business world, he turns away from the lake to face the city that rises up before him to meet his dreams of power.

From its founding, Chicago has been a river city as well as a lake city. The Chicago River, running west from the lake just north of the Loop, then forking into a north and south branch, has always been important to the commercial life of the town, even if its prominence diminished with the decline of water traffic. The river is often mentioned in Chicago writing (in dime novels set in the city, criminals are constantly conspiring in warehouses along the river), but there are few evocative descriptions or tributes. Unlike the lake, whose natural beauty appears to be so different from the city proper, the Chicago River has become so integrated into the cityscape that it has lost its identity to urban technology. Unimposing in size, lacking the romantic appeal of a Hudson River or Golden Gate, it has been repeatedly befouled, dredged, bridged, tunneled, and straightened. In the 1890s the direction of its current was even changed when, for the sake of better sanitation and transportation, the Chicago Sanitary and Ship Canal was built.

In a short poem by Charlton Lawrence Edholm that was published early this century, the river speaks of the way it has been abused and exploited beyond recognition: "No outcast of the gutters / Slinks by more soiled than I, / Polluted within and without!" The river's sole recompense, it explains, is that it bears upon its "shackeled breast" the commerce of the world, an observation that has become less true over the years. Besides, this is no comfort for the poet, who must look to the Hudson, the Rhine, the Danube, or the Nile if he wants inspiration. The river finally claims, however, that it has its own special form of expression, which is just as eloquent as that of more beautiful and stately rivers: "But the broad ships that weight my breast / Are like iron medals with these words wrought: FOR SERVICE." Nevertheless, this Chicago Liffey still awaits its Joyce.

Other potentially significant features of Chicago were the physical reminders of its frontier past. Many people today do not realize that for a large portion of its early nineteenth-century history, Chicago was a settlement on the western frontier. The outstanding symbol and reminder of that history was Fort Dearborn, the garrison that was built in 1803 where the Chicago River crosses Michigan Avenue, and later rebuilt after local soldiers and settlers were massacred on the lakefront in 1812 while retreating from hostile Indians. Although abandoned by the government in 1836, the fort stood until the late 1850s, an index of how far the city had come in so short a time.

There is a substantial imaginative literature of Fort Dearborn and the frontier past. A good deal of this has been written by women, perhaps, as Sidney H. Bremer suggests, because Chicago's female writers—in contrast to many leading male novelists—were in many cases not newcomers but members of established families and more aware of the continuities between past and present (Bremer also asserts that female writers were more sensitive to the presence of nature, including the lake, in city life). But most of the city's residents had roots elsewhere, and their outlook was toward the future and not the past. San Franciscans of the turn of the century still invoked the spirit of the Argonauts, their heroic name for the forty-niners, as essential to their vitality in the present, but the "western" spirit of Chicago, to the extent that it persisted at all, was best summed up in the stockyards, where the drovers and the packers met in the biggest cow town in the world. Although the facts of the case are hazy, the late Mayor Richard Daley let it be known that as a young man he worked on horseback in the yards. By that time his "western" experience was part of being Chicago urban ethnic, and the relics of the Indian days were curiosities not central to the collective consciousness of this city of immigrants.

The Great Chicago Fire of 1871 was certainly the most legendary event in all of Chicago history, and it inspired a large literary outpouring, including eyewitness accounts, pulp sensationalism (one enterprising company put out a "Burning of Chicago" songster before the cinders were cool), popular histories (including the tales of Mrs. O'Leary's cow), and all sorts of fiction and verse, including E. P. Roe's *Barriers Burned Away*. No less a light than John Greenleaf Whittier devoted a poem to the conflagration. He began:

> *Men said at vespers: "All is well!"*
> *In one wild night the city fell;*
> *Fell shrines of prayer and marts of gain*
> *Before the fiery hurricane.*

Whittier read the fire as a great purging of Chicago's evils ("How shrivelled in thy hot distress / The primal sin of selfishness!"), and he predicted a newer and better city of God and man. In the more dominant ideology of boosterism, the fire was viewed not as a judgment on this modern city of the plain, but as a test of Chicago's will to survive. Of course, in this rhetoric the town rose "Phoenix-like" (as was said over and over again) from the ashes to prevail. But like the city's frontier heritage, the fire was not part of the active memory of most Chicagoans by the 1890s, nor certainly was it important to those writers who came to the city from elsewhere and wrote about Chicago as the embodiment of the new age. By the time of the World's Columbian Exposition of 1893, the fire was mainly a milestone that marked the beginning of the history of the modern city.

One additional important element in Chicago writing of the turn of the century was what might be called the view from the streets. "The first impression which a stranger receives on arriving in Chicago," W. T. Stead wrote in 1894, "is that of the dirt, the danger and the inconvenience of the streets." Like most American cities laid out in the nineteenth century, Chicago adopted the unimaginative gridiron pattern beloved by real-estate developers. The flatness of the site only emphasized the monotony of the grid, especially as the city stretched further north and south along the lake and westward out into the prairie. The inescapability and lack of variety in the pattern have reinforced the sense some have had of the city as an endless web that confuses and entraps the individual.

But to others, being on the street, especially in the downtown and other busy areas, was one of the most appealing aspects of city life. Here were crowds, color, noise. No one had a better sense of this world than did Dreiser, who described Chicago street life as a "constant and varying panorama." When Eugene Witla arrives in Chicago early in Dreiser's autobiographical novel, *The "Genius,"* he finds a room and immediately sets out to look around. He tells his landlady, "I want to see the streets." The view from and of the streets is especially important in the work of the most noted journalists of the turn of the century. Finley Peter Dunne's Mr. Dooley comments on Chicago from his saloon on Archer Avenue. This boulevard serves him well as a revelation of the tragicomedy of life, as a reminder of the necessity of irony, and as a general source of urban wisdom. One of his maxims is, "There's no better place to see what's goin' on thin the Ar-rchey Road," and he firmly believes, "There's more life on a Saturday night in th' Ar-rchy Road thin in all th' books fr'm Shakespeare to th' rayport iv th' drainage trustees." George Ade was another champion of street smarts. His columns in the *Chicago Record* were called "Stories of the Streets and Of the Town," and one of his major creations is Artie, the forthright and capable common man who is always genuine, loyal to his friends, and thoroughly at one with Chicago. Ade contrasts this outgoing fellow with his shy and reflective friend Miller: "Miller and Artie got along famously together. Miller was the listener and Artie was the entertainer. Miller read books and Artie read the town." Ade, another reader of the town, obviously implies that Artie has the better text.

Despite these and other examples, the view from the streets was not used as extensively and with such depth as a way of comprehending the city as a total entity as were the train, the new large buildings, and the stockyards. The richer use of the streets in Chicago literature comes after the First World War (along with the full flower of the city's association with gangsterism), in studies of individuals who become wandering consciousnesses moving uncertainly against the coordinates of the urban grid. They are prefigured in the work of European novelists in the nineteenth century, and in the work of Eliot and Joyce early in the twentieth. These characters come most fully to life in Chicago literature as statements on the urban condition in the characters of Farrell, Wright, and Bellow.

Notes

CHAPTER ONE

1. See, for example, James Fullarton Muirhead's *America The Land of Contrasts: A Briton's View of His American Kin*, 4th ed. (New York: John Lane Co., 1911), p. 207: "In some respects Chicago deserves the name City of Contrasts, just as the United States is the Land of Contrasts." Muirhead's remarks were based on his travels in the United States in the early 1890s. See also the rich collection of travelers' observations in Bessie Louise Pierce, ed., *As Others See Chicago: Impressions of Visitors, 1673–1933* (Chicago: University of Chicago Press, 1933).

2. G. W. Steevens, *The Land of the Dollar*, 4th ed. (Edinburgh: William Blackwood, 1900), pp. 144–45.

3. Julian Street, *Abroad at Home: American Ramblings, Observations, and Adventures of Julian Street* (New York: Century, 1914), p. 139.

4. The most remarkable "guide" to Chicago was the noted British journalist W. T. Stead's *If Christ Came to Chicago: A Plea for the Union of All Who Love in the Service of All Who Suffer* (Chicago: Laird & Lee, 1894), a carefully researched and fervently written survey of the city's social and moral ills that began with the question of what would be Christ's response if he visited Chicago of the 1890s. Like Steevens and Muirhead, Stead wrote, "It is impossible to describe Chicago as a whole. It is a congeries of different nationalities, a compost of men and women of all manners and languages" (p. 127).

183

5. The *Dial* at this point was true to its mission of "dealing with literary interests in a just, dignified, and authoritative manner." Some of the ways in which it carried out this mission included attacking Chicago's materialism and supporting the institutions and forms of traditional high culture. See *Dial* 13 (1892): 127.

6. Edward Eggleston, *The Hoosier Schoolmaster: A Story of Backwoods Life in Indiana* (New York: Grosset & Dunlap, 1913), p. 29.

7. Stanley Waterloo, "'Who Reads a Chicago Book,'" *Dial* 13 (1892): 207.

8. See Sherwood Anderson, "An Apology for Crudity," in *Sherwood Anderson's Notebook* (New York: Boni & Liveright, 1926), pp. 196, 198. This is an example of the attitude Lionel Trilling criticizes in his noted essay, "Reality in America," when he complains, "In the American metaphysic, reality is always material reality, hard, resistant, unformed, impenetrable." See *The Liberal Imagination: Essays on Literature and Society* (New York: Viking, 1950), p. 13.

9. Theodore Dreiser, *The Titan,* ed. Philip L. Gerber (New York: World, 1972), p. 6. Here, in his autobiographies, and in a number of passages from *Sister Carrie* and *The "Genius,"* Dreiser consistently described the city as a siren that sang to him, prompting him to capture its song in his words. For example, Dreiser stated in *Dawn*, his account of his early years, that he felt privileged to have seen a city such as Chicago in the making. Though his family's first Chicago apartment exposed them to rats and filth, its windows framed "a constant and varying panorama" which struck the creative chord in Dreiser's soul, urging him to write. "Would that I were able to suggest in prose the throb and urge and sting of my first days in Chicago!" he proclaimed. "A veritable miracle of pleasing sensations and astounding and fascinating scenes. The spirit of Chicago flowed into me and made me ecstatic." Later he explained that he seemed to hear this spirit speaking to him: "I am the pulsing urge of the universe! You are a part of me, I of you! All that life or hope is or can be or do, this I am, and it is here before you! Take of it! Live, live, satisfy your heart! Strive to be what you wish to be now while you are young and of it! Reflect its fire, its tang, its color, its greatness! Be, be, wonderful or strong or great, if you will but be!" For these and similar passages, see *Dawn* (New York: Horace Liveright, 1931), pp. 156–59, 298; and *A Book about Myself* (New York: Boni & Liveright, 1922), pp. 1–3.

10. "The winds give strength and penetration and alertness," Garland added. "The mighty stretches of woods lead to breadth and generosity of intellectual conception." See *Crumbling Idols: Twelve Essays on Art and Literature* (Chicago and Cambridge: Stone & Kimball, 1894), pp. 155–56. Alfred Kazin calls *Crumbling Idols* "one of the windiest critical

documents of the new era." He adds, "Yet precisely because it was hortatory and shrill, Garland acted as the bandmaster of realism. His service was to announce its coming, to suggest its emotional importance and its sterling Americanism, to open the common mind to vistas of nationalism, freedom, and democracy in which Lincoln and Ibsen, Howells and the Declaration of Independence, were somehow commingled." See *On Native Grounds: An Interpretation of Modern American Prose Literature* (New York: Harcourt, Brace, 1942), p. 37.

11. W. D. Howells, "Certain of the Chicago School of Fiction," *North American Review* 176 (1903): 738–39.

12. Warner Berthoff, *The Ferment of Realism: American Literature, 1884–1919* (New York: Free Press, 1965), pp. 1–2. Berthoff adds, "Insofar as it constituted a movement at all, American literary realism was concerned less with problems of artistic definition and discovery than with clearing the way to a more profitable exercise of individual ambition."

13. Along these same lines, Street described Chicago as "a young demigod, product of a union between Rodin's 'Thinker' and the Wingèd Victory of Samothrace . . . ," *Abroad at Home,* p. 139.

14. John F. Kasson, *Civilizing the Machine: Technology and Republican Values in America 1776–1900* (New York: Grossman, 1976), p. 57.

15. Will Payne, *Jerry the Dreamer* (New York: Harper & Bros., 1896), p. 204.

Chapter Two

1. Jane Addams, *Twenty Years at Hull-House* (New York: New American Library, 1961), pp. 255, 91. The book was first published in 1910 by the Phillips Publishing Company and Macmillan after appearing in part in the *American Magazine* and *McClure's.*

2. Ibid., p. 98.

3. *Twenty Years at Hull-House,* along with much of Addams's other writings, reveals how essential to the development of her social thought was her wide reading. Her own prose is full of allusions to the Brownings, Hawthorne, Pater, Carlyle, Ruskin, Morris, Aristotle, Maeterlinck, Gray, Eliot, Hugo, Tolstoy, Shakespeare, Goethe, Whitman, and Wordsworth. Most of these allusions are employed to deal with specific local issues in terms of timeless lessons explored and illuminated by great writers. As Allen F. Davis and others have pointed out, Addams's use of literature as a source of moral authority was a common response of many nineteenth-century English and American intellectuals "when they became disillusioned and perplexed by the church" and with the

general failure of middle-class life. See *American Heroine: The Life and Legend of Jane Addams* (New York: Oxford University Press, 1973), p. 16; and Christopher Lasch, "Jane Addams: The College Woman and the Family Claim," in *The New Radicalism in America: The Intellectual as a Social Type* (New York: Vintage Books, 1965), pp. 3–37. Davis's biography of Addams offers an excellent history of Hull-House. See also his *Spearheads for Reform: The Social Settlements and the Progressive Movement* (New York: Oxford University Press, 1967).

4. *Twenty Years at Hull-House*, pp. 170–71.

5. Ibid., p. 268. Hull-House made similar efforts in art and music. The settlement opened an art gallery in 1891, sponsored art classes, and encouraged the handicrafts among industrial workers who often felt that their labor had little meaning. In addition to its music school, Hull-House also hosted concerts of various kinds. Once again, the highest aim of such projects was a social one. Addams noted how people of all faiths were drawn into a program of Christmas music, and she remarked, "In the deep tones of the memorial organ erected at Hull-House, we realize that music is perhaps the most potent agent for making the universal appeal and inducing men to forget their differences." See *Twenty Years at Hull-House*, pp. 263–64.

6. Jane Addams, "A Modern Lear," in *The Social Thought of Jane Addams*, ed. Christopher Lasch (Indianapolis: Bobbs-Merrill, 1965), pp. 111, 123. The essay was first published in *Survey* in 1912. According to Davis and Lasch, Addams could not readily publish it in journals normally eager to accept her work.

7. *Twenty Years at Hull-House*, p. 59, W. T. Stead observed in like manner, "But a new generation is springing up of men and women born in the lap of luxury, shielded from childhood from all the rude blasts of adverse fortune, and endowed neither by precept or example with any ideas as to their duties to the community in which they live." See *If Christ Came to Chicago*, p. 116.

8. *Twenty Years at Hull-House*, pp. 63–64. The relevant passage from DeQuincey can be found in *The English Mail-Coach and Other Essays*, ed. John E. Jordan (London: J. M. Dent, 1961), p. 36.

9. *The Spirit of Youth and the City Streets* (Urbana: University of Illinois Press, 1972). This is a reprint of the 1909 edition published by Macmillan.

10. James D. Hart, *The Popular Book: A History of America's Literary Taste* (Berkeley: University of California Press, 1961), p. 121.

11. E. P. Roe, *Barriers Burned Away* (New York: Dodd, Mead, 1872), pp. 238, 486.

12. For more on Fuller's life, see the biography by Bernard Bowron, Jr., *Henry B. Fuller of Chicago: The Ordeal of a Genteel Realist in Ungenteel America* (Westport, Conn.: Greenwood Press, 1974).

13. Henry B. Fuller, *With the Procession* (Chicago: University of Chicago Press, 1967), pp. 199, 201, 203–4. The book was originally published by Harper & Bros. in 1895. Compare Fuller's observations with Stead's remarks, published a year earlier: "This vast and heterogeneous community, which has been collected together from all quarters of the known world, knows only one common bond. Its members came here to make money. They are staying here to make money. The quest of the almighty dollar is their Holy Grail" (*If Christ Came to Chicago,* p. 127).

14. Henry B. Fuller, *The Cliff-Dwellers* (New York: Harper & Bros., 1893), pp. 95, 97.

15. Ibid., p. 104.

16. Ibid., p. 50. After explaining that by Chicago's standards McDowell is the city's proper laureate, Fuller adds immediately: "We of Chicago are sometimes made to bear the reproach that the conditions of our local life draw us towards the sordid and the materialistic." He then replies to this charge with a mock counterargument: "Now, the most vital and typical of our human products is the real-estate agent: is he commonly found tied down by earth-bound prose" (p. 105)? This "most artistic" of Chicagoans demonstrates how boorish and greedy Chicago is in subverting the highest imaginative efforts of its citizens to the cause of making money. Those in search of the finest Chicago fiction, Fuller might say, would be best advised to read the real-estate listings.

17. *With the Procession,* p. 58.

18. Ibid., p. 57.

19. Ibid., pp. 115, 117–18.

20. Ibid., p. 120.

21. Henry B. Fuller, "The Downfall of Abner Joyce," in *Under the Skylights* (New York: Appleton & Co., 1901), p. 3.

22. Ibid., pp. 4, 13.

23. Ibid., pp. 88, 139, 136.

24. Henry B. Fuller, "Little O'Grady vs. the Grindstone," in *Under the Skylights,* p. 150.

25. Ibid., p. 174.

26. Ibid., pp. 198, 289.

27. Henry B. Fuller, "Dr. Gowdy and the Squash," in *Under the Skylights,* pp. 328–29. Gowdy appears to be based on the popular Congregationalist minister Frank Gunsaulus, pastor of the Plymouth Congregational Church from 1887 to 1899, then of the Central Church for the next twenty years. Gunsaulus was an art collector who lectured widely on literature and music as well as religion. He published poetry, fiction, and biography in addition to theology.

28. Ibid., p. 333. In his edition of Garland's diaries, Donald Pizer explains that the Central Art Association was organized in 1894 "in

order to encourage the creation and appreciation of a native Western art." Garland evidently took Fuller's jabs at him well. He commented on "Dr. Gowdy and the Squash": "It is capital satire; just the right tone, and hit off art conditions here most happily. It had a little of me, a good deal of the Central Art Association, the [Art] Institute and also a good deal of himself [Fuller] and his controversy with colonels of militia and wholesale grocers on art matters. He is doing a most diverting history of the art colony [*Under the Skylights*]. This story is only a part of it." See *Hamlin Garland's Diaries*, ed. Donald Pizer (San Marino, Calif.: Huntington Library, 1968), pp. 14–15.

29. "Dr. Gowdy and the Squash," p. 381.

30. In 1918 Fuller published *On the Stairs* (Boston: Houghton, Mifflin), another study of art and business in Chicago. This book has less texture and detail than his earlier Chicago fiction (in an "Author's Note," Fuller himself states that his book "may seem less a Novel than a Sketch of a Novel or a Study for a Novel"). It is even more dispirited than his previous work about the plight of those with a sensibility like Fuller's, and less critical of Chicago's commercial culture than of his own attitudes. The story follows the intertwining lives of two men from their school days together to middle age. The Fuller character is born to greater wealth and opportunity, but he slowly and surely becomes a pathetic, isolated, and embittered man, dabbling self-indulgently in various aesthetic projects and viewing life as a spectator while his counterpart pursues Chicago's opportunities and becomes a successful financier. By the end of the book, the first man is helpless and alone. He has lost the family business and home due to careless management of his affairs. Much worse, his ex-wife has married his former schoolmate, who has virtually adopted his grown son.

31. Quoted by Blake Nevius in *Robert Herrick: The Development of a Novelist* (Berkeley: University of California Press, 1962), p. 85. Professor Nevius's book is a sympathetic study of this often unsympathetic man.

32. Robert Herrick, "The Background of the American Novel," *Yale Review* 3 n.s. (1914): 231–32.

33. Robert Herrick, "Myself" (Robert Herrick Papers, Box 3, Folder 10, University of Chicago Archives), pp. 77, 78. Nevius believes that this was probably written in 1915.

34. Robert Herrick, *The Common Lot* (New York: Macmillan, 1913), pp. 30, 6, 87. The novel was first published in 1904.

35. Ibid., p. 262.

36. Ibid., pp. 257, 55.

37. Ibid., p. 335.

38. Ibid., p. 420.

39. Ibid., pp. 408–9.
40. Will Payne, *Jerry the Dreamer*, pp. 13, 15.
41. Ibid., pp. 47, 50.
42. Ibid., p. 252.
43. Ibid., p. 291.

CHAPTER THREE

1. Sidney H. Bremer, "Lost Continuities: Alternative Urban Visions in Chicago Novels," *Soundings* 64 (1981), 39. Some of the writers Bremer mentions are Elia Peattie, Clara Burnham, Susan Glaspell, Edith Wyatt, Clara Laughlin, and Alice Gerstenberg. Bremer argues persuasively that the work of these women has been undervalued by literary and cultural historians.

2. For more on the influence of *The Portrait of a Lady* on *The Gospel of Freedom*, see Blake Nevius, *Robert Herrick*, p. 80.

3. Robert Herrick, *The Gospel of Freedom* (New York: Macmillan, 1898), p. 80. Herrick and Berenson were both in the exceptional group of students who worked on the *Harvard Monthly*. This group also included, among others, George Santayana and Robert Morss Lovett (see n. 10). Herrick visited Berenson in Florence in 1896 and transcribed whole conversations with his host directly into his novel. In spite of the fact that Herrick violated Berenson's hospitality and made him the model for what Berenson himself called "a very odious character," the two men remained friends. When the Berensons visited Chicago for two weeks early in 1904, they had a very pleasant visit with the Herricks, who in turn stopped at the Villa I Tatti two years later. In Chicago, Berenson met Jane Addams (who dined with him at the Herricks'), Robert Lincoln, J. Ogden Armour, and Mrs. Potter Palmer. See Nevius, *Robert Herrick*, pp. 66–67; and Ernest Samuels, *Bernard Berenson: The Making of a Connoisseur* (Cambridge: Harvard University Press, 1979), pp. 29–30, 266–69, 422–25.

4. *The Gospel of Freedom*, pp. 89–90.

5. Ibid., pp. 125, 130.

6. Ibid., p. 149.

7. Robert Herrick, *The Memoirs of an American Citizen* (Cambridge: Harvard University Press, 1963), p. 94. The novel was originally published by Macmillan in 1905.

8. Ibid., p. 140.

9. Ibid., p. 191.

10. Robert Morss Lovett, *A Wingèd Victory* (New York: Duffield & Co., 1907), p. 218. Lovett, an active scholar, political journalist, and critic, was another Harvard graduate who came to Chicago in 1893 to

join the University of Chicago faculty. See *All Our Years: The Autobiography of Robert Morss Lovett* (New York: Viking, 1948).

11. Ibid., pp. 273, 311.

12. Ibid., pp. 250, 349, 356–57.

13. Ibid., p. 415.

14. Ibid., pp. 165, 415, 423.

15. Ibid., pp. 414, 426.

16. Ibid., p. 414. In a continuation of his general remarks on the state of American literature, cited earlier, Robert Herrick argued that the contemporary interest in women suffrage (he was writing in 1914) was only one aspect of the changing status and developing self-consciousness of women. "Of much more immediate significance," he maintained, "is the way in which women are being absorbed in the economic machine of our industrialism, as breadwinners, as competitors of men, and in the freer strata of society as independent creators." Herrick pointed out how rich this movement was as a subject for the modern novelist: "No one can stand in our city streets mornings and evenings and watch the hurrying throng of working women," he claimed, "without a feeling that a wealth of imaginative material lies here close at hand, if we only knew the daily experiences, the life stories of these women units in the struggle." See "The American Novel," *Yale Review* 3 n.s. (1914): 434–35. While the working woman is underrepresented in the literature of the period, she does figure importantly in the writings of Jane Addams, some of Fuller's earlier work (see Cornelia McNabb of *The Cliff-Dwellers*, discussed in Chapter 6), in Will Payne's novels, and in much of Dreiser.

17. Theodore Dreiser, *Sister Carrie,* ed. Neda M. Westlake et al. (Philadelphia: University of Pennsylvania Press, 1981), p. 4. I use this "new" text because it is superior to the previous standard edition as a fuller exposition of Dreiser's ideas. Where important differences arise in interpretation because of the different text, they will be noted.

18. "Even without practise, she could sometimes restore dramatic situations she had witnessed by recreating, before her mirror, the expressions of the various faces taking part in the scene. She loved to modulate her voice after the conventional manner of the distressed heroine, and repeat such pathetic fragments as appealed most to her sympathies. Of late, seeing the airy grace of the ingénue in several well-constructed plays, she had been moved to secretly imitate it, and many were the little movements and expressions of the body which she indulged in from time to time in the privacy of her chamber. On several occasions when Drouet had caught her admiring herself, as he imagined, in the mirror, she was doing nothing more than recalling some

little grace of the mouth or the eyes which she had witnessed in another. Under his airy accusation she mistook this for vanity and accepted the blame with a faint sense of error, though as a matter of fact it was nothing more than the first subtle outcroppings of an artistic nature, endeavoring to recreate the perfect likeness of some phase of beauty which appealed to her. In such feeble tendencies, be it known, such outworkings of desire to reproduce life, lies the basis of all dramatic art" (*Sister Carrie*, pp. 157–58).

19. Ibid., pp. 192–93, 455. The "mash notes" that beseech Carrie once she is a star please her because they are acknowledgments of her power, and by this time she realizes that they are more a recognition of the attractions of her performance than of her real personality: "Adulation, being new in any form, pleased her. Only she was sufficiently wise to distinguish between her old condition and her new one. She had not had fame or money before. Now they had come. She had not had adulation and affectionate propositions before. Now they had come. Wherefore? She smiled to think that men should suddenly find her so much more attractive. In the least way it incited her to coolness and indifference" (pp. 455–56).

20. Ibid., p. 177.

21. Ibid., pp. 485–86.

22. For more on the revisions involving Ames, see the "Historical Commentary" section of the University of Pennsylvania edition, especially pp. 514–19.

23. Will Payne, *Mr. Salt* (Boston: Houghton, Mifflin, 1903), p. 107.

24. Ibid., p. 107.

25. Ibid., pp. 314–15.

26. Ibid., p. 107.

27. Willa Cather, *The Song of the Lark* (Boston: Houghton Mifflin, 1943), p. 268. The text cited is the revised 1937 edition, though the passages quoted are substantially the same in the 1915 edition.

28. Ibid., pp. v, 252.

29. Ibid., pp. 252–55.

30. Ibid., pp. v–vi.

31. Ibid., pp. vi, 551.

32. Ibid., pp. 509, 580–81. While the sources of *The Song of the Lark* include Cather's own youth and some of her experiences as an adult, the direct inspiration for Thea was the career of the opera star Olive Fremstad, whom Cather first met in 1913 while preparing an article for *McClure's*. For more on the Cather-Fremstad association, see E. K. Brown, *Willa Cather: A Critical Biography,* completed by Leon Edel (New York: Alfred A. Knopf, 1953), pp. 184–88.

CHAPTER FOUR

1. Potter briefly reviews Stagmar's early life. The reader learns that Stagmar was abandoned at three to make his own way in the world, and so he developed a very bitter view of existence. He somehow taught himself to read, and one day he found a discarded novel, which he devoured with great effect: "The writer's instinct had been born in him." Even in his young, impressionable years, he was impatient with the quality of most literature because it was not realistic. After reading a piece of cheap escapist fiction, Stagmar threw it to the ground, exclaiming, "It ain't true. Such things don't happen, and I know it. The men that write about 'em are lyin.' I'm sick of the lot of 'em. Why can't they write the truth?" When he later encountered a worthy literary model in Thackeray's *Pendennis*, he realized that he "had found the work he was to do" (Robert Dolly Williams [Margaret Horton Potter], *A Social Lion* [Chicago: R. R. Donnelley & Sons, 1899]), pp. 170, 96–98. Potter was only eighteen the year *A Social Lion* was published. She wrote a book a year over the next decade, including less realistic works such as *Uncanonized: A Romance of English Monachism* and *Istar of Babylon: A Phantasy*. She married the prominent lawyer John D. Black in 1902. Potter died in 1911, her thirtieth year.

2. For a direct and concise discussion along these lines, see "Chicago's Higher Evolution," *Dial* 13 (1892):205–6.

3. Edward Everett Cassady surveys the treatment of the businessman by the American writer in "The Business Man in the American Novel: 1865–1903" (Ph.D. diss., University of California, Berkeley, 1939). For a much briefer overview, see Henry Nash Smith, "The Search for a Capitalist Hero," in *The Business Establishment*, ed. Earl F. Cheit (New York: Wiley, 1964), pp. 77–112. On success literature, see John G. Cawelti, *Apostles of the Self-Made Man: Changing Concepts of Success in America* (Chicago: University of Chicago Press, 1965). Finally, for the comments on the relationship between the writer and the businessman by two leading American authors of the day, see William Dean Howells, "The Man of Letters as a Man of Business," in *Literature and Life* (New York: Harper & Bros., 1911), pp. 1–35; and Henry James, "The Question of the Opportunities," in Morton Dauwen Zabel, ed., *Literary Opinion in America*, vol. 2, 3d ed. rev. (New York: Harper & Row, 1962), pp. 51–55.

4. Some leading critical opinion is less forgiving of the novel's faults. In *On Native Grounds*, for example, Alfred Kazin concedes Norris's "mastery of episode," but calls the book "a mediocre counterpiece to the stock novel of finance that became popular six years later" (pp. 100–101).

5. Frank Norris, *The Pit: A Story of Chicago* (New York: Grove Press, 1956), p. 34. This is a reprint of the 1903 Doubleday edition.

6. Frank Norris, "The True Reward of the Novelist," in *The Responsibilities of the Novelist and Other Literary Essays* (New York: Greenwood Press, 1968), p. 20.

7. *The Pit*, pp. 60–63.

8. Ibid., p. 63.

9. Ibid., pp. 33–34.

10. Ibid., pp. 17, 72. Landry Court, whom the reader is clearly meant to trust (he eventually marries Page after his brief infatuation with Laura), says of Corthell, "He's a good sort, and I like him well enough, but he's the kind of man that gets up a reputation for being clever and artistic by running down the very one particular thing that every one likes, and cracking up some book or picture or play that no one has heard of." He continues, "I say it's pure affectation, that's what it is, pure affectation" (pp. 56–57).

11. Ibid., pp. 35, 64–65. Jadwin is so much more substantial than his rival in every way. Large and forceful, he "would have made two of Corthell . . ." (p. 33). He is a self-made man who has moved progressively from farming in Michigan to the livery business to real estate and grain speculation. He is one of the entrepreneurs who built Chicago, while Corthell lives off inherited wealth that makes possible his exquisite home, his studio in the Fine Arts Building, his exotic travels, and his work for the new Art Institute.

12. Ibid., p. 65. Much later, when Laura is upset that Jadwin has apparently abandoned her to defend his corner in wheat, she realizes that the characteristic that made him decide to leave her and return to the Pit is curiously the root of his attraction. "How keep him to herself when the great conflict impended?" she wonders. "She knew how the thunder of the captains and the shoutings appealed to him. She had seen him almost leap to his arms out of her embrace." That the Pit can pull him from her is, paradoxically, a sign of his virility: "He was all the man she had called him, and less strong, less eager, less brave, she would have loved him less" (p. 316). T. J. Jackson Lears analyzes the cult of chivalry, the martial ideal, heroic violence, and force in American literature and culture at the turn of the century, including the work of Norris, in *No Place of Grace: Antimodernism and the Transformation of American Culture, 1880–1920* (New York: Pantheon Books, 1981), pp. 107–17, 128–32. Norris describes the businessman as chivalric hero, and compares modern trade and commercial competition to war, in the essay "The Frontier Gone at Last," in *Responsibilities of the Novelist,* pp. 67–81.

13. Ibid., p. 387. To be sure, Norris belabors the whirlpool and bat-

tleground metaphors, though he effectively describes the irregular rhythm of the trading floor. The third chapter of the book is an excellent depiction of a typical day in the Pit, and it serves as a backdrop for later scenes of more tumultuous action.

14. Ibid., pp. 92–93. In a related earlier passage, Norris describes what happens to normal men once they are on the floor of the Pit: "The gentle-mannered fellow, clean-minded, clean-handed, of the breakfast or supper table was one man. The other, who and what was he? Down there in the murk and grime of the business district raged the Battle of the Street, and therein he was a being transformed, case hardened, supremely selfish, asking no quarter; no, nor giving any" (p. 64).

15. Ibid., p. 84. "The newspapers, not only of Chicago, but of every city in the Union, exploited him for 'stories.' The history of his corner, how he had effected it, its chronology, its results, were told and retold, till his name was familiar in the homes and at the firesides of uncounted thousands. 'Anecdotes' were circulated concerning him, interviews—concocted for the most part in the editorial rooms—were printed. His picture appeared. He was described as a cool, calm man of steel, with a cold and calculating grey eye, 'piercing as an eagle's'; as a desperate gambler, bold as a buccaneer, his eye black and fiery—a veritable pirate; as a mild, small man with a weak chin and a deprecatory demeanour; as a jolly and roistering 'high roller,' addicted to actresses, suppers, and to bathing in champagne" (pp. 332–33). While Norris derides these fabricated stories, they are not far from his own efforts to mythologize the speculator.

16. Ibid., pp. 395–96. *The Pit* is the second volume of Norris's uncompleted *Trilogy of the Wheat*, whose major purpose was to dramatize his conception of the production, distribution, and consumption of wheat as elemental processes which no man or group of men could master. In the two books he did complete, *The Octopus* and *The Pit*, Norris the Romantic Naturalist reserved his most energetic writing for those passages in which the wheat destroys the plans and lives of those—including Jadwin—who delude themselves into thinking that they can master it. See, for example, the death of Behrman at the end of *The Octopus*. He is quite literally drowned and crushed by the wheat that has been purchased at the cost of many other fortunes, hopes, and lives. Still, there is no doubt that Norris admires Jadwin for facing such a force, however petty Jadwin's actions are against the force of the wheat, and that he sees Jadwin's attempt to control a corner as one of heroic defiance of the limits of human experience.

17. *Responsibilities of the Novelist*, p. 21. For an excellent treatment of the aesthetics of power in Naturalist writing, see Harold Kaplan,

Power and Order: Henry Adams and the Naturalist Tradition in American Fiction (Chicago: University of Chicago Press, 1981).

18. *The Pit*, p. 259.

19. Ibid., p. 216.

20. Ibid., p. 125. Laura favored Jadwin over Corthell from the beginning because he treated her as a companion as well as a woman. "And between them," Norris writes, "it was more a give-and-take affair, more equality, more companionship. Corthell spoke only of her heart and to her heart. But Jadwin made her feel—or rather she made herself feel when he talked to her—that she had a head as well as a heart" (p. 35).

21. In an amusing and touching sequence, Jadwin proudly takes his broker and close friend Gretry for a tour. In the gallery—which is full of ivory statuettes, snuff boxes, and sixteenth-century fans purchased for the Jadwins—he grandly points to their Bougereau. Gretry looks at the bathing nymphs and comments, "This is what the boys down on the Board would call a bar-room picture." Of "one of the inevitable studies of a cuirassier" by Detaille, Gretry observes, "Queer the way these artists work." He moves closer to the canvas and notes, "Look at it close up and it's just a lot of little daubs, but you get off a distance . . . and you see now. Hey—see how the thing bunches up. Pretty neat, isn't it?" Jadwin's favorite object in the gallery is a built-in organ, "large enough for a cathedral," to which he has had attached a player roll. He pumps out the overture to *Carmen* as he talks to Gretry. The snatches of words Gretry makes out through the strains of mechanical music reveal the ludicrous helter-skelter mix of industry and art in this Chicago millionaire's mansion. As Jadwin pumps and brags about his acquisitions, the broker only hears "Toréador . . . horse power . . . Madam Calvé . . . electric motor . . . fine song . . . storage battery" (pp. 199–201).

22. Ibid., p. 255.

23. Larzer Ziff points out that "the vital tension" in the book is not between bulls and bears but, as has been argued here, between the Pit and the opera, the masculine business world and the art world associated with women. Ziff writes, "The American businessman, Norris shows, excludes his wife from his characteristically most forceful moments, leaving her open to seek gratification in lovers, or to pursue art or social work as substitutes for sexual fulfillment." Ziff calls *The Pit* "the first profound business novel because it rightly examines the psychic consequences of the commercialization of American life." See *The American 1890's: Life and Times of a Lost Generation* (New York: Viking Press, 1966), p. 273. Howard Horwitz analyzes the relationship between what he calls "the marriage and speculation plots" in *The Pit*

in "'To Find the Value of X': *The Pit* as a Renunciation of Romance,'" in Eric J. Sundquist, ed., *American Realism: New Essays*, (Baltimore: Johns Hopkins University Press, 1982), pp. 215–37.

24. *The Pit*, pp. 294, 292. See Kenneth S. Lynn's reading of *The Pit*, in light of the conflict between Norris's parents over whether their son should become an artist or a businessman, in *The Dream of Success: A Study of the Modern American Imagination* (Boston: Little, Brown, 1955), pp. 201–7.

25. *The Pit*, p. 311.

26. Ibid., p. 312. For a fuller discussion of Laura's "theatricality" and its importance in *The Pit*, see Don Graham, *The Fiction of Frank Norris: The Aesthetic Context* (Columbia: University of Missouri Press, 1978), pp. 123–56.

27. *The Pit*, p. 21.

28. Ibid., p. 22.

29. Ibid., p. 404.

30. In marrying a businessman in the hopes of becoming his "partner," and, that failing, in taking up with an artist, Laura resembles Adela Anthon in Herrick's *The Gospel of Freedom*. Wilbur is a more minor character than Jadwin, however, and his world is dishonest in a way Jadwin's is not. Unlike Erard, Corthell is not an evil fraud. But both books discuss the place of art in Chicago, the dilemma of the ambitious and intelligent woman of wealth in the city, and the ways the relationships between men, women, art, and life in Chicago intersect. In one of the best comprehensive readings of *The Pit*, Donald Pizer points out the similarities between Norris's novel, Zola's *La Curée* and *L'Argent*, and Harold Frederic's *The Market Place*. See *The Novels of Frank Norris* (Bloomington: Indiana University Press, 1966), pp. 163–64.

31. *The Financier* was published in 1912 by Harper & Brothers and revised in 1927 for Boni & Liveright, while *The Titan* was issued by John Lane in 1914. Dreiser began *The Stoic* shortly after the other books, but it was still uncompleted at the time of his death. It was published posthumously in 1947. *The Financier* follows Cowperwood's youth and early career in Philadelphia, *The Titan* his life in Chicago, and *The Stoic* his final years in New York and London. Citations here are to the World Publishing single-volume edition of the *Trilogy* (New York, 1972), with an introduction by Philip L. Gerber.

32. Gerber has extensively traced Dreiser's use of Yerkes's life. See chapter 4 of his *Theodore Dreiser* (New York: Twayne, 1964), "Financier, Titan, and Stoic: A Trilogy of Desire*," pp. 87–110; "Dreiser's Financier: A Genesis," *Journal of Modern Literature* 1 (1971): 354–74; "The Alabaster Protegé: Dreiser and Berenice Fleming," *American Literature* 43 (1971): 217–30; "The Financier Himself: Dreiser and C. T.

Yerkes," *PMLA* 88 (1973): 112–21; and "Frank Cowperwood: Boy Financier," *Studies in American Fiction* 2 (1974): 165–74. Jack E. Wallace offers a somewhat different view of the sources of the *Trilogy* and argues for what he calls "an essentially coherent comic structure" in the novels in "The Comic Voice in Dreiser's Cowperwood Narrative," *American Literature* 53 (1981): 56–71. There are some close similarities also between Dreiser's autobiographies, his autobiographical novel *The "Genius,"* and the *Trilogy*. Robert Penn Warren suggests that Dreiser was perhaps trying to invent a genre in which "all the outer facts are certified and the inner facts are imaginatively extrapolated from that evidence, and the whole, outer and inner, is offered as a document." Warren discusses the form of the *Trilogy* and issues of business and art in *Homage to Theodore Dreiser* (New York: Random House, 1971), pp. 76–77. For Norris's more limited use of actual people and events, see Charles Kaplan, "Norris's Use of Sources in *The Pit*," *American Literature* 25 (1953): 75–84.

33. *The Titan*, p. 59.

34. Some critics have argued that Dreiser's conception of the businessman as artist is unconvincingly presented, and that the large portions of the *Trilogy* that chronicle Cowperwood's financial manipulations are dull. Michael Millgate, for example, asserts, "When, however, Dreiser attempts to define this special artistic quality of Cowperwood's mind he can do no more than make large but ineffectual gestures." See "Theodore Dreiser and the American Financier," *Studi Americani* 7 (1961): 133–45. Kenneth Lynn calls *The Titan* a "fabulous bore" in *The Dream of Success* (p. 56).

35. *The Financier*, p. 43.

36. *The Titan*, p. 4.

37. Ibid., p. 169.

38. Warren discusses this point in *Homage to Theodore Dreiser*, pp. 80–81.

39. Theodore Dreiser, "The American Financier," in *Hey Rub-a-Dub-Dub: A Book of the Mystery and Wonder and Terror of Life* (New York: Boni & Liveright, 1920), pp. 81, 82, 88, 90.

40. Dreiser reaffirms the Romantic separation of art from fixed moral systems when he acknowledges that the businessman-artist may be "an advocate of every conceivable vice in order to twist his brain into some strange phantasmagorical tendency." He includes "so-called vice and crime and destruction and so-called evil" in "the universal creative process" ("The American Financier," p. 90), repeating aspects of Keats's remarks on the nature of poetic genius and character: " . . . it enjoys light and shade; it lives in gusto, be it foul or fair, high or low, rich or poor, mean or elevated—It has as much delight in conceiving an Iago

as an Imogen." See *The Letters of John Keats*, ed. Hyder Edward Rollins, vol. 1 (Cambridge: Harvard University Press, 1958), p. 387.

41. Quoted by Robert H. Elias in *Theodore Dreiser: Apostle of Nature*, emended ed. (Ithaca: Cornell University Press, 1970), pp. 175–76. Elias adds, "Of course, since the artistic element was to be found in the inscrutability, and the inscrutability became evident only when an individual was the victim of the whim of life's forces, it remained for the artist as artist to appreciate the plight. With the eye of the outsider the artist observed the Lucifers and Michaels of the world and gave their struggle relevance." Dreiser's image of the financier-artist as satanic creator is, of course, deeply rooted in the Romantic tradition.

Richard Lehan offers one of the fullest of several discussions of Dreiser as a Romantic. Lehan believes that Spencerian and Romantic ideas warred within Dreiser and his characters, and that Dreiser (and Cowperwood) never reconciled the material and spiritual in their lives. While Dreiser may not personally have made such a reconciliation, he did see in the *Trilogy* a way through the material to the spiritual by means of the beautiful. Lehan's analysis is in *Theodore Dreiser: His World and His Novels* (Carbondale and Edwardsville: Southern Illinois University Press, 1969).

42. *The Titan*, p. 72; *The Stoic*, pp. 6–7. In a famous review of *The "Genius"* that surveyed Dreiser's career to 1915, Stuart P. Sherman called the first two books of the *Trilogy* "a sort of huge club-sandwich composed of slices of business alternating with erotic episodes," but these elements are better integrated that Sherman suggests. They reflect the power of Dreiser's hero and his urge to be something more than a successful businessman. See "The Barbaric Naturalism of Mr. Dreiser," in Alfred Kazin and Charles Shapiro, eds., *The Stature of Theodore Dreiser: A Critical Survey of the Man and His Work* (Bloomington: Indiana University Press, 1955), p. 78. Walter Blackstock correctly states that Cowperwood's love affairs are a way of gratifying the financier's "intensely artistic" nature. See "Dreiser's Dramatizations of Art, the Artist, and the Beautiful in American Life," *Southern Quarterly* 1 (1962): 81; and Ernest Griffin, "Sympathetic Materialism: A Re-Reading of Theodore Dreiser," *Humanities Association Bulletin* 20 (1969): 56–68. Kenneth S. Lynn also notes the "artistic" nature of Cowperwood's women.

43. *The Financier*, p. 162. Walter Benn Michaels ingeniously explores the relationship between Cowperwood's business dealings and love affairs in "Dreiser's *Financier*: The Man of Business as a Man of Letters," in Eric J. Sundquist, ed., *American Realism*, pp. 278–95.

44. *The Titan*, p. 201.

45. *The Stoic*, p. 256.

46. *The Financier,* pp. 468–69.

47. Russell also describes Yerkes's traction companies as being over-capitalized and shoddy. Of one company, he writes, "If its sole business had been to make the American city a symbol around the world for all things detestable and dishonest it could hardly have done more to achieve that result." See *Lawless Wealth: The Origin of Some Great American Fortunes* (New York: B. W. Dodge & Co., 1908), pp. 39, 272–73, 49. W. T. Stead attacks Yerkes and his streetcars in *If Christ Came to Chicago,* pp. 198–201, 112–15.

48. *The Stoic,* p. 246.

49. Evidently the text is as coherent as it is partly thanks to Anderson's friends among the writers of the Chicago Renaissance, notably Floyd Dell, who helped get the book revised and published. Dell's assistance is discussed in *Sherwood Anderson's Memoirs: A Critical Edition,* ed. Ray Lewis White (Chapel Hill: University of North Carolina Press, 1969), pp. 22–23, 334–36; and in William A. Sutton, *The Road to Winesburg: A Mosaic of the Imaginative Life of Sherwood Anderson* (Metuchen, N.J.: Scarecrow Press, 1972), pp. 286–87.

50. Sherwood Anderson, *Windy McPherson's Son* (Chicago: University of Chicago Press, 1965), p. 227. This edition is based on the 1922 revised text.

51. These other versions include, among others, Payne's *Jerry the Dreamer,* Dreiser's *The "Genius"* (and, to a lesser extent, *Sister Carrie*), Dell's *Moon-Calf* and *The Briary-Bush,* and Cather's *The Song of the Lark.* These novels are similar in their discussions of artistic awakening to such classics as Joyce's *A Portrait of the Artist as a Young Man* and Lawrence's *Sons and Lovers.*

52. The Alger parallel is conscious and explicit. Anderson explains that Sam's work as a newsboy gives him "both a living and a kind of standing in the town's life," for all the people in this late nineteenth-century American corn-shipping village believe in the conventions of popular success fiction: "To be a newsboy or a bootblack in a small novel-reading American town is to make a figure in the world. Do not all of the poor newsboys in the books become great men and is not this boy who goes among us so industriously day after day likely to become such a figure? Is it not a duty we of the town owe to future greatness that we push him forward" (p. 17). While Anderson's tone is ironic, he is quite serious about the power of such popular mythologies.

53. Tall, bearded, handsome, financially independent, and jauntily tailored, Telfer "made a figure that might have passed unnoticed on the promenade before some fashionable summer hotel, but that seemed a breach of the laws of nature when seen on the streets of a corn-shipping town in Iowa." He regrets that he has ended up as "a village cut-up, a

pot-house wit, a flinger of idle words into the air of a village intent upon raising corn" (pp. 5, 61). As the leader of a group of townsmen who gather around the drugstore to discuss ideas and events, Telfer is part of a tradition in American letters going back at least to the worthies who gather around the tavern in "Rip Van Winkle."

54. Ibid., p. 7.

55. Telfer adds that the so-called starving genius is "not only incapable in money getting but also incapable in the very art for which he starves," while the "great men" in "real life" are "more likely to ride in carriages on Fifth Avenue and have country places on the Hudson" (pp. 69–70). Later, in his stylized autobiography, *A Story Teller's Story* (New York: Viking Press, 1969; first published by B. W. Huebsch in 1924), Anderson argued that the artist is rarely a financial success and is demeaned when he is concerned with selling his work. See pp. 5, 308, 320.

56. From the traveling salesmen, Sam "got into his nostrils a whiff of the city and, listening to them, he saw the great ways filled with hurrying people, the tall buildings touching the sky, the men running about intent upon money making, and the clerks going on year after year on small salaries, getting nowhere, a part of, and yet not understanding, the impulses and motives of the enterprises that supported them." *Windy McPherson's Son*, pp. 65, 67, 106.

57. Ibid., pp. 125, 142–43. Anderson was as capable of overwriting as Norris or Dreiser, and sometimes his rhetoric loads more on to his subject than it can hold: "And summer and winter a million hens laid the eggs that were gathered there, and the cattle on a thousand hills sent their yellow butter fat packed in tubs and piled upon trucks to add to the confusion" (p. 125). Anderson first came to Chicago in 1896, worked in a warehouse, and lived in a rooming house on the West Side. His first impressions, recalled much latter in his *Memoirs*, were more mixed than Sam's, and his excitement was more tempered by the squalor he saw. In other writings virtually contemporary with *Windy*, he condemned the city as a denial of life. See, for example, *Marching Men* (1917) and *Mid-American Chants* (1918). An excerpt from the latter: "You know my city—Chicago triumphant—factories and marts and the roar of machines—horrible, terrible, ugly and brutal." "Song of Industrial America," *Mid-American Chants* (New York: B. W. Huebsch, 1923), p. 16.

58. Anderson repeatedly stresses the violence of Sam's world. Sam soon learns to watch for the "vague, uncertain look" that marks the weaker businessman (this, too, recalls scenes from Dreiser, in which Cowperwood sizes up other businessmen as weaklings), and he takes advantage of his rivals "as a successful prize fighter watches for a

similar vague, uncertain look in the eyes of an opponent." He views other businessmen "only as so many individuals that might some day test their ability against his own," and he surveys the urban scene as "the old Norse marauders looked at the cities sitting in their splendour on the Mediterranean." As he is rising in business, those who oppose him are "secretly marked for slaughter." At times Sam seems to have no loyalty but to his ambition of power, looking upon his company as "a great tool" with which, he thinks, "I will pry my way into the place I mean to occupy among the big men of this city and this nation" (pp. 113, 118, 126, 141).

59. Ibid., pp. 148–50, 178.

60. Ibid., p. 79.

61. Ibid., p. 219.

62. Ibid., p. 232.

63. Ibid., pp. 220, 236–37. Anderson does not say, even at this point, that Sam's failed experiment with Sue was a waste of time. He asserts that Sam's exposure to art and ideas makes him a better businessman: "Now with the fires of youth still in him and with the training and discipline that had come from two years of reading, of comparative leisure and of thought, he was prepared to give the Chicago business world a display of that tremendous energy that was to write his name in the industrial history of the city as one of the first of the western giants of finance." To follow this path, Sam tells Sue, is "to be myself now and lead my own life in my own way." He continues, "I cannot stand idly by and let life go past" (pp. 220–21).

64. Ibid., p. 263.

65. Ibid., pp. 299–300. Anderson wrote in his *Memoirs,* "The artist, any man born artist as I was, and caught as I was and, I dare say, as all such men are caught, has this hunger always to remake, to recreate. There is this shapeless thing all about him everywhere and the fingers ache to reshape it" (251).

66. *Windy McPherson's Son,* pp. 329–330.

67. Anderson wrote in a letter in 1937: "I rather think that modern life and, in fact, any life wherein most people are compelled to be driven by the profit motive makes it impossible for all of us to be anything else but grotesque." See *Letters of Sherwood Anderson,* ed. Howard Mumford Jones and Walter B. Rideout (Boston: Little, Brown, 1953), p. 376. Anderson told Waldo Frank in November of 1918, "I suspect that the thing needed is quite simple—a real desire on the part of a few people to shake off the success disease, to really get over our American mania for 'getting on.' It has got to be pretty deep-seated if it gets us anywhere." Quoted by Sutton in *The Road to Winesburg,* p. 84. Earlier in the same year, Anderson wrote Van Wyck Brooks about his own desire for escape,

a wish that he transferred to the hero of his novel: "God damn it, Brooks, I wish my books would sell for one reason. I want to quit working for a living and go wander for five years in our towns. I want to be a factory hand again and wander from place to place." See *Letters*, p. 31.

68. A sample of some of his work, this from 1903: "As a man travels about he realizes more and more, that the business man is the very front and center of things American. He is the man on horseback in our national life. He knows, and I pray you, doubt not, that he dictates the whole works." Anderson asked rhetorically, "And what manner of man is he, this American business man? Is he a better, cleaner and braver man than the warriors and scholars who have cast their big shadows in the past?" The answer: "You can be sure he is." Anderson did add, however, that the businessman "may have occasionally a bad dose of dollarism." Quoted in Sutton, *The Road to Winesburg*, p. 110.

According to Anderson, he was invited to Philadelphia for an interview with the *Saturday Evening Post*, which featured the "romance of business," but he turned the opportunity down. He claimed that years later, just after he published *Windy*, the Curtis Company asked him to write novels for them that began as *Windy* did but didn't "stumble" the same way at the end. He said that they offered him a great deal of money, but he again turned them down. Recollected in his *Memoirs* (pp. 211–15), this story—true or not—is another episode in Anderson's long inner struggle between a desire for artistic freedom and the pursuit of wealth. Sutton includes Anderson's correspondence with Waldo Frank on the same subject. Frank warned that Curtis would probably not publish Anderson's work: "The idea of a literary Odyssey through the West would appeal to them, doubtles —but your gospel of defeat, your golden discovery of unfinancial gods, your subtle revolutionary visions would give them the creeps if they began to catch on." See *The Road to Winesburg*, p. 327.

69. To do him justice, Windy tries to turn his talent for spinning stories to a profit. As a younger man, one of his unsuccessful ventures was as a traveling entertainer. This part of Windy's career was also taken from Irwin Anderson's life. Windy turns local schoolhouses into temporary stages, singing comic songs and pattering through magic lantern shows, earning little but the applause of a few farmers and townfolk. See *Windy McPherson's Son*, p. 79.

70. Ibid., pp. 31, 233.

71. *A Story Teller's Story*, p. 26. There is often a dreamy quality to many of Anderson's heroes, including those who succeed in the world's terms, such as Hugh McVey of *Poor White*.

72. As noted in Chapter 1, Anderson at times sounded like Stanley Waterloo and Hamlin Garland, who twenty and thirty years earlier

championed a literature that reflected common life in the American hinterland, even if this literature might be crude. In his *Memoirs,* Anderson explained that during the mid-teens in Chicago he came to realize that being true to American materials also meant working within the boundaries of American speech, "the language of the streets of American towns and citites, the language of the factories and warehouses where I had worked, of laborers' rooming houses, the saloons, the farms." Influenced by Gertrude Stein, he tried to redefine American literary art: "There was a kind of painting I was seeking in my prose, word to be laid against word in just a certain way, a kind of word color, an arch of words and sentences, the color to be squeezed out of simple words, simple sentence construction" (p. 338). The question of influences in Anderson's work (including authors from whom he learned as well as those whose writing he affected) is a difficult one, however, and it is not made easier by Anderson's inconsistent and unreliable remarks on the subject.

73. Note, for example, Norris's handling of Corthell. As for Dreiser, see his treatment of Harold Sohlberg, a violinist with whose wife Cowperwood has an affair. Sohlberg backs down after a show of anger when he finds out about the liaison and allows Cowperwood to humiliate him with proof of his own indiscretions. When Aileen finds out, she attacks Mrs. Sohlberg, and the two husbands respond very differently to Mrs. Sohlberg's screams: "Cowperwood, always the man of action as opposed to nervous cogitation, braced up on the instant like taut wire," while "Sohlberg the artist, responding like a chameleon to the various emotional complexions of life, began to breathe stertorously, to blanch, to lose control of himself." Later, a promising young poet is described as "a mere breath of romance" beside the "real," the "strange, terrible, fascinating" Cowperwood. See *The Titan,* pp. 148, 239.

74. *Memoirs,* pp. 317–19. What they wanted to join, however, was a different America and Chicago than those at hand. "I wanted, as all men do, to belong," Anderson confessed near the end of *A Story Teller's Story.* "To what? To an America alive, an America that was no longer a despised cultural foster child of Europe, with unpleasant questions always being asked about its parentage, to an America that had begun to be conscious of itself as a living home-making folk, to an America that had at last given up the notion that anything worth while could ever be got by being in a hurry, by being dollar rich, by being merely big and able to lick some smaller nation with one hand tied behind its broad national back" (p. 395). Irving Howe discusses the characteristic loneliness and yearning for some ideal community that brought writers like Anderson from the small towns of the Midwest to Chicago, where they formed little bohemias and tried to express in their work some sense of

their loneliness and formulate some escape from it. See *Sherwood Anderson* (New York: William Sloane Associates, 1951), pp. 59–64.

75. *A Story Teller's Story*, pp. 202, 219, 254.

76. Anderson was obsessed with finding the right words. He admitted repeatedly that he was in love with words, that he felt physical pleasure in having at hand piles of paper and bottles of ink and pencils so that he could write his words. "Through long years of the baffling uncertainty," he wrote, "that only such men as myself can ever know, I am to creep with trembling steps forward in a strange land, following the little words, striving to learn all the ways of the ever-changing words, the smooth-lying little words, the hard, jagged, cutting words, the round, melodious, healing words" (*A Story Teller's Story*, pp. 19–20, 66).

77. As noted, earlier, some critics maintain that Jadwin and Cowperwood are uninteresting in spite of all their creators' efforts to say otherwise.

78. *The Titan*, p. 167.

Chapter Five

1. George Rogers Taylor, *The Transportation Revolution 1815–1860* (New York: Rinehart & Co., 1951), p. 86.

2. Carl W. Condit, *Chicago, 1910–1929: Building, Planning, and Urban Technology* (Chicago: University of Chicago Press, 1973), p. 40. This book and Harold M. Mayer and Richard C. Wade's *Chicago: Growth of a Metropolis* (Chicago: University of Chicago Press, 1969), to which I am generally indebted, are the main sources of the figures cited here.

3. Lois Wille studies the Illinois Central and its place in the long effort to make the lakefront into public park land in *Forever Open, Clear and Free: The Historic Struggle for Chicago's Lakefront* (Chicago: Regnery, 1972), pp. 26–37. The Illinois Central agreed in 1912 to depress its tracks as part of the construction of Grant Park.

4. Condit, *Chicago, 1910–1929*, p. 38.

5. Condit writes, "The construction of the Union Loop had results without exact parallel in the history of the American city." Noting that the pattern of waterways had fixed the urban core into a rectangle defined by the lake and the two branches of the Chicago River, and that the construction of railroad terminals closed the south side of the rectangle, he explains that "the Loop threw a tight ring around the inner heart, so to speak." This had important advantages and disadvantages. "All elements of the core—all offices, stores, theaters, and other commercial and recreational facilities, all financial, administrative, and municipal institutions—lie within a ten-minute walk of one or another of

the ten Loop stations." But the Union Loop also has had "a strangling effect," producing a higher density of pedestrian and vehicular traffic at peak times than the streets can bear, as well as blighting the surrounding area with its noise and shadow (*Chicago, 1910–29,* pp. 39–40).

6. Unfortunately for Mamie, the realities of urban opportunity soon dispel the romance. She becomes a kind of failed Sister Carrie, working in the basement of a department store and wondering "if there is a bigger place the railroads run to from Chicago where maybe there is / romance / and big things / and real dreams / that never go smash." "Mamie" is collected in *The Complete Poems of Carl Sandburg,* rev. and expanded ed. (New York: Harcourt Brace Jovanovich, 1970), p. 17. It first appeared in *Chicago Poems* in 1916.

7. Floyd Dell, *The Briary-Bush* (New York: Alfred A. Knopf, 1921), p. 3. G. Thomas Tanselle examines Dell's career in "Faun at the Barricades: The Life and Works of Floyd Dell" (Ph.D diss., Northwestern University, 1959). In his introduction to *Windy McPherson's Son,* Wright Morris (himself the son of a railroad man in small-town Nebraska) speaks of the centrality of Chicago rather than places like New York and Europe in the midwestern imagination: "If you were born, like Anderson, in the sprawling Midwest, Chicago was the place to go and where you went. Those faded maps on the walls of small railroad stations illustrated this mindless movement at a glance: all the lines led to Chicago. There they stopped." See "Windy McPherson's Son the Storyteller's Story," introduction to Sherwood Anderson's *Windy McPherson's Son* (Chicago: University of Chicago Press, 1965), p. xii.

8. In 1883, representatives of major railroads appropriately met in Chicago to agree on standard time zones. Marjorie Kriz describes their convention in "'The Day of Two Noons'—Achieving Standard Time," *Chicago History* 7 (Spring 1978): 12–21.

9. Paul Bourget, *Outre-Mer: Impressions of America* (London: T. Fisher Unwin, 1895), pp. 115–16.

10. Quoted by Bessie L. Pierce in *As Others See Chicago,* p. 280.

11. Julian Ralph, *Our Great West* (New York: Harper & Bros., 1893), pp. 30–31.

12. Waldo Frank, *Our America* (New York: Boni & Liveright, 1919), pp. 118, 119. Frank devoted a portion of the Chicago chapter to the writers of the city.

13. W. T. Stead, *If Christ Came to Chicago,* pp. 194–95.

14. Theodore Dreiser, *Dawn,* pp. 301–2.

15. Michael Cowan offers a brief but comprehensive survey of the American writer's vision of the city, including a discussion of the view from the train, in "Walkers in the Street: American Writers and the Modern City," *Prospects* 6 (1981): 281–311.

16. Leo Marx, *The Machine in the Garden: Technology and the Pastoral Ideal in America* (New York: Oxford University Press, 1964), p. 229.

17. Ralph Waldo Emerson, *The Journals and Miscellaneous Notebooks of Ralph Waldo Emerson,* vol. 4 (1832–34), ed. Alfred R. Ferguson (Cambridge: Belknap Press, 1964), p. 226. See also John F. Kasson, *Civilizing the Machine,* p. 115. Henry James, *The American Scene,* ed. Leon Edel (Bloomington: Indiana University Press, 1968), p. 465.

18. As Cowan notes, Howells made exceptionally effective use of the view of New York from the train. See *A Hazard of New Fortunes,* ed. Don L. Cook et al. (Bloomington: Indiana University Press, 1976), pp. 76–77, 182–84, 305–6.

19. There have been several intriguing studies of the nature of the experience of riding the train, including some of the artist's use of the view from the train. See, for example, Wolfgang Schivelbusch, *The Railway Journey: Trains and Travel in the 19th Century,* trans. Anselm Hollo (New York: Urizen Books, 1979); Susan Danly Walther, "The Railroad in the Industrial Landscape: 1900–1950," in *The Railroad in the American Landscape: 1850–1950* (Wellesley, Mass.: Wellesley College Museum, 1981), pp. 52–66; and Walker Evans, *Many Are Called* (Boston: Houghton Mifflin, 1966). Walther's essay examines American painting and photography, while Evans's book includes photographs of the faces of riders on the subway in the late 1930s and early 1940s.

20. Louis H. Sullivan, *The Autobiography of an Idea* (New York: Dover, 1956), p, 197. The book was first published in 1924.

21. Hamlin Garland, *A Son of the Middle Border* (New York: Grosset & Dunlap, 1917), pp. 261, 268–69.

22. Theodore Dreiser, *Dawn,* pp. 295–96.

23. Waldo Frank, *Our America,* pp. 117–18.

24. Robert Herrick, *The Gospel of Freedom,* pp. 101–4.

25. Hamlin Garland, *Rose of Dutcher's Coolly,* ed. Donald Pizer (Lincoln: University of Nebraska Press, 1969), pp. 90, 92, 95. This text is reproduced from the 1895 edition published by Stone & Kimball in Chicago. These passages, and the relative candor with which Garland discussed Rose's sexuality throughout the book, shocked reviewers. Four years later, Garland brought out a revised and less "offensive" text. See Pizer's introduction to the reissued 1895 edition, pp. vii–xxiv. Rose is another female artist in Chicago fiction. She wishes to be a writer, but her supposed talent is never convincingly conveyed by Garland, and her courtship increasingly takes over central interest to the exclusion of other issues. This is true also of Bert Leston Taylor's *The Charlatans* (1906), which begins with heroine Hope Winston coming in on the

train to study piano in Chicago. Taylor switches from a realistic handling of life in the city (including a discussion of musical training in Chicago) to a fairy tale about this country maid who finds her prince, a music critic.

26. *Rose of Dutcher's Coolly*, pp. 180–83.

27. Dreiser was not above some creative "borrowing." His description of Drouet and his methods of winning the attentions of attractive women (including those he meets on the train) was adapted in part from George Ade's *Fables in Slang*. For more on Dreiser's plagiarism, see the Pennsylvania edition of *Sister Carrie*, p. 558–59; and Jack Salzman, "Dreiser and Ade: A Note on the Text of *Sister Carrie*," *American Literature* 40 (1969): 544–48. Ellen Moers's *Two Dreisers* (New York: Viking Press, 1969) is a superb comprehensive examination of the sources of *Sister Carrie* and Dreiser's other writings. The differences between Rose and Carrie should not be overlooked. Both are attractive young women seeking their fortune in Chicago, but Rose is more intelligent and certain of her purpose, and less dissatisfied with her home life.

28. These quotations are all from the first chapter of the Pennsylvania edition of *Sister Carrie*, pp. 3–12. This version is a little longer than the previously standard edition, but it is substantially the same. Philip Fisher discusses the imaginative dimensions of the train and other physical features of Carrie's world in "Acting, Reading, Fortune's Wheel: *Sister Carrie* and the Life History of Objects," in Eric J. Sandquist, ed., *American Realism*, pp. 259–77.

29. The passage continues: "The little low one and two story houses, quite new as to wood, were frequently unpainted and already smoky— in places grimy. At grade-crossings, where ambling street-cars and wagons and muddy-wheeled buggies waited, he noted how flat the streets were, how unpaved, how sidewalks went up and down rhythmically—here a flight of steps, a veritable platform before a house, there a long stretch of boards laid flat on the mud of the prairie itself. What a city! Presently a branch of the filthy, arrogant, self-sufficient little Chicago River came into view, with its mass of sputtering tugs, its black, oily water, its tall, red, brown, and green grain-elevators, its immense black coal-pockets and yellowish-brown lumber yards." *The Titan*, pp. 2, 1, 3–4.

30. Dreiser makes this meaning of Cowperwood's entry into Chicago clearer at the end of *The Financier*, when he describes more briefly the same trip that opens *The Titan*: "It was only three months later that a train, speeding through the mountains of Pennsylvania and over the plains of Ohio and Indiana, bore to Chicago and the West the young financial aspirant who, in spite of youth and wealth and a notable vigor of body, was a solemn, conservative speculator as to what his future

might be. The West, as he had carefully calculated before leaving, held much. He had studied the receipts of the New York Clearing House recently and the disposition of bank-balances and the shipment of gold, and had seen that vast quantities of the latter metal were going to Chicago. He understood finance accurately. The meaning of gold shipments was clear. Where money was going *trade was*—a thriving, developing life. He wished to see clearly for himself what this world had to offer" (p. 499).

31. *The Titan*, pp. 3, 5.

32. Ibid., pp. 223, 472.

Chapter Six

1. Siegfried Giedion, *Space, Time, and Architecture: The Growth of a New Tradition*, 5th ed. (Cambridge: Harvard University Press, 1967), p. 347. The precise attribution of the invention of balloon framing is disputed, but not its identification with the rise of Chicago.

2. Carl Condit, *The Chicago School of Architecture: A History of Commercial and Public Building in the Chicago Area, 1875–1925* (Chicago: University of Chicago Press, 1964), p. 1. Once again, I have relied on Professor Condit's historical information and critical judgment.

3. Alan Trachtenberg writes, "For the railroad stations inserted at the heart of cities an emblem of the immense fact that 'distance' had become a matter of time rather than space, that (after 1883) all times were now one. Like a giant clock seated in the city's midst, the terminal represented regulation, system, obedience to schedule. By necessity, its spaces were provisional: not habitations or places of continuous labor but sites of comings and goings. In its housing of multiple structures keyed to each other, the terminal stood as a virtual model of the new form of the urban: not so much a distinctive 'place' as a place for movement, for transactions made against an infallible clock." See *The Incorporation of America: Culture and Society in the Gilded Age* (New York: Hill & Wang, 1982), pp. 120–21.

4. Even Frank Merriwell notes on his arrival in Chicago that "when it came to 'sky-scrapers,' New York could not hold a candle to Chicago." This remark is from Burt L. Standish [Gilbert Patten], *Frank Merriwell in Chicago; or, Meshed by Mysteries* (New York: Street & Smith, 1896), p. 20. For more on dime novels set in Chicago, see Carl S. Smith, "Fearsome Fiction and the Windy City; or, Chicago in the Dime Novel," *Chicago History* 7 (Spring 1978): 2–11.

5. Louis H. Sullivan, *Kindergarten Chats and Other Writings* (New York: George Wittenborn, 1947), p. 140. *Kindergarten Chats* was first published serially in 1901. This text is from the 1918 revised edition.

6. For a more extensive survey of the achievement of Burnham and Root in Chicago, see Condit, *The Chicago School of Architecture,* pp. 95–107.

7. Quoted by Harriet Monroe in *John Wellborn Root: A Study of His Life and Work* (Park Forest, Ill.: Prairie School Press, 1966), pp. 79, 89. Monroe was Root's sister-in-law, and her biography of him was first published by Macmillan in 1896. See also Donald Hoffman, *The Architecture of John Wellborn Root* (Baltimore: Johns Hopkins University Press, 1973).

8. *John Wellborn Root,* pp. 106–7.

9. On Sullivan's career, see Hugh Morrison, *Louis Sullivan: Prophet of Modern Architecture* (New York: Norton, 1935); and Sherman Paul, *Louis Sullivan: An Architect in American Thought* (Englewood Cliffs, N.J.: Prentice-Hall, 1962).

10. *Kindergarten Chats,* p. 30.

11. Sullivan, *The Autobiography of an Idea,* p. 264.

12. *Kindergarten Chats,* p. 107.

13. Ibid., pp. 181, 213. "The Tall Office Building Artistically Considered" appeared in *Lippincott's* in March 1896.

14. Carl Sandburg, "Good Morning, America," in *Complete Poems,* p. 320. This poem was originally published in book form in 1928. See also Sandburg's "Again?" in which he argues that for all the Woolworth family's efforts to surpass "Babel, the Nineveh Hanging Gardens, Karnak" with their building, the truth is that it was constructed by "women buying mousetraps,

> *Wire cloth dishrags, ten cent sheet music,*
> *They paid for it; the electric tower*
> *Might yell an electric sign to the inbound*
> *Ocean liners, 'Look what the washerwomen*
> *Of America can do with their nickels,' or*
> *'See what a nickel and a dime can do,' . . .*
>
> —*Complete Poems,* p. 368

15. Ibid., pp. 439, 491. *The People, Yes* appeared in 1936.

16. Ibid., pp. 31–32. This poem was published in 1916 in *Chicago Poems,* Sandburg's first book of poetry.

17. Ibid., pp. 109–10. This poem was included in *Cornhuskers* (1918).

18. Fuller continues this view of the cityscape as an unnatural natural world. He compares the tallest structures to Yosemite's El Capitan, but in this case the falling rain is no ethereal cascade like the famed Bridal Veil Falls but "is woven by the breezes of lake and prairie from the warp of soot-flakes and the woof of damp-drenched smoke." The

terrain is treeless save for the "forest of chimneys," shrubless except for the "gnarled carpentry of the awkward frame-works which carry the telegraph," arid despite the water tanks that "squat on the high angles of alley walls" and the pools of tar and gravel that "ooze and shimmer" on the rooftops. Finally, it is airless except for its "swathing mists of coal-smoke" (*The Cliff-Dwellers*, pp. 1–5).

19. Steevens, *The Land of the Dollar*, pp. 145–46.

20. Bourget, *Outre-Mer*, p. 118. Bourget was impressed by these buildings, however, and in the same paragraph he sounded like Louis Sullivan: "The simple power of necessity is to a certain degree a principle of beauty; and these structures so plainly manifest this necessity that you feel a strange emotion in contemplating them. It is the first draught of a new sort of art,—an art of democracy made by the masses and for the masses, an art of science, where the invariability of natural laws gives to the most unbridled daring the calmness of geometrical figures."

21. *The Cliff-Dwellers*, p. 5.

22. Edmund Wilson contends that the book's structure anticipates that of later innovative novels such as John Dos Passos's *Manhattan Transfer*. Wilson's remarks are in "Henry Blake Fuller: The Art of Making It Flat," *New Yorker* (23 May 1970): 116.

23. *The Cliff-Dwellers*, pp. 38, 43, 44.

24. Ibid., pp. 60, 63.

25. Ibid., pp. 69, 70.

26. As he calls out the numbers of the floors, the elevator operator has an air of authority that suits his importance as driver of this vehicle of aspiration: "He wore a blue uniform with gilt buttons and he had a gold band on his cap. He was as important as Ingles himself—perhaps more so" (p. 116).

27. Ibid., p. 298. This scene compares with Jerry Drew's attack on Sidney Bane in *Jerry the Dreamer*.

28. Ibid., p. 324.

29. Henry B. Fuller, "The Upward Movement in Chicago," *Atlantic Monthly* 80 (1897): 534, 541–42. In some rare moments, Fuller was more hopeful. A respected minor character in *The Cliff-Dwellers* defends Chicago to a visitor from Boston. It is interesting to note that he uses architectural imagery to make his point: "You have seen the foundations. . . . It has taken fifty years to put them in, but the work is finally done and well done. And now we are beginning to build on these foundations. We might have put up our building first and then put in the underpinning afterwards. That is the common way, but ours will be found to have its advantages." He argues that Chicago *is* a civilized

place that erects libraries as well as banks, developing character as well as making money. "Chicago is Chicago," he concludes. "It is the belief of all of us. It is inevitable; nothing can stop us now" (pp. 238, 243). Fuller's fear of the consequences of democracy also is reflected in the strain of nativism that surfaces in his writing. See Guy Szuberla, "Henry Blake Fuller and the 'New Immigrant,'" *American Literature* 53 (1981): 246–65.

30. Herrick, "The Background of the American Novel," pp. 224–25.

31. Herrick, *The Common Lot*, p. 168.

32. Norris, *The Pit*, pp. 40, 41, 420–21.

33. *The Times* (London), 21 October 1887, p. 4.

34. A. T. Andreas, *A History of Chicago*, vol. 3 (Chicago: A. T. Andreas, 1886), p. 319.

35. Tallmadge was, however, very impressed with the trading room: "Truthfully expressed in the exterior, and abiding in memory's eye as full of color from the stained glass windows; with many marble mosaics and frescoes and mahogany; full of motion from the frantic traders; full of noise as wheat, corn, hogs and lard varied a point or two, and full of tobacco smoke whose blue haze, pierced by the shafts of sunlight through the lofty windows, gave an eerie splendor to the scene." See *Architecture in Old Chicago* (Chicago: University of Chicago Press, 1941), p. 167.

36. Frank Lloyd Wright, *An Autobiography* (New York: Duell, Sloan, & Pierce, 1943), p. 88.

37. Montgomery Schuyler, *American Architecture and Other Writings*, ed. William H. Jordy and Ralph Coe, vol. 1 (Cambridge: Harvard University Press, 1961), p. 94. Schuyler's remarks were first published in 1891.

38. Dreiser, *Sister Carrie*, pp. 17, 27.

39. Ibid., pp. 29, 31.

40. Ibid., pp. 22, 23.

41. Ibid., pp. 339, 353, 449.

42. Herrick, *The Common Lot*, p. 193.

43. Upton Sinclair, *The Jungle* (New York: Doubleday, Page, 1906), pp. 277–78, 337.

44. Norris, *The Pit*, p. 7.

45. For more on the statistics of this building, see David F. Burg, *Chicago's White City of 1893* (Lexington: University Press of Kentucky, 1976), pp. 95–97. Diagrams showing the capacity of the floor space in relation to other major buildings appeared in "The Area of the Liberal Arts Building at Chicago," *American Architect and Building News* 42 (1893): 151.

46. Harriet Monroe, *Chosen Poems* (New York: Macmillan, 1935), p. 75. See also her autobiography, *A Poet's Life: Seventy Years in a Changing World* (New York: Macmillan, 1938).

47. Edgar Lee Masters, *A Book of Verses* (Chicago: Way & Williams, 1898), p. 123.

48. Henry Van Brunt, "The Columbian Exposition and American Civilization," *Atlantic Monthly* 71 (1893): 577.

49. Garland accompanied his parents into the electrically illuminated Court of Honor one evening, "and as lamps were lit and waters of the lagoon began to reflect the gleaming walls of the great palaces with their sculptured ornaments, and boats of quaint shape filled with singers came and went beneath the arching bridges, the wonder and the beauty of it all moved these dwellers of the level lands to tears of joy which was almost as poignant as pain." For people set in their ways, however, Chicago and the Fair were overpowering. Dazzled by this sudden vision of splendor, Garland's elderly mother soon could not take any more and asked to go home. His father lasted a little longer, but he soon declared that he, too, had enough. To the young person who identified his future with that of Chicago, as Garland did, the scene was purely inspiring. See *A Son of the Middle Border,* pp. 458–61.

50. Dreiser, *A Book About Myself,* pp. 246, 247.

51. Sullivan, *The Autobiography of an Idea,* pp. 324, 322. Sullivan's Transportation Building, with its celebrated Golden Door, contrasted sharply with the style and color of the major buildings of the Court of Honor.

52. Montgomery Schuyler, "Last Words About the World's Fair," *Architectural Record* 3 (1893–94): 300.

53. William Dean Howells, *Letters of an Altrurian Traveller,* ed. Clara M. Kirk and Rudolf Kirk (Gainesville, Fla.: Scholars' Facsimiles & Reprints, 1961), p. 23.

54. Henry Adams, *The Education of Henry Adams,* ed. Ernest Samuels (Boston: Houghton Mifflin, 1973), pp. 339–40.

55. Clara Louise Burnham, *Sweet Clover: A Romance of the White City* (Boston: Houghton, Mifflin, 1894), p. 155.

56. Ibid., pp. 180–81, 230.

57. Ibid., pp. 201–2.

58. Ibid., pp. 385, 410.

59. Chicago *Tribune,* 8 January 1894, p. 11.

60. Chicago *Tribune,* 9 January 1894, p. 1; 10 January 1894, p. 1.

61. Chicago *Tribune,* 6 July 1894, p. 7. News of the Pullman Strike and of troops in the city pushed the reports of the destruction of the Court of Honor off the front page.

62. Herrick, "Myself," pp. 48–49. Van Harrington, the narrator and hero of Herrick's *Memoirs of an American Citizen*, likewise acknowledges that the Fair was a "triumph of beauty," but calls the economic crisis that surrounded Jackson Park "the skeleton that lay at the feast" (pp. 147–48).

63. Robert Herrick, *The Web of Life* (New York: Macmillan, 1900), pp. 57, 172.

64. Payne, *Mr. Salt*, pp. 56–59, 139–40.

65. Thomas S. Hines's *Burnham of Chicago: Architect and Planner* (New York: Oxford University Press, 1974) is an excellent analysis of Burnham's career. On his influence and his creative context, see also Manio Manieri-Elia, "Toward an 'Imperial City': Daniel H. Burnham and the City Beautiful Movement," and Francesco Dal Co, "From Parks to the Region: Progressive Ideology and the Reform of the American City," in Giorgio Ciucci et al., *The American City: From the Civil War to the New Deal*, trans. Barbara Luigia La Penta (Cambridge: M.I.T. Press, 1979), pp. 1–291.

66. Daniel H. Burnham and Edward H. Bennett, *Plan of Chicago*, ed. Charles Moore (New York: Da Capo Press, 1970), pp. 4, 1. This is a reprint of the 1909 edition.

67. Ibid., pp. v, 80.

CHAPTER SEVEN

1. Bessie Louise Pierce, *A History of Chicago*, vol. 3 (New York: Alfred A. Knopf, 1957), pp. 109, 111. Professor Pierce's fourth chapter, "The Economic Empire of Chicago: Livestock and Meat Packing" (pp. 108–44), has been very useful in providing information for this chapter. An interesting and colorful, if not entirely reliable, survey of the history and daily operations of the stockyards is W. Joseph Grand's *Illustrated History of the Union Stockyards: Sketch-Book of Familiar Faces and Places at the Yards* (Chicago: n.p., 1901). Another source of information here has been the Commission on Chicago Historical and Architectural Landmarks pamphlet, *Union Stock Yard Gate* (Chicago, 1976).

2. Siegfried Giedion, *Mechanization Takes Command: A Contribution to Anonymous History* (New York: Oxford University Press, 1948), p. 218.

3. *The United States with an Excursion into Mexico: A Handbook for Travellers*, ed. Karl Baedeker (New York: DaCapo Press, 1971), p. 286. This is a facsimile of the edition published in New York and Leipzig in 1893. Its author was James Fullarton Muirhead, author of *America The Land of Contrasts*.

4. Charles Edward Russell, *The Greatest Trust in the World* (New York: Ridgway-Thayer, 1905), p. 212.

5. Upton Sinclair, *The Autobiography of Upton Sinclair* (New York: Harcourt, Brace & World, 1962), p. 118.

6. Charles J. Bushnell, *The Social Problem at the Chicago Stock Yards* (Chicago: University of Chicago Press, 1902), pp. xiv, xi–xii.

7. Bourget, *Outre-Mer*, p. 120.

8. *From Max Weber: Essays in Sociology*, ed. H. H. Gerth and C. Wright Mills (New York: Oxford University Press, 1946), p. 15.

9. Rudyard Kipling, *From Sea to Sea: Letters of Travel*, pt. 2 (Garden City: Doubleday, Page, 1923), pp. 139, 153.

10. H. L. Mencken, "Civilized Chicago," Chicago *Sunday Tribune*, 28 October 1917, pt. 8, p. 5.

11. W. L. George, *Hail, Columbia!* (New York: Harper & Bros., 1921), p. 48.

12. Norman Mailer, *Miami and the Siege of Chicago* (New York: New American Library, 1968), p. 90.

13. Herrick, *The Memoirs of an American Citizen*, pp. 50, 72.

14. Arthur Jerome Eddy, *Ganton & Company* (Chicago: A. C. McClurg, 1908), p. 10. Eddy (1859–1920) was an attorney whose writings included not only works on the laws of monopoly, trade, taxes, and property, but also on contemporary social and economic conditions, travel, and art. In addition to fiction and drama, he published books on Whistler, cubism and postimpressionism, and aesthetics.

15. Ibid., p. 50.

16. Ibid., p. 385.

17. Ibid., pp. 405–7.

18. According to John Tebbel, the letters were a primary impetus for the growth of the *Post*'s circulation in this period. See *George Horace Lorimer and the Saturday Evening Post* (Garden City, N.Y.: Doubleday, 1948), p. 28. In his early years at the *Post*, Lorimer published the business fiction of, among others, Herrick, Norris, and Payne.

19. George Horace Lorimer, *Letters from a Self-made Merchant to His Son* (Boston: Small, Maynard, 1902), p. 143.

20. George Horace Lorimer, *Old Gorgon Graham* (New York: Doubleday, Page, 1904), p. 9.

21. *Letters from a Self-made Merchant to His Son*, p. 3.

22. *Old Gorgon Graham*, p. 291.

23. In his *Autobiography*, Sinclair spoke about the key fault of the book, the way the plot gets lost in a long-winded socialist polemic at the end. Sinclair explained, "The last chapters were not up to standard, because both my health and my money were gone, and a second trip to

Chicago, which I had hoped to make, was out of the question. I did the best I could—and those critics who didn't like the ending ought to have seen it as it was in manuscript!" (p. 114). Michael Brewster Folsom discusses the writing of the novel in "Upton Sinclair's Escape from *The Jungle:* The Narrative Strategy and Suppressed Conclusion of America's First Proletarian Novel," *Prospects* 4 (1979): 237–66.

24. Sinclair, *The Jungle,* pp. 27, 28.

25. Ibid., pp. 28–29, 37, 40.

26. Ibid., pp. 44, 152. Charles Bushnell also singled out the fertilizer works as the worst place in the stockyards. "In one week during November, 1900," he wrote in *The Social Problem at the Chicago Stock Yards,* "in one plant alone, 126 men were employed, and at the end of the week all but six had deserted—even in the face of extreme difficulty of securing work and maintaining a livelihood" (p. 75). Jurgis stays in the fertilizer plant for a while only because at this point he must have work at all costs.

27. *The Jungle,* pp. 42, 39, 38, 47.

28. Ibid., p. 41.

29. Ibid., p. 337.

30. Ibid., pp. 376–77. There are, not unexpectedly, several other "factory" novels of the period not set in the stockyards that are also critical of Chicago's "dark Satanic mills" and the socioeconomic order that contains them. See, for example, the work of I. K. Friedman (1870–1931), especially *By Bread Alone* (New York: McClure, Phillips, 1901), which studies labor strife in the vividly described steel mills.

31. *The Jungle,* pp. 153, 190.

32. Lorimer believed that Sinclair was a "notoriety-seeker," and he offered space in his magazine to J. Ogden Armour, his former boss's son, for a series favorable to the packers. This was published in a book a few months after *The Jungle* appeared, as *The Packers, the Private Car Lines, and the People* (Philadelphia: H. Altemus Co., 1906).

33. *The Autobiography of Upton Sinclair,* p. 126.

CHAPTER EIGHT

1. Floyd Dell, "Chicago in Fiction," *Bookman* 38 (1913): 275.

2. Blake Nevius, *Robert Herrick,* pp. 88, 90.

3. See Raymond Williams, *The Country and the City* (New York: Oxford University Press, 1973); Max Byrd, *London Transformed: Images of the City in the Eighteenth Century* (New Haven: Yale University Press, 1978); and Morton and Lucia White, *The Intellectual versus the City* (Cambridge: Harvard University Press and M.I.T. Press, 1962).

4. John Higham, "The Reorientation of American Culture in the 1890's," in *Writing American History: Essays on Modern Scholarship* (Bloomington: Indiana University Press, 1970), pp. 73–102.

5. Helen Lefkowitz Horowitz argues, for example, that the trustees of several of the leading cultural institutions of Chicago "turned to cultural philanthropy not so much to satisfy personal aesthetic or scholarly yearnings as to accomplish social goals. Disturbed by social forces they could not control and filled with idealistic notions of culture, these businessmen saw in the museum, the library, the symphony orchestra, and the university a way to purify their city and to generate a civic renaissance." Horowitz gives more credit to the city's business elite than did most Chicago novelists, some of whose work she examines. See *Culture and the City: Cultural Philanthropy in Chicago from the 1880s to 1917* (Lexington: University Press of Kentucky, 1976), p. x. In *City People: The Rise of Modern City Culture in Nineteenth-Century America* (New York: Oxford University Press, 1980), Gunther Barth traces the rise of such popular urban institutions as the apartment building, the metropolitan press, the department store, the ball park, and the vaudeville house. Barth states that these institutions "mirrored faithfully the struggle of city people with change and chance," and that the popular culture "furnished answers to everyday needs until the problems it addressed disappeared in the face of new realities" (pp. 5, 234). See also Neil Harris, "Museums, Merchandising, and Popular Taste: The Struggle for Influence," in Ian M. G. Quimby, ed., *Material Culture and the Study of American Life* (New York: W. W. Norton, 1978), pp. 140–74.

6. Raymond Williams points out the historical importance of the idea of culture and art as a refuge and as a "mitigating and rallying alternative" to the industrial world in *Culture and Society, 1780–1950* (New York: Columbia University Press, 1958), p. xvi.

7. William Hale "Big Bill" Thompson was Chicago's colorful mayor for much of the period between the mid-teens and the early 1930s. See also the passage from Bellow's *The Dean's December* (New York: Harper & Row, 1982): "Well, there's low-down Chicago and there's high-up Chicago. There's Big Bill Thompson, and then there's Aristotle, who has also had a longtime association with the city, which amuses a great many people" (p. 228). Bellow's remarks, like many of those by Chicago realists earlier this century, recall George Santayana's comments on the division in America between the spirit of "aggressive enterprise" and the genteel tradition. See "The Genteel Tradition in American Philosophy," in *The Genteel Tradition: Nine Essays by George Santayana*, ed. Douglas L. Wilson (Cambridge: Harvard University Press, 1967), p. 40.

8. Saul Bellow, "Chicago and American Culture: One Writer's View," *Chicago Guide* 22, no. 5 (May 1973): 84, 86, 87. See also Bellow's brief autobiographical essay about his early career, "Starting Out in Chicago," *American Scholar* 44 (1974–75): 71–77.

9. Bellow continues: "Because they were, after all, *not* strong? A tempting answer, but perhaps too easy. A critical lady looking at one of Whistler's paintings said, 'I don't see things as you do.' The artist said, 'No, ma'am, but don't you wish you could?' A delicious snub but again too easy. The struggle was not the artist's struggle with the vulgar. That was pure nineteenth century. Things were now far worse than that." See *The Dean's December*, pp. 237, 241, 264–65.

10. Ibid., pp. 1, 42, 264.

11. The remarks on the modern city of one of Bellow's characters recalls Dell's article: "It's no longer a location, it's only a condition." Ibid., p. 237. Interestingly enough, Bellow (again like others) shows a special affection for the Chicago of *his* youth, the period before World War II, when, he feels, Chicago's culture was much more rich and attractive.

Bibliography

*Selected Bibliography and Guide
to Further Reading*

This bibliography is intended to supplement the notes by pointing out some of the sources that have been important in writing this book and by offering a few suggestions for further reading. With some exceptions, works that are cited in the text and notes are not repeated, nor have biographies, autobiographies, and studies of the works of individual writers been included. One should keep in mind also that this book deals with a fraction of Chicago writers and writing in the period it examines. Those interested in the full range of Chicago writing, or in specific categories within this range—whether utopian, feminist, historical, genteel, political, proletarian, aesthetic, romantic, juvenile, ethnic, or any of numerous other types—can find a wealth of examples worth pursuing.

Chicago History and Literature

Of Chicago histories, Harold M. Mayer and Richard C. Wade's *Chicago: Growth of a Metropolis* (Chicago: University of Chicago Press, 1969), and Bessie Louise Pierce's *A History of Chicago* (New York: Alfred A. Knopf, 1937–57), which ends in 1893, have been most important here. Mayer and Wade concentrate on the physical development of the city, while Pierce goes into much more detail on economic, social, political, and cultural affairs. Pierce also edited an excellent anthology of travelers' accounts, *As Others See Chicago: Impressions of Visitors, 1673–1933* (Chicago: University of Chicago Press, 1933). Perry Duis's *Chicago: Creating New Traditions* (Chicago: Chicago Historical Society, 1976), which accompanied a Bicentennial exhibition of the same title at the Chicago Historical Society, is a graceful and handsomely illustrated overview of Chicago's leadership in several areas of American life in the late nineteenth and early twentieth centuries. On the growth of the city, Homer Hoyt's *One Hundred Years of Land Values in Chicago: The Relationship of the Growth of Chicago to the Rise in Its Land Vaues, 1830–1933* (Chicago: University of Chicago Press, 1933) is of wider interest than its title might suggest. Of several multi-volume histories of Chicago published between the 1880s and 1920, I have relied most on A. T. Andreas's *History of Chicago: From the Earliest Period to the Present Time*, 3 vols. (Chicago: A. T. Andreas, 1884–86). There are several more recent popular and often highly anecdotal histories, including the newly reissued *Fabulous Chicago* (New York: Atheneum, 1981), by Emmett Dedmon. A few Chicago writers of the period covered here tried their hand at impressionistic descriptions and histories of the city. See, for example, *Chicago* (Boston: Houghton Mifflin, 1917), by Hobart Chatfield-Taylor, a versatile author and one of the spokesmen for genteel Chicago, and *The Tale of Chicago* (New York: Putnam's, 1933), by Edgar Lee Masters. David Lowe's *Lost Chicago* (Boston: Houghton Mifflin, 1975) and *Chicago Interiors: Views of a Splendid World* (Chicago: Contemporary Books, 1979), and Herman Kogan and Lloyd Wendt's *Chicago: A Pictorial History* (New York: Dutton, 1958) join Mayer and Wade as good published sources of photographs.

I have elsewhere acknowledged my great debt to Carl Condit for his books on Chicago architecture. Most vital to this study have been *The Chicago School of Architecture: A History of Commercial and Public Building in the Chicago Area, 1875–1925* (Chicago: University of Chicago Press, 1964), and *Chicago, 1910–1929: Building, Planning, and Urban Technology* (Chicago: University of Chicago Press, 1973). See also Thomas E. Tallmadge, *Architecture in Old Chicago* (Chicago: University of Chicago Press, 1941). Condit's more general works on American building have also been important, as have other fine architectural histories. These include John Burchard and Albert Bush-Brown, *The Architecture of America: A Social and Cultural History* (Boston: Little, Brown, 1961); James Marston Fitch, *American Building: The Historical Forces That Shaped It*, rev. ed. Boston: Houghton Mifflin, 1966); Siegfried Giedion, *Space, Time, and Architecture: The Growth of a New*

Tradition (Cambridge: Harvard University Press, 1949); Vincent Scully, *American Architecture and Urbanism* (New York: Praeger, 1969); and Christopher Tunnard and Henry Hope Reed, *American Skyline: The Growth and Form of Our Cities and Towns* (New York: New American Library, 1956). On the physical layout of Chicago and many other American cities, see John W. Reps, *The Making of Urban America: A History of City Planning in the United States* (Princeton: Princeton University Press, 1965). Early issues of the *Inland Architect*, which began publication in Chicago in 1883, are a good source of statements of the ideology of the Chicago School. On the Columbian Exposition, the major recent full-length studies are David F. Burg, *Chicago's White City of 1893* (Lexington: University Press of Kentucky, 1976), and Reid Badger, *The Great American Fair: The World's Columbian Exposition and American Culture* (Chicago: Nelson Hall, 1979). On issues surrounding domestic architecture in Chicago, see Gwendolyn Wright, *Moralism and the Model Home: Domestic Architecture and the Cultural Conflict in Chicago, 1873–1913* (Chicago: University of Chicago Press, 1980).

There are several examinations of special topics in Chicago cultural life at the turn of the century. In *Culture and the City: Cultural Philanthropy in Chicago from the 1880s to 1917* (Lexington: University Press of Kentucky, 1976), Helen Lefkowitz Horowitz examines the founding of some of Chicago's leading cultural institutions and the motives of their benefactors. For more on Chicago's elite, see Frederic Cople Jaher, *The Urban Establishment: Upper Strata in Boston, New York, Charleston, Chicago, and Los Angeles* (Urbana: University of Illinois Press, 1982). Richard Sennett analyzes the middle class and social mobility in changing Chicago in *Families against the City: Middle Class Homes of Industrial Chicago, 1872–1890* (Cambridge: Harvard University Press, 1970). On poverty and reform, see Thomas Lee Philpott, *The Slum and the Ghetto: Neighborhood Deterioration and Middle-Class Reform, Chicago 1880–1930* (New York: Oxford University Press, 1978). Herman Kogan and Lloyd Wendt offer a popular account of Chicago's colorful political scene early this century in *Lords of the Levee: The Story of Bathhouse John and Hinky Dink* (Indianapolis: Bobbs-Merrill, 1943; reissued by Indiana University Press in 1967 as *Bosses in Lusty Chicago*). There are also many works that focus on different neighborhoods and ethnic groups in the city, such as Harvey W. Zorbaugh, *Gold Coast and Slum: A Sociological Study of Chicago's Near North Side* (Chicago: University of Chicago Press, 1929); and Allan H. Spear, *Black Chicago: The Making of a Negro Ghetto, 1890–1920* (Chicago: University of Chicago Press, 1967). Many articles in the early issues of the *American Journal of Sociology*, which was founded at the University of Chicago in 1895 and edited for its first three decades by Albion W. Small, relate to the city's cultural life in general. Some of the most interesting observations of Chicago's distinguished group of urban sociologists were collected by Robert Park, Ernest W. Burgess, and Roderick D. McKenzie in *The City* (Chicago: University of Chicago Press, 1925; reissued with an introduction by Morris Janowitz in 1967). This book includes a bibliography by Louis Wirth. The writings of Thorstein Veblen, who was at the University of Chicago from 1892 to 1906, closely parallel and illuminate the fiction of the period, as do the reflections on urban life of other leading American and European social thinkers of the time.

Much has been written on Chicago literature. Histories of the city often devote sections or chapters to the city's cultural institutions, its newspapers and magazines, and its importance as a publishing center, but there are also works that specifically examine the lives of Chicago writers as a group, categorize and analyze their writing, and place it in American literary history. The fullest taxonomic survey of the varieties of Chicago fiction up to the 1930s is Lennox Bouton Grey's massive "Chicago and 'The Great American Novel': A Critical Approach to the American Epic" (Ph.D. diss., University of Chicago, 1935). See also Clarence A. Andrews's more recent *Chicago in Story: A Literary History* (Iowa City: Midwest Heritage Publishing Co., 1982). On a smaller scale, see Hugh D. Duncan's *The Rise of Chicago as a Literary Center from 1885 to 1920: A Sociological Essay in American Culture* (Totowa, N.J.: Bedminster Press, 1964). Most critical discussions of Chicago writers center on the Chicago literary renaissance of the turn of the century and after (which included some authors who did not write about the city per se), when the city became the center of literary experimentation in America and an appealing place for self-consciously innovative writers to live and work. The best study of this movement is Bernard Duffey's *The Chicago Renaissance in American Letters: A Critical History* (East Lansing: Michigan State College Press, 1954). Duffey surveys the overlapping generations of realists and rebels between the 1890s and World War I as he discusses the social history of Chicago literature, the literary magazines (such as the *Dial, Poetry, Chap-Book,* and the *Little Review*), the newspapers, and related developments in the arts. He also offers insightful critiques of leading Chicago writers and their work, as well as an excellent guide to sources. See also Dale Kramer, *Chicago Renaissance: The Literary Life in the Midwest, 1900–1930* (New York: Appleton-Century, 1966), plus the many memoirs of writers who spent a significant portion of their lives in the city.

There are a few studies of special aspects of Chicago literary history.

Bibliography

On the little magazines and the city's cultural life, see Ellen Williams, *Harriet Monroe and the Poetry Renaissance: The First Ten Years of Poetry, 1912–1922* (Urbana: University of Illinois Press, 1977). Alson Jesse Smith, in *Chicago's Left Bank* (Chicago: Regnery, 1953), speaks of the city's bohemias. For the image of Chicago in early popular fiction, see Carl S. Smith, "Fearsome Fiction and the Windy City; or, Chicago in the Dime Novel," *Chicago History* 7 (Spring 1978): 2–11. On the distinctive contribution of Chicago's female novelists, special attention should be paid to Sidney H. Bremer, "Lost Continuities: Alternative Urban Visions in Chicago Novels, 1890–1915," *Soundings* 64 (1981): 29–51.

Finally, some broadly synthetic discussions of turn-of-the-century Chicago life make bold connections between different areas of creative urban experience. In *Altgeld's America: The Lincoln Ideal versus Changing Realities* (New York: Funk & Wagnalls, 1958), Ray Ginger ties together major developments in politics, social reform, the arts, education, law, and ideology through the careers of several leading figures. A more broadly ambitious, if less coherent, work is Hugh D. Duncan's ponderously titled *Culture and Democracy: The Struggle for Form in Society and Architecture in Chicago and the Middle West during the Life and Times of Louis H. Sullivan* (Totowa, N.J.: Bedminster Press, 1965). Duncan makes sometimes brilliant observations on the dynamics of art and society in Chicago at the turn of the century. He links the work of major architects, authors, philosophers, and sociologists in their collective attempt to find new ways of thinking, speaking, and acting that were appropriate to modern city life. See also Kenny J. Williams, *In the City of Men: Another Story of Chicago* (Nashville: Townsend Press, 1974); and the Chicago sections of Robert C. Bray, *Rediscoveries: Literature and Place in Illinois* (Urbana: University of Illinois Press, 1982.

BACKGROUNDS

A full bibliography of urban history is much too extensive to list here. For general background, I have relied on Arthur M. Schlesinger, *The Rise of the City, 1878–1898* (New York: Macmillan, 1933); Constance Green, *The Rise of Urban America* (New York: Harper & Row, 1965); Blake McKelvey, *The Urbanization of America, 1865–1915* (New Brunswick, N.J.: Rutgers University Press, 1963); and Sam Bass Warner, *The Urban Wilderness: A History of the American City* (New York: Harper & Row, 1972). In the course of his long career, Lewis Mumford has offered some of the most imaginative analyses of urban culture. See, in particular, *The Culture of Cities* (New York: Harcourt, Brace,

1938); and *The City in History: Its Origins, Its Transformations, and Its Prospects* (New York: Harcourt, Brace & World, 1961). Two recent and highly helpful studies of the evolution of urban thought and institutions are Thomas Bender, *Toward an Urban Vision: Ideas and Institutions in Nineteenth-Century America* (Lexington: University Press of Kentucky, 1975); and Gunther Barth, *City People: The Rise of Modern City Culture in Nineteenth-Century America* (New York: Oxford University Press, 1980). There are several readers and anthologies in urban studies that contain entries of special interest to the student of literature. See, for example, Alan Trachtenberg, Peter Neill, and Peter C. Bunnell, eds., *The City: American Experience* (New York: Oxford University Press, 1971).

Some of the leading analyses of major developments in American cultural history of the late nineteenth and early twentieth centuries are particularly useful to understanding the development of Chicago and modern urban industrial culture. Among the most interesting are Burton J. Bledstein, *The Culture of Professionalism: The Middle Class and the Development of Higher Education in America* (New York: W. W. Norton, 1976); Alfred D. Chandler, Jr., *The Visible Hand: The Managerial Revolution in American Business* (Cambridge: Harvard University Press, 1977); Thomas C. Cochran and William Miller, *The Age of Enterprise: A Social History of Industrial America*, rev. ed. (New York: Harper & Row, 1961); Neil Harris, introduction to *The Land of Contrasts: 1880–1901* (New York: Braziller, 1970); Samuel P. Hays, *The Response to Industrialism, 1885–1914* (Chicago: University of Chicago Press, 1957); John Higham, "The Reorientation of American Culture in the 1890's," in *Writing American History: Essays on Modern Scholarship* (Bloomington: Indiana University Press, 1970); Richard Hofstadter, *The Age of Reform: From Bryan to F.D.R.* (New York: Alfred A. Knopf, 1955); T. J. Jackson Lears, *No Place of Grace: Antimodernism and the Transformation of American Culture, 1880–1920* (New York: Pantheon Books, 1981); Henry F. May, *The End of American Innocence: A Study of the First Years of Our Own Time, 1912–1917* (New York: Alfred A. Knopf, 1959); Lewis Mumford, *The Brown Decades: A Study of the Arts in America, 1865–1895* (New York: Harcourt, Brace, 1931); Alan Trachtenberg, *The Incorporation of America: Culture and Society in the Gilded Age* (New York: Hill & Wang, 1982); and Robert H. Wiebe, *The Search for Order, 1877–1920* (New York: Hill & Wang, 1967). Trachtenberg devotes his last chapter to the World's Columbian Exposition.

Most general works on American literary history of the late nineteenth and early twentieth centuries discuss Chicago writing. Of most relevance here are Warner Berthoff, *The Ferment of Realism: American*

Literature, 1884–1919 (New York: Free Press, 1965); Maxwell Geismar, *Rebels and Ancestors: The American Novel, 1890–1915* (Boston: Houghton Mifflin, 1953); Harold Kaplan, *Power and Order: Henry Adams and the Naturalist Tradition in American Fiction* (Chicago: University of Chicago Press, 1981); the opening chapter of Alfred Kazin, *On Native Grounds: An Interpretation of Modern American Prose Literature* (New York: Harcourt, Brace, 1942); Kenneth S. Lynn, *The Dream of Success: A Study of the Modern American Imagination* (Boston: Little, Brown, 1955); Jay Martin, *Harvests of Change: American Literature, 1865–1914* (Englewood Cliffs, N.J.: Prentice-Hall, 1967); Vernon L. Parrington, *The Beginnings of Critical Realism in America, 1860–1920,* vol. 3 of *Main Currents in American Thought* (New York: Harcourt, Brace, 1930); Donald Pizer, *Realism and Naturalism in Nineteenth-Century American Literature* (Carbondale: Southern Illinois University Press, 1966); Charles C. Walcutt, *American Literary Naturalism: A Divided Stream* (Minneapolis: University of Minnesota Press, 1956); and Larzer Ziff, *The American 1890's: Life and Times of a Lost Generation* (New York: Viking Press, 1966). For a brief but incisive recent characterization of American realism, see Eric J. Sundquist, "The Country of the Blue," introduction to *American Realism: New Essays* (Baltimore: Johns Hopkins University Press, 1982).

RELATED WORKS

There is a varied group of scholarly works that, in method as much as in subject, have proved useful in the formulation of some of the ideas and methods of this book. Among other studies of the city and the American mind, see Michael H. Cowan, *City of the West: Emerson, America, and Urban Metaphor* (New Haven: Yale University Press, 1967); Martin Green, *The Problem of Boston: Some Readings in Cultural History* (New York: W. W. Norton, 1966); David R. Weimer, *The City as Metaphor* (New York: Random House, 1966); and Morton and Lucia White, *The Intellectual versus the City: From Thomas Jefferson to Frank Lloyd Wright* (Cambridge: Harvard University Press and M.I.T. Press, 1962). Kevin Starr's *Americans and the California Dream, 1850–1915* (New York: Oxford University Press, 1973), while only partly about urban writing (when Starr discusses literary San Francisco), is a consistently engaging handling of the literature of place.

Several outstanding books deal with European and British cities, some combining literary analysis and cultural history with great effectiveness. Chief among these works are Max Byrd, *London Transformed: Images of the City in the Eighteenth Century* (New Haven:

Yale University Press, 1978); Donald Fanger, *Dostoyevsky and Romantic Realism: A Study of Dostoyevsky in Relation to Balzac, Dickens, and Gogol* (Cambridge: Harvard University Press, 1965); Steven Marcus, *Engels, Manchester, and the Working Class* (New York: Random House, 1974); Carl E. Schorske, *Fin-de-Siècle Vienna: Politics and Culture* (New York: Alfred A. Knopf, 1980); and, most sweeping in its scope, Raymond Williams, *The Country and the City* (New York: Oxford University Press, 1973). Williams's *Culture and Society, 1780–1950* (New York: Columbia University Press, 1958) has also been of great help in understanding how Chicago writers saw their own work as artists in relation to the new industrial city. See also Malcolm Bradbury, "The Cities of Modernism," in *Modernism, 1890–1930,* ed. Malcolm Bradbury and James McFarlane (Atlantic Highlands, N.J.: Humanities Press, 1978); and Irving Howe, "The City in Literature," in *The Critical Point: On Literature and Culture* (New York: Horizon Press, 1973).

For provocative discussions of the imaginative dimensions of major developments in technology in the nineteenth and twentieth centuries, see Siegfried Giedion, *Mechanization Takes Command: A Contribution to Anonymous History* (New York: Oxford University Press, 1948); John F. Kasson, *Civilizing the Machine: Technology and Republican Values in America, 1776–1900* (New York: Grossman, 1976), and *Amusing the Million: Coney Island at the Turn of the Century* (New York: Hill & Wang, 1978); Leo Marx, *The Machine in the Garden: Technology and the Pastoral Ideal in America* (New York: Oxford University Press, 1964); and Alan Trachtenberg, *Brooklyn Bridge: Fact and Symbol* (New York: Oxford University Press, 1965). I have benefited greatly from several studies of images of the city and their importance to individual and collective urban experience. See especially Kevin Lynch, *The Image of the City* (Cambridge: Technology Press and Harvard University Press, 1960), and *Managing the Sense of a Region* (Cambridge: M.I.T. Press, 1976); and, with particular reference to Chicago, Anselm L. Strauss, *Images of the American City* (Glencoe, Ill.: Free Press, 1961). On the significance of the perception of environment, see Yi-Fu Tuan, *Topophilia: A Study of Environmental Perception, Attitudes, and Values* (Englewood Cliffs, N.J.: Prentice-Hall, 1974).

Index

227

Index

Bourget, Paul, 104–5, 106, 130, 157
Boyington, W. W., 137
Bremer, Sidney H., 40–41, 179
Breton, Jules, 54
Brett, George P., 170
Briary-Bush, The (Dell), 103–4
Brooks, Van Wyck, 201–2
Brueghel, Pieter, 72
Buildings. *See* Architecture
Burnett, Frances Hodgson, 141
Burnham, Clara Louise: *Sweet Clover: A Romance of the White City*, 144–46, 149
Burnham, Daniel, 125, 140, 143, 149–50, 152–53
Bushnell, Charles J., 156–57, 164

Cather, Willa: *The Song of the Lark*, 8, 53–56, 60–61; mentioned, 3, 41, 175
Central Art Association, 31, 187–88
Charlatans, The (Taylor), 206–7
Chatelaine of La Trinité, The (Fuller), 22
Chevalier of Pensieri-Vani, The (Fuller), 22
"Chicago" (Sandburg), 58, 61–62, 158, 174
Chicago: Growth of a Metropolis (Mayer and Wade), 101
Chicago: The Marvelous City of the West (Flinn), 152, 154–55
"Chicago and 'The Great American Novel'" (Grey), xi
Chicago Board of Trade, 58, 60, 94 (pictured), 103, 135–38
Chicago Plan of 1909, 178
Chicago Record, 181
Chicago Renaissance, 88, 199
Chicago River, 61, 73, 150, 152, 178–79
Chicago Stock Exchange, 52, 126
Chicago Tribune, 146
Chimes (Herrick), 33
City Beautiful movement, 149
Cliff-Dwellers, The (Fuller): architecture in, 129–34, 135; art and society in, 22–24, 28, 30, 33, 35
Clybourne, Archibald, 152
Columbian Exposition. *See* World's Columbian Exposition
"Columbian Ode" (Monroe), 142, 178
Commercial Club, 149
Condit, Carl, 101–2, 122

Common Lot, The (Herrick): architecture in, 135, 139; art and society in, 34–37, 38, 39; female central character in, 40, 43, 44, 51
Cooper, James Fenimore, 4
Crane, Stephen, 171
Criticism and Fiction (Howells), 15, 20
Crumbling Idols (Garland), 4, 5

Daley, Richard, 180
Dante, 166
Daumier, Honoré, 73
Davis, Allen F., 185–86
Dawn (Dreiser), 110–12, 113, 115, 120
Dean's December, The (Bellow), 175–76
Dell, Floyd, 103–4, 171
DeQuincey, Thomas, 19–20, 41
Dewey, John, 172
Dial, 4
Dickens, Charles, 12, 38, 73, 171
Donne, John, 128
Dostoyevsky, Fyodor, 12
Dow, Jenny, 17
"Downfall of Abner Joyce, The" (Fuller), 28–29, 30. See also *Under the Skylights*
"Dr. Gowdy and the Squash" (Fuller), 31–33. See also *Under the Skylights*
Dreiser, Sara White, 51, 116
Dreiser, Theodore: "The American Financier," 74; assessment of, 6, 172, 173, 175; on business and art, 70–78, 84–85, 90; *Dawn,* 110–12, 115, 120; *The Financier,* 57, 70–73, 207–8; *The "Genius,"* 115, 120, 181; and railroad, 106–7, 110–12, 113, 115–20; *Sister Carrie,* 49–51, 52–53, 55–56, 75, 115–19, 138–39, 172, 178; *The Titan,* 5, 6, 61–62, 70, 73–74, 119–20; *Trilogy of Desire,* 57, 70–78, 81, 84–85, 173; and view from the streets, 181; on World's Columbian Exposition, 142–43; mentioned, 3, 8, 22, 29, 83, 88, 89, 176
Dunne, Finley Peter, 181

Eddy, Arthur Jerome: *Ganton & Company,* 160–61, 163, 164
Edholm, Charlton Lawrence, 179
Education of Henry Adams, The (Adams), 40, 144

228

Index

Index

James, Henry: *The American Scene,* 104, 108–9, 123; *The Portrait of a Lady,* 42; mentioned, 133, 171, 172
Jenney, William LeBaron, 126
Jerry the Dreamer (Payne), 37–39, 53
Joyce, James, 12, 179, 181
Jungle, The (Sinclair), 139, 152, 154, 156, 164–70, 178

Kasson, John F., 9
Kazin, Alfred, 192
King Lear (Shakespeare), 18
Kipling, Rudyard, 158, 166–67

Lake Michigan, 177–78
Lancet, 156
Land of the Dollar, The (Steevens), 1–2, 6, 7
Lawless Wealth (Russell), 77, 155
Lears, T. J. Jackson, 193
Lehan, Richard, 198
Letters from a Self-Made Merchant to His Son (Lorimer), 162–64
Lewis, Sinclair, 59, 85, 175
Life on the Mississippi (Twain), 1
Lincoln, Abraham, 127
"Literary imagination," defined, xi
"Little O'Grady vs. the Grindstone" (Fuller), 29–31. See also *Under the Skylights*
London, Jack, 170
Daily Mail (London), 1
Times (London), 136–37
Loop, and railroads, 102–3, 104
Lorimer, George Horace, 161–64, 168, 170
Lovett, Robert Morss: *A Wingèd Victory,* 46–49; mentioned, 172
Lynch, Kevin, 177

McGovern, Terry, 81
Machine in the Garden, The (Marx), 108
MacMonnies, Frederick, 140
Mailer, Norman, 159
Main-Travelled Roads (Garland), 28
"Mamie" (Sandburg), 101, 103
Marx, Leo, 10, 108
Masters, Edgar Lee, 11, 142
Mayer, Harold M., 101
Memoirs (Anderson), 87, 88
Memoirs of an American Citizen, The (Herrick), 44–46, 60, 160, 164

Mencken, H. L., 158–59
"Metropolis and Mental Life, The" (Simmel), 15
Miami and the Siege of Chicago (Mailer), 159
Mid-American Chants (Anderson), 200
Midway, and World's Columbian Exposition, 143–44, 145, 146
Millgate, Michael, 197
"Modern Lear, A" (Addams), 18
Monroe, Harriet: "Columbian Ode," 142, 178
Moon-Calf (Dell), 103–4
Morris, Nelson, 153, 155
Morris, Wright, 205
Mr. Salt (Payne), 51–53, 55–56, 60–61, 148–49
Muirhead, James Fullarton, 183
"My Kinsman, Major Molineux" (Hawthorne), 114

Napoleon, 65
Naturalism, 70, 88, 132
Nevius, Blake, 171
Norris, Frank: on architecture, 135–38; assessment of, 172, 173; and Dreiser, compared, 70–71; *The Octopus,* 70, 194; *The Pit,* 57, 60–70, 76, 77, 79, 80, 84–85, 140, 163, 178; "The True Reward of the Novelist," 57; mentioned, 3, 8, 88, 89, 90
North American Review, 6
Norton, Charles Eliot, 22
Nouvelle Revue Français, 106

Octopus, The (Norris), 70, 194
Old Gorgon Graham: More Letters from a Self-made Merchant to His Son (Lorimer), 162
Olmsted, Frederick Law, 140
On the Stairs (Fuller), 188
Our America (Frank), 106, 112

Packingtown. *See* Stockyards
Page, Walter Hines, 170
Payne, Will: *Jerry the Dreamer,* 37–39, 53; *Mr. Salt,* 51–53, 55–56, 60–61, 148–49; mentioned, 69, 79
People, Yes, The (Sandburg), 127–28
Pierce, Bessie Louise, 154
Pioneer (train), 101

230

Index

Index